S0-CFR-035

PENGUIN BOOKS

A WRITER'S NOTEBOOK

William Somerset Maugham was born in 1874 and lived in Paris until he was ten. He was educated at King's School, Canterbury, and at Heidelberg University. He afterwards walked the wards of St Thomas's Hospital with a view to practice in medicine, but the success of his first novel, *Liza of Lambeth* (1897), won him over to letters. Something of his hospital experience is reflected, however, in the first of his masterpieces, *Of Human Bondage* (1915), and with *The Moon and Sixpence* (1919) his reputation as a novelist was assured.

His position as one of the most successful playwrights on the London stage was being consolidated simultaneously. His first play, *A Man of Honour* (1903), was followed by a procession of successes just before and after the First World War. (At one point only Bernard Shaw had more plays running at the same time in London.) His theatre career ended with *Sheppey* (1933).

His fame as a short-story writer began with *The Trembling of a Leaf*, sub-titled *Little Stories of the South Sea Islands*, in 1921, since when he published more than ten collections.

Somerset Maugham's general books are fewer in number. They include travel books, such as *On a Chinese Screen* (1922) and *Don Fernando* (1935), essays, criticism, and the self-revealing *The Summing Up* (1938). *A Writer's Notebook* comes into this category.

Mr Maugham lived on the Riviera, from which he retired temporarily during the war. During his life he travelled in almost every part of the world. He became a Companion of Honour in 1954 and died in 1965.

A Writer's Notebook

W. SOMERSET MAUGHAM

PENGUIN BOOKS

Penguin Books Ltd, Harmondsworth, Middlesex, England
Viking Penguin Inc., 40 West 23rd Street, New York, New York 10010, U.S.A.
Penguin Books Australia Ltd, Ringwood, Victoria, Australia
Penguin Books Canada Ltd, 2801 John Street, Markham, Ontario, Canada L3R 1B4
Penguin Books (N.Z.) Ltd, 182–190 Wairau Road, Auckland 10, New Zealand

First published in Great Britain by William Heinemann Ltd 1949
First published in the United States of America by Doubleday & Company, Inc., 1949
Published in Penguin Books in Great Britain 1967
Published in Penguin Books in the United States of America by arrangement with
Doubleday & Company, Inc., 1984
Reprinted 1987

Printed and bound in Great Britain by
Cox & Wyman Ltd, Reading
Set in Monotype Times

In
Loving Memory of my Friend
FREDERICK GERALD HAXTON
1892–1944

PREFACE

The *Journal* of Jules Renard is one of the minor masterpieces of French literature. He wrote three or four one-act plays, which were neither very good nor very bad; they neither amuse you much nor move you much, but when well acted they can be sat through without ennui. He wrote several novels, of which one, *Poil de Carotte*, was very successful. It is the story of his own childhood, the story of a little uncouth boy whose harsh and unnatural mother leads him a wretched life. Renard's method of writing, without ornament, without emphasis, heightens the pathos of the dreadful tale, and the poor lad's sufferings, mitigated by no pale ray of hope, are heartrending. You laugh wryly at his clumsy efforts to ingratiate himself with that demon of a woman and you feel his humiliations, you resent his unmerited punishments, as though they were your own. It would be an ill-conditioned person who did not feel his blood boil at the infliction of such malignant cruelty. It is not a book that you can easily forget.

Jules Renard's other novels are of no great consequence. They are either fragments of autobiography or are compiled from the careful notes he took of people with whom he was thrown into close contact, and can hardly be counted as novels at all. He was so devoid of the creative power that one wonders why he ever became a writer. He had no invention to heighten the point of an incident or even to give a pattern to his acute observations. He collected facts; but a novel cannot be made of facts alone; in themselves they are dead things. Their use is to develop an idea or illustrate a theme, and the novelist not only has the right to change them to suit his purpose, to stress them or leave them in shadow, but is under the necessity of doing so. It is true that Jules Renard had his theories; he asserted that his object was merely to state, leaving the reader to write his own novel, as it were, on the data presented to him, and that to attempt to do anything else was literary fudge. But I am always suspicious of a novelist's theories; I have never known them to be anything other than a justification of his own shortcomings. So a writer who has no gift for the contrivance of a plausible story will tell you that storytelling is the least important part of the novelist's equipment, and if he is devoid of humour he will moan that humour is the death of

7

fiction. In order to give the glow of life to brute fact it must be transmuted by passion, and so the only good novel Jules Renard wrote was when the passion of self-pity and the hatred he felt for his mother charged his recollections of his unhappy childhood with venom.

I surmise that he would be already forgotten but for the publication after his death of the dairy that he kept assiduously for twenty years. It is a remarkable work. He knew a number of persons who were important in the literary and theatrical world of his day, actors like Sarah Bernhardt and Lucien Guitry, authors like Rostand and Capus, and he relates his various encounters with them with an admirable but caustic vivacity. Here his keen powers of observation were of service to him. But though his portraits have verisimilitude, and the lively conversation of those clever people has an authentic ring, you must have, perhaps, some knowledge of the world of Paris in the last few years of the nineteenth century and the first few years of the twentieth, either personal knowledge or knowledge by hearsay, really to appreciate these parts of the journal. His fellow writers were indignant when the work was issued and they discovered with what acrimony he had written of them. The picture he paints of the literary life of his day is savage. They say dog does not bite dog. That is not true of men of letters in France. In England, I think, men of letters bother but little with one another. They do not live in one another's pockets as French authors do; they meet, indeed, infrequently, and then as likely as not by chance. I remember one author saying to me years ago: 'I prefer to live with my raw material.' They do not even read one another very much. On one occasion, an American critic came to England to interview a number of distinguished writers on the state of English literature, and gave up his project when he discovered that a very eminent novelist, the first one he saw, had never read a single book of Kipling's. English writers judge their fellow craftsmen; one they will tell you is pretty good, another they will say is no great shakes, but their enthusiasm for the former seldom reaches fever-heat, and their disesteem for the latter is manifested rather by indifference than by detraction. They do not particularly envy someone else's success, and when it is obviously unmerited, it moves them to laughter rather than to wrath. I think English authors are self-centred. They are, perhaps, as vain as any others, but their vanity is satisfied by the appreciation of a private circle. They are not inordinately affected by adverse criticism, and with one or two exceptions do not go out of their way to ingratiate themselves with the reviewers. They live and let live.

Things are very different in France. There the literary life is a merciless conflict in which one gives violent battle to another, in which one clique attacks another clique, in which you must be always on your guard against the gins and snares of your enemies, and in which, indeed, you can never be quite sure that a friend will not knife you in the back. It is all against all, and, as in some forms of wrestling, anything is allowed. It is a life of bitterness, envy and treachery, of malice and hatred. I think there are reasons for this. One, of course, is that the French take literature much more seriously than we do, a book matters to them as it never matters to us, and they are prepared to wrangle over general principles with a vehemence that leaves us amazed – and tickled, for we cannot get it out of our heads that there is something comic in taking art so seriously. Then, political and religious matters have a way of getting themselves entangled with literature in France, and an author will see his book furiously assailed, not because it is a bad book, but because he is a Protestant, a nationalist, a communist or what not. Much of this is praiseworthy. It is well that a writer should think not only that the book he himself is writing is important, but that the books other people are writing are important too. It is well that authors, at least, should think that books really mean something, and that their influence is salutary, in which case they must be defended, or harmful, in which case they must be attacked. Books can't matter much if their authors themselves don't think they matter. It is because in France they think they matter so much that they take sides so fiercely.

There is one practice common to French authors that has always caused me astonishment, and that is their practice of reading their works to one another, either when they are in process of writing them, or when they have finished them. In England writers sometimes send their unpublished works to fellow craftsmen for criticism, by which they mean praise, for rash is the author who makes any serious objections to another's manuscript; he will only offend, and his criticism will not be listened to; but I cannot believe that any English author would submit himself to the excruciating boredom of sitting for hours while a fellow novelist read him his latest work. In France it seems to be an understood thing that he should, and what is stranger, even eminent writers will often rewrite much of their work on the strength of the criticism they may have thus received. No less a person than Flaubert acknowledges that he did so as a result of Turgenev's remarks, and you can gather from André Gide's *Journal* that he has often profited in the same way. It has puzzled me; and the explanation that I have offered to myself is that the French, because writing is an honourable profession (which it has never been in England), often adopt it without having any marked creative power; their keen intelligence, their sound education and their background of an age-long culture enable them to produce work of a high standard, but it is the result of resolution, industry and a well-stored, clever brain rather than of an urge to create, and so criticism, the opinions of well-intentioned persons, can be of considerable use. But I should be surprised to learn that the great producers, of whom Balzac is the most eminent example, put themselves to this trouble. They wrote because they had to, and having written, thought only of what they were going to write next. The practice proves, of course, that French authors are prepared to take an immense deal of trouble to make their works as perfect as may be, and that, sensitive as they are, they have less self-complacency than many of their English fellow craftsmen.

There is another reason why the antagonisms of authors in France are more envenomed than in England; their public is too small to support their great number: we have a public of two hundred millions; they have one of forty. There is plenty of room for every English writer; you may never have heard of him, but if he has any gift at all, in any direction, he can earn an adequate income. He is not very rich, but then he would never have adopted the profession of letters if riches had been his object. He acquires in time his body of faithful readers, and since in order to get the publishers' advertisements the papers are obliged to give a good deal of space to reviews, he is accorded a sufficient amount of attention in the public Press. He can afford to look upon other writers without envy. But in France few writers can make a living by writing novels; unless they have private means or some other occupation that enables them to provide for their needs, they are forced to resort to journalism. There are not enough book-buyers to go round, and the success of one author can greatly attenuate the success of another. It is a struggle to get known; it is a struggle to hold one's place in the public esteem. This results in frantic efforts to attract the benevolent attention of critics, and it is to the effect their reviews may have that must be ascribed the anxiety felt even by authors of reputation when they know that a notice is to appear in such and such a paper, and their fury when it is not a good one. It is true that criticism carries greater weight in France than it does in England. Certain critics are so influential that they can make or mar a book. Though every person of culture in the world reads French, and French books are read not only in Paris, it is only the opinion of Paris, of its writers, its critics, its intelligent public, that the French author really cares about. It is because literary ambition is centred in that one place that it is the scene of so much strife and heart-burning. And it is because the financial rewards of authorship are so small that there is so much eagerness, so much scheming to win the prizes that are every year awarded to certain books, or to enter into one or other of the academies which not only set an honourable seal on a career but increase an author's market value. But there are few prizes for the aspiring writer, few vacancies in the academies for the established one. Not many people know how much bitterness, how much bargaining, how much intrigue goes to the awarding of a prize or the election of a candidate.

But, of course, there are authors in France who are indifferent to money and scornful of honours, and since the French are a generous people, these authors are rewarded with the unqualified respect of all. That is why, indeed, certain writers who, judged by any reasonable standards, are evidently of no great consequence enjoy, especially among the young, a reputation that is incomprehensible to the foreigner. For unfortunately talent and originality do not always attend nobility of character.

Jules Renard was very honest, and he does not draw a pretty picture of himself in his *Journal*. He was malignant, cold, selfish, narrow, envious and ungrateful. His only redeeming feature was his love for his wife; she is the only person in all these volumes of whom he consistently speaks with kindness. He was immensely susceptible to any fancied affront, and his vanity was outrageous. He had neither charity nor good will. He splashes with his angry contempt everything he doesn't understand, and the possibility nevers occurs to him that if he doesn't the fault may lie in himself. He was odious, incapable of a generous gesture, and almost incapable of a generous emotion. But for all that the *Journal* is wonderfully good reading. It is extremely amusing. It is witty and subtle and often wise. It is a notebook kept for the purposes of his calling by a professional writer who passionately sought truth, purity of style and perfection of language. As a writer no one could have been more conscientious. Jules Renard jotted down neat retorts and clever phrases, epigrams, things seen, the sayings of

11

people and the look of them, descriptions of scenery, effects of sun-shine and shadow, everything, in short, that could be of use to him when he sat down to write for publication; and in several cases, as we know, when he had collected sufficient data he strung them together into a more or less connected narrative and made a book of them. To a writer this is the most interesting part of these volumes; you are taken into an author's workshop and shown what materials he thought worth gathering, and how he gathered them. It is not to the point that he lacked the capacity to make better use of them.

I forget who it was who said that every author should keep a note-book, but should take care never to refer to it. If you understand this properly, I think there is truth in it. By making a note of something that strikes you, you separate it from the incessant stream of impres-sions that crowd across the mental eye, and perhaps fix it in your memory. All of us have had good ideas or vivid sensations that we thought would one day come in useful, but which, because we were too lazy to write them down, have entirely escaped us. When you know you are going to make a note of something, you look at it more attentively than you otherwise would, and in the process of doing so the words are borne in upon you that will give it its private place in reality. The danger of using notes is that you find yourself inclined to rely on them, and so lose the even and natural flow of your writing which comes from allowing the unconscious that full activity which is somewhat pompously known as inspiration. You are also inclined to drag in your jottings whether they fit in or not. I have heard that Walter Pater used to make abundant notes on his reading and re-flection and put them into appropriate pigeon-holes, and when he had enough on a certain subject, fit them together and write an essay. If this is true, it may account for the rather cramped feeling one has when one reads him. This may be why his style has neither swing nor vigour. For my part, I think to keep copious notes is an excellent practice and I can only regret that a natural indolence has prevented me from exercising it more diligently. They cannot fail to be of service if they are used with intelligence and discretion.

It is because Jules Renard's *Journal* in this respect so pleasantly engaged my attention that I have ventured to collect my own notes and offer them to the perusal of my fellow writers. I hasten to state that mine are not nearly so interesting as his. They are much more interrupted. There were many years in which I never kept notes at all. They do not pretend to be a journal; I never wrote anything about my meetings with interesting or famous people. I am sorry that I didn't. It would doubtless have made the following pages more amusing if I had recorded my conversations with the many and distinguished writers, painters, actors and politicians I have known more or less intimately. It never occurred to me to do so. I never made a note of anything that I did not think would be useful to me at one time or another in my work, and though, especially in the early notebooks, I jotted down all kinds of thoughts and emotions of a personal nature, it was only with the intention of ascribing them sooner or later to the creatures of my invention. I meant my notebooks to be a storehouse of materials for future use and nothing else.

As I grew older and more aware of my intentions, I used my notebooks less to record my private opinions, and more to put down while still fresh my impressions of such persons and places as seemed likely to be of service to me for the particular purpose I had in view at the moment. Indeed, on one occasion, when I went to China, vaguely thinking that I might write a book upon my travels, my notes were so copious that I abandoned the project and published them as they were. These, of course, I have omitted from this volume. I have likewise omitted everything I have elsewhere made use of, and if I have left in a phrase or two here and there that a diligent reader of my works recalls, it is not because I am so pleased with it that I want to repeat it, but from inadvertence. On one or two occasions, however I have deliberately left in the facts that I noted down at the time and that gave me the idea for a story or novel, thinking it might entertain the reader who chanced to remember one or the other, to see on what materials I devised a more elaborate piece. I have never claimed to create anything out of nothing; I have always needed an incident or a character as a starting point, but I have exercised imagination, invention and a sense of the dramatic to make it something of my own.

My early notebooks were largely filled with pages of dialogue for plays that I never wrote, and these, because I thought they could interest no one, I have also left out, but I have not left out a considerable number of remarks and reflections that seem to me now exaggerated and foolish. They are the expression of a very young man's reaction to real life, or what he thought was such, and to liberty, after the sheltered and confined existence, perverted by fond fancies and the reading of novels, which was natural to a boy in the class in which I was born; and they are the expression of his revolt from the ideas and conventions of the environment in which he had been brought

13

up. I think I should have been dishonest with the reader if I had suppressed them. My first notebook is dated 1892; I was then eighteen. I have no wish to make myself out more sensible than I was. I was ignorant, ingenuous, enthusiastic and callow.

My notebooks amounted to fifteen stoutish volumes, but by omitting so much, as I have above described, I have reduced them to one no longer than many a novel. I hope the reader will accept this as a sufficient excuse for its publication. I do not publish it because I am so arrogant as to suppose that my every word deserves to be perpetuated. I publish it because I am interested in the technique of literary production and in the process of creation, and if such a volume as this by some other author came into my hands I should turn to it with avidity. By some happy chance what interests me seems to interest a great many other people; I could never have expected it, and I have never ceased to be surprised at it; but it may be that what has happened so often before will happen again, and some persons may be found who will discover here and there in the following pages something to interest them. I should have looked upon it as an impertinence to publish such a book when I was in the full flow of my literary activity; it would have seemed to claim an importance for myself which would have been offensive to my fellow writers; but now I am an old man, I can be no one's rival, for I have retired from the hurly-burly and ensconced myself not uncomfortably on the shelf. Any ambition I may have had has long since been satisfied. I contend with none not because none is worth my strife, but because I have said my say and I am well pleased to let others occupy my small place in the world of letters. I have done what I wanted to do and now silence becomes me. I am told that in these days you are quickly forgotten if you do not by some new work keep your name before the public, and I have little doubt that it is true. Well, I am prepared for that. When my obituary notice at last appears in *The Times*, and they say: 'What, I thought he died years ago,' my ghost will gently chuckle.

1892

In this year I entered the Medical School of St Thomas's Hospital. I spent five years there. I carefully set down the dates on which I started my first notebooks, and these dates will, I hope, serve as an extenuation of their contents. My later notebooks are undated, indeed many of my notes were scribbled on a scrap of paper or the back of an envelope, and I have had to determine when they were written by their subject matter. It may be that here and there I am a year or two out; I do not think it is of any consequence.

Considering how foolishly people act and how pleasantly they prattle, perhaps it would be better for the world if they talked more and did less.

Music-hall songs provide the dull with wit, just as proverbs provide them with wisdom.

Good luck always brings merit, but merit very seldom brings good luck.

Maxims of the Vicar.
A parson is paid to preach, not to practise.

Only ask those people to stay with you or to dine with you, who can ask you in return.

'Do unto others as you would they should do unto you.' An excellent maxim – for others.

He always answered the contentions of the temperance people by saying that 'God has ordered us to make use of the things of this world,' and he exemplified his reply by keeping himself well supplied with whisky and liqueurs, which, however, he kept carefully locked up in the sideboard. 'It is not good for all people to drink spirits,' he said, 'in fact it is a sin to put temptation in their way; and besides, they would not appreciate them at their true value.'

These observations fell from the lips of my uncle who was Vicar of Whitstable; I took them seriously, but looking back on them now, I am inclined to think that he was exercising at my expense a humour which I never suspected him of possessing.

Reading does not make a man wise; it only makes him learned. Respectability is the cloak under which fools cover their stupidity.

No action is in itself good or bad, but only such according to convention.

An old maid is always poor. When a spinster is rich she is an unmarried woman of a certain age.

Genius should use mediocrity as ink wherewith to write its name in the annals of the world.

Genius is talent provided with ideals.

Genius starves while talent wears purple and fine linen.

The man of genius of to-day will in fifty years' time be in most cases no more than a man of talent.

A visit to a picture gallery with a friend is, perhaps, the severest test you can put him to. Most people, on going to a gallery, leave politeness and courtesy, with their umbrellas and sticks, at the door. They step in stripped of their veneer, and display their dispositions in all their nakedness. Then you will find them dogmatic and arrogant, flippant and foolish, impatient of contradiction and even of difference of opinion. Neither do they then seek to hide their opinion of you; for the most part it is a very unfavourable one.

The man who in these conditions listens tolerantly to your opinion and allows that you may be as right as he, is a friend indeed.

But, first of all, are you perfectly convinced of my friendship, are you so assured of it that I may speak to you of the most personal subject?

Certainly, my dear boy, a heart as true as yours has the right to say the most unpleasant things. Go on.

Brooks. He is a man under the middle size, broad and sturdy

and well-shaped; with a beautiful head, a good nose, and a broad, high forehead; but his face, clean-shaven, narrows down to a pointed chin; his eyes are pale blue, slightly expressionless; his mouth is large and his lips are thick and sensual; his hair is curly but getting thin; and he wears it long. He has a look of refinement and a romantic air.

When he went up to Cambridge he got into a set of men with money and of sporting tastes, among whom his intelligence was deemed exceptional; an opinion which was shared by his tutor and the master of his college. He ate his dinners and read for the Bar. He took a second class. When he went to London, he dressed at an expensive tailor's, kept a mistress, was elected to the Reform, which his friends made him join under the impression that he had in him the makings of a politician. His friends were reading men, and he went through a course of English classics in a light, amateurish manner. He admired George Meredith and was scornful of the three-volume novel. He became a diligent reader of the weekly sixpennies, of the literary monthlies and the quarterlies. He went a good deal to the theatre and to the opera. Other evenings he spent either in a friend's room or at some old-fashioned inn, drinking whisky and smoking, discussing far into the night life and death, fate, Christianity, books and politics. He read Newman, and was impressed by him, and the Roman Catholicism which he found at Brompton intensely attracted him. Then he fell ill and, on recovering, went to Germany. Here he met people whose pursuits and predilections were different from those of his former companions. He began to learn German, and with this object, read the German classics. He added an admiration of Goethe to his old admiration of Meredith and Newman. On going to Italy for a short holiday, he fell in love with the country and, after a few more months in Germany, returned to it.

He read Dante and Boccaccio; but he came in contact with men, scholars, who had a passion for the classic writers of Greece and Rome, and found that they did not think very highly of the dilettante spirit in which he worked. Always very easily influenced, every new impression producing its effect on him, he quickly adopted the outlook of his new friends; he began to read Greek and Latin.

He professes a great admiration for the beautiful; he will rave over a Botticelli, snow-covered Alps, the sun setting over the sea, all the things which are regularly and commonly admired; but will not see the simple beauties that are all around him. He is not a humbug; he admires what he admires sincerely and with real enthusiasm; but he can see beauty only if it is pointed out to him. He can discover nothing for himself. He intends to write, but for that he has neither energy, imagination, nor will. He is mechanically industrious, but intellectually lazy. For the last two years he has been studying Leopardi with the purpose of translating some of his works, but as yet has not set pen to paper. Because he has lived so much alone, he has acquired a great conceit of himself. He is scornful of the philistine. He is supercilious. Whenever anyone starts a conversation he will utter a few platitudes with an air of profound wisdom as if he had settled the question and there was nothing more to be said. He is extremely sensitive and is hurt if you do not accept his own opinion of himself. He has a craving for admiration. He is weak, vain and profoundly selfish; but amiable when it costs him nothing to be so and, if you take care to butter him up, sympathetic. He has good taste and a genuine feeling for literature. He has never had an original idea in his life, but he is a sensitive and keen-sighted observer of the obvious.

How happy life would be if an undertaking retained to the end the delight of its beginning, if the dregs of a cup of wine were as sweet as the first sip.

However much you may dislike a relation, and whatever ill you may yourself say of him, you do not like others to say anything which shows him in a ridiculous or objectionable light; since the discredit thrown on your relation reflects upon yourself and wounds your vanity.

At the hospital. Two men were great friends; they lunched together, worked together and played together: they were inseparable. One of them went home for a few days, and in his absence the other got blood-poisoning at a post-mortem and forty-eight hours later died. The first came back; he'd made an appointment to meet his friend in the P.M. room; when he went in he found him lying on a slab naked and dead.

'It gave me quite a turn,' he said when he told me.

I had just come from London. I went into the dining-room and there I saw my old aunt sitting at her table and at work. The lamp was lit. I went up to her and touched her on the shoulder; she gave a little cry and then, seeing it was I, sprang up and put her thin arms round my neck and kissed me.

'Ah, darling boy,' she said, 'I thought I should never see you again.' Then, with a sigh, she leaned her poor old head on my breast: 'I feel so sad, Willie; I know that I am passing away; I shall never see the winter out. I had wished that your dear uncle might go first, so that he might be spared the grief of my death.'

The tears came into my eyes and began to run down my cheeks. Then I knew that I had been dreaming, for I remembered that my aunt had been dead nearly two years, and that, almost before she had slept out the beauty-sleep of death, my uncle had married again.

Last year there was a bad storm in St Ives' Bay and an Italian ship was caught in it. The ship was going down; a rocket was sent, but the sailors didn't seem to know how to use the apparatus; they were in sight of land, with every possibility of saving themselves, and were helpless. Mrs Ellis told me that she stayed at her cottage window, looking at the ship as it sank; the agony was so terrible that at last she felt she could bear it no longer and she went into the kitchen and there spent the night praying.

Most people are such fools that it really is no great compliment to say that a man is above the average.

How ugly most people are! It's a pity they don't try to make up for it by being agreeable.

She's unmarried. She told me that in her opinion marriage was bound to be a failure if a woman could only have one husband at a time.

How the gods must have chuckled when they added Hope to the evils with which they filled Pandora's box, for they knew very well that this was the cruellest evil of them all, since it is Hope that lures mankind to endure its misery to the end.

This morning Caserio Santo, the assassin of President Carnot, was executed; the papers are full of phrases such as: Santo died like a coward.

But surely he didn't; it is true that he trembled so that he could scarcely walk to the scaffold, and his last words were spoken in so weak a voice as hardly to be audible, but these words were the assertion of his faith: *Vive l'Anarchie*. He was faithful to his principles to the last; his mind was as free from cowardice and as firm as when he struck the blow which he knew must be expiated by his own death. That he trembled and could scarcely speak are the signs of the physical terror of death, which the bravest may feel, but that he spoke the words he did shows strange courage. The flesh was weak, but the spirit unconquerable.

1894

These last days everyone has been in a singular state of excitement about a possible war between the English and the French.

A week ago nothing was heard of it; no one dreamt of such an event; but last Saturday the papers began to mention that there were strained relations between the two countries. Even then no word of war was spoken, and when it was suggested everyone laughed at the absurdity. On the following day the papers were more explicit; the cause of the trouble was Madagascar, which the French wished to annex. The papers talked of grave complications and began to suggest that it might be necessary to fight; but still among private people it was looked upon as a groundless scare, for they argued that the French would never be so foolish as to provoke a war; and now to-day, Wednesday, the third of October, the town was startled by an announcement that a Cabinet council had been hastily summoned, the ministers, who were all away, having been suddenly called back to London.

As the day wore on the excitement increased: people talked of the growing jealousy of the French and of their intrigues in Siam and the Congo; papers were eagerly bought, and the articles on the subject, which were accompanied with maps of Madagascar, read. On the Exchange there has been a panic; stocks have fallen and war has been the subject of every conversation: the city men have been talking of volunteering. Wherever you go people ask for news. Everyone is anxious. There is no ill will towards the French, but a firm determination to fight if need be. The Government does not arouse confidence, for it is well known to be divided; and although there is trust in Lord Rosebery, it is common knowledge that some of the other members of the Cabinet are in disagreement with him, and it is thought that they may hinder him from doing anything. There is a general feeling that if England submits to another rebuff from France the Government will be overthrown. The anxiety, the dread of war are great, and there is a general consensus of opinion that though it may be delayed, such is the greed, pride and jealousy of the French, it must eventually break out. But if it does, few people will know its cause; why exactly there should be trouble about Madagascar, no one has the slightest idea.

This evening I went to see some men, and on my way passed two postmen talking of the common topic. When I arrived I found my friends in the same agitated state as everyone else. We spoke of nothing else. We compared the feeling between the French and Germans before the war of 1870 with the feeling now. We talked of Crécy and Agincourt, of Pitt and Wellington. There was a long discussion about the first movements of the war: we talked about what would happen if the French landed an army on the English coast; where they would land; what would be their movements; and how they would be prevented from taking London.

October 4th. The scare is over. The reason of the Cabinet

council has been explained, namely to provide for the safety of British subjects in Pekin, and consequently matters have resumed their former state. The public, however, is somewhat indignant at having been so misled; they ask what need there was to keep secret the motive for suddenly summoning a council, especially as it must have been foreseen that a panic would be caused and a great deal of money lost on the Exchange. The journalists who have been the chief agents in the trouble are angry that they should have been led into such foolishness.

Annandale. I noticed that he had turned two statuettes that were in his room with their faces to the wall, and I asked him why. He said there was so much more character in the back of things.

Annandale: 'I often think life must be quite different to a man called Smith; it can have neither poetry nor distinction.'

He is fond of reading the Bible. 'There always seems to me something so exceedingly French about some of the characters.'

Yesterday evening he made an old joke and I told him I'd heard it a good many times before. Annandale: 'It's quite unnecessary to make new jokes. In fact, I think I rather despise the man who does. He is like the miner who digs up diamonds, but I am the skilful artist who cuts them, polishes them and makes them delightful to the eye of women.'

Later he said: 'I don't see why people shouldn't say what they think of themselves merely because it happens to be complimentary. I'm clever, I know it, and why shouldn't I acknowledge it?'

While I was at St Thomas's Hospital, I lived in furnished rooms at 11 Vincent Square, Westminster. My landlady was a character. I have drawn a slight portrait of her in a novel called Cakes and Ale, *but I did no more than suggest her many excellences. She was kind and she was a good cook. She had common sense and a Cockney humour. She got a lot of fun out of her lodgers. The following are notes I made of her conversation.*

Mrs Foreman went to a concert at the Parish Hall last night with Miss Brown who lets lodgings at number 14. Mr Harris, who keeps the pub round the corner was there: '"Why, that's

Mr Harris," says I, "I'm blowed if it ain't." Miss Brown puts up 'er eyeglass and squints down, and says: "So it is, it's Mr Harris himself." "He is dressed up, ain't he?" says I. "Dressed! Dressed to death and kill the fashion, I call it!" says she. "And you can see his clothes ain't borrowed; they fits him so nice," says I. "'Tain't everyone 'as a suit of dress-clothes, is it?" says she.'

Then to me: 'I tell yer, he did look a caution; he had a great big white flower in his button-hole; and wot with his ole white flower, an' his ole red face, he did look a type and no mistake.'

'Ah yes, I wanted a little boy, and the Lord, He gave me my wish: but I wish He hadn't now; I should 've like to have a little girl, and I should have taught her scrubbin' and the pianoforte and black-leadin' grates and I don't know what all.'

Telling me of a long word someone had used: 'Such an aristocratic word, you know; why, it sounded as if it would break your jaw coming out.'

'Oh, it'll all come right in the end when we get four balls of worsted for a penny.'

'He does look bad: I think he's going home soon.'

My fire was out when I came in, and Mrs Foreman relit it. 'Ask the fire to burn up while I'm away, won't you? And don't look at it, will you? You'll see how nicely it'll burn if you don't.'

'I don't think our boy is very affectionate: he never has been, not even from his childhood. But he knows why I spoil him; he gets up to such hanky-panky-tricks. We do love him. Oh, he is a lump of jam! I feel I could eat him when I'm hungry; some parts of his body are so nice and soft; I could bite them.'

There are two kinds of friendship. The first is a friendship of animal attraction; you like your friend not for any particular qualities or gifts, but simply because you are drawn to him. '*C'est mon ami parce que je l'aime parce que c'est mon ami.*' It is unreasoning and unreasonable; and by the irony of things it is probable that you will have this feeling for someone quite unworthy of it. This kind of friendship, though sex has no active part in it, is really akin to love: it arises in the same way, and it is not improbable that it declines in the same way.

The second kind of friendship is intellectual. You are attracted by the gifts of your new acquaintance. His ideas are unfamiliar; he has seen sides of life of which you are ignorant; his experience is impressive. But every well has a bottom and finally your friend will come to the end of what he has to tell you: this is the moment decisive for the continuation of your friendship. If he has nothing more in him than his experience and his reading have taught him, he can no longer interest or amuse you. The well is empty, and when you let the bucket down, nothing comes up. This explains why one so quickly makes warm friendships with new acquaintances and as quickly breaks them: also the dislike one feels for these persons afterwards, for the disappointment one experiences on discovering that one's admiration was misplaced turns into contempt and aversion. Sometimes, for one reason or another, however, you continue to frequent these people. The way to profit by their society then is to make them yield you the advantages of new friends; by seeing them only at sufficiently long intervals to allow them to acquire fresh experiences and new thoughts. Gradually the disappointment you experienced at the discovery of their shallowness will wear off, habit brings with it an indulgence for their defects and you may keep up a pleasant friendship with them for many years. But if, having got to the end of your friend's acquired knowledge, you find that he has something more, character, sensibility and a restless mind, then your friendship will grow stronger, and you will have a relationship as delightful in its way as the other friendship of physical attraction.

It is conceivable that these two friendships should find their object in one and the same person; that would be the perfect friend. But to ask for that is to ask for the moon. On the other hand, when, as sometimes happens, there is an animal attraction on one side and an intellectual one on the other, only discord can ensue.

When you are young friendship is very important, and every new friend you make is an exciting adventure. I do not remember who the persons were who occasioned these confused reflections, but since extreme youth is apt to make general rules from single instances, I surmise that I had found my feeling for someone to whom I was drawn unreciprocated, and that somebody else, whose mind had interested me, proved less intelligent than I had thought.

I do not know that in the ordinary affairs of life philosophy is of much more use than to enable us to make a virtue of necessity. By showing us the advantages of a step which we are forced to take, but would not of our own free will, it consoles us a little for its unpleasantness. It helps us to do with equanimity what we would rather not do.

In love one should exercise economy of intercourse. None of us can love for ever. Love will be stronger and last longer if there are impediments to its gratification. If a lover is prevented from enjoying his love by absence, difficulty of access, or by the caprice or coldness of his beloved, he can find a little consolation in the thought that when his wishes are fulfilled his delight will be intense. But love being what it is, should there be no such hindrances, he will pay no attention to the considerations of prudence; and his punishment will be satiety. The love that lasts longest is the love that is never returned.

It is doubtless true that we owe many of our virtues to Christianity, but it is equally true that we owe to it some of our vices. The love of self is the mainspring of every man's action, it is the essence of his character; and it is fair to suppose that it is necessary for his preservation. But Christianity has made a vice of it. It has decided that man should have neither love, nor care, nor thought for himself, but only for his soul, and by demanding of him that he should behave otherwise than as his nature prompts, has forced him into hypocrisy. It has aroused a sense of guilt in him when he follows his natural instincts, and a feeling of resentment when others, even though not at his expense, follow theirs. If selfishness were not regarded as a vice no one would be more inconvenienced by it than he is by the Law of Gravity; no one would expect his fellow-men to act otherwise than according to their own interests; and it would seem reasonable to him that they should behave as selfishly as in point of fact they do.

It is a good maxim to ask of no one more than he can give without inconvenience to himself.

The belief in God is not a matter of common sense, or logic, or argument, but of feeling. It is as impossible to prove the existence of God as to disprove it. I do not believe in God. I see no need of such an idea. It is incredible to me that there should be an after-life. I find the notion of future punishment outrageous and of future reward extravagant. I am convinced that when I die, I shall cease entirely to live; I shall return to the earth I came from. Yet I can imagine that at some future date I may believe in God; but it will be as now, when I don't believe in Him, not a matter of reasoning or of observation, but only of feeling.

If you once grant the existence of God, I do not see why you should hesitate to believe in the Resurrection, and if you once grant the supernatural I do not see why you should put limits to it. The miracles of Catholicism are as well authenticated as those of the New Testament.

The evidence adduced to prove the truth of one religion is of very much the same sort as that adduced to prove the truth of another. I wonder that it does not make the Christian uneasy to reflect that if he had been born in Morocco he would have been a Mahometan, if in Ceylon a Buddhist; and in that case Christianity would have seemed to him as absurd and obviously untrue as those religions seem to the Christian.

The Professor of Gynaecology. He began his course of lectures as follows: Gentlemen, woman is an animal that micturates once a day, defecates once a week, menstruates once a month, parturates once a year and copulates whenever she has the opportunity.

I thought it a prettily-balanced sentence.

1896

I don't suppose anyone's life is ruled by his philosophy; his philosophy is an expression of his desires, instincts and weaknesses. The other night, talking to B., I got him to tell me the system of ideas he had devised to give sense to his life.

The highest object in life, he said, is to bring out one's own personality and that one does by following one's instincts, by letting oneself be carried on the waves of human things and by submitting oneself to all the accidents of fate and fortune. Then finally one is purified by these accidents as by fire and thus made fit for a future life. The power of loving that he has in him persuades him that there is a God and an immortality. He believes that Love, taken on its sensual as well as on its spiritual side, purifies. There is no happiness in this world, nothing but moments of contentment, and the lack of happiness and the immense desire of it afford another proof of immortality. He denies the need of self-sacrifice, asserting that the beginning, middle and end of all endeavour is the development of oneself; but he is not unwilling to allow that self-sacrifice may at times conduce to this.

I asked him to explain the promiscuity of his amours. It vexed him a little, but he answered that his sexual instincts were very strong, and that he was really only in love with an ideal. He found traits and characteristics to love in many different persons, and by the number of these built up his ideal just as a sculptor, taking a feature here, a feature there, a fine form, a fine line, might finally create a figure of perfect beauty.

But it is obvious that in the development of oneself and the following of one's instincts, one is certain to come in contact with other people. So I asked B. what he would say to a man whose instinct it was to rob or murder. He answered that society found the instinct harmful and therefore punished the man for it.

'But then,' I said, 'what if he follows his instinct, so as not to infringe any of the laws of society, but yet so as to do harm to others? Thus he may fall in love with a married woman, persuade her to leave her home, husband and family, and come to live with him; and then getting tired of her or falling in love with someone else, leave her.'

To this his reply was: 'Well, then I should say that he may follow his instincts only so far as to do no harm to other people.'

In which case obviously the theory falls to the ground. These, it is plain, are the ideas of a weak man, who has not the strength to combat his desires, but yields like a feather to every wind that blows. And indeed B. has no will, no self-restraint, no courage against any of the accidents of fortune. If he cannot smoke he is wretched; if his food or his wine is bad he is upset; a wet day shatters him. If he doesn't feel well, he is silent, cast down and melancholy. The slightest cross, even a difference of opinion, will make him angry and sullen. He is a selfish creature, indifferent to other people's feelings, and the only thing that makes him behave with a semblance of decency is his conventional view of the conduct proper to an English gentleman. He would not cross the road to help a friend, but he would never fail to rise to his feet when a woman entered the room.

People are never so ready to believe you as when you say things in dispraise of yourself; and you are never so much annoyed as when they take you at your word.

You worry me as if I was a proverb you were trying to turn into an epigram.

Anyone can tell the truth, but only very few of us can make epigrams.

In the nineties, however, we all tried to.

'Do you know French?'

'Oh, well, you know, I can read a French novel when it's indecent.'

Cockney.

'You are a 'andsome woman.' 'Yes, abaht the feet.'

'You've said that before.' 'Well, I say it be'ind now.'

'A 'andsome young man with a Roman shiped eye an' a cast in 'is nose.'

'How about our Sunday boots now?'

'You're very clever! 'Ow many did yer mother 'ave like you?'

'Yus, I've 'ad fifteen children, an' only two 'usbinds ter do it on.'

'Ah, wot a blessin' it 'ud be for your family if the Lord see fit ter tike yer.'

'I've 'ad two 'usbinds in my time, an' I 'ope to 'ave another before I die.'

'I do love yer, Florrie.' 'Pore feller, wot you must suffer!'

A woman may be as wicked as she likes, but if she isn't pretty it won't do her much good.

'Oh, I should hate to be old. All one's pleasures go.'

'But others come.'

'What?'

'Well, for instance, the contemplation of youth. If I were your age I think it not improbable that I should think you a rather conceited and bumptious man: as it is I consider you a charming and amusing boy.'

I can't for the life of me remember who said this to me. Perhaps my Aunt Julia. Anyhow I'm glad I thought it worth making a note of.

There is a pleasant irony in the gilded youth who goes to the devil all night and to eight o'clock Mass next morning.

At a dinner party one should eat wisely but not too well, and talk well but not too wisely.

The intellect is such a pliable and various weapon that man, provided with it, is practically bereft of all others; but it is a weapon of no great efficacy against instinct.

The history of human morals is very well brought to light in the course of literature: the writer, with whatever subject he deals, displays the code of morals of his own age. That is the great fault of historical novels; the characters portrayed, while they do acts which are historical, comport themselves according to the moral standard of the writer's time. The inconsequence is obvious.

People often feed the hungry so that nothing may disturb their own enjoyment of a good meal.

In moments of great excitement the common restraints of civilisation lose their force, and men return to the old law of a tooth for a tooth.

It is a false idea of virtue which thinks it demands the sacrifice of inclination and consists only in this sacrifice. An action is not virtuous merely because it is unpleasant to do.

The life of most men is merely a ceaseless toil to prepare food and home for their offspring; and these enter the world to perform exactly the same offices as their progenitors.

The more intelligent a man is the more capable is he of suffering.

If women exhibit less emotion at pain it does not prove that they bear it better, but rather that they feel it less.

That love is chiefly the instinct for the propagation of the species shows itself in the fact that most men will fall in love with any woman in their way, and not being able to get the first woman on whom they have set their heart, soon turn to a second.

It is but seldom that a man loves once and for all; it may only show that his sexual instincts are not very strong.

As soon as the instinct of propagation has been satisfied, the madness which blinded the lover disappears and leaves him with a wife to whom he is indifferent.

I do not know what is meant by abstract beauty. The beautiful is that which excites the aesthetic sense in the artist. What is beautiful to an artist to-day will be beautiful to all and sundry in ten years. Not so many years ago everyone would have said that nothing was more hideous than factory chimneys with black smoke belching from them; but certain artists discovered in them a decorative quality and painted them; they were laughed at at first, but little by little people saw beauty in their pictures and then looking at what they had painted saw beauty there too. It does not now require great perspicacity to receive as great a thrill of delight from a factory with its chimneys as from a green field with its flowers.

People wonder at the romantic lives of poets and artists, but they should rather wonder at their gift of expression. The occurrences which pass unnoticed in the life of the average man in the existence of a writer of talent are profoundly interesting. It is the man they happen to that makes their significance.

Men have an extraordinarily erroneous opinion of their position in nature; and the error is ineradicable.

If the good were only a little less heavy-footed!

The philosopher is like a mountaineer who has with difficulty climbed a mountain for the sake of the sunrise, and arriving at the top finds only fog; whereupon he wanders down again. He must be an honest man if he doesn't tell you that the spectacle was stupendous.

To-day reasons are hardly necessary to refute Christianity; there is a feeling in the air against it, and since religion is itself a feeling, feeling is the instrument to cope with it. One man has faith and the other hasn't; and there perhaps is the end of it: their respective arguments are only rationalisations of their feelings.

Those who live for the world and work for the world naturally demand the world's approval. But the man who lives for himself neither expects nor is affected by the world's approval. If he is indifferent to Tom, Dick and Harry, why should he care what they think of him?

The power of great joy is balanced by an equal power of great sorrow. Enviable is the man who feels little, so that he is un-affected either by the extremes of bliss or of grief. In the greatest happiness there is still an after-taste of bitterness, while misery is unalloyed.

No man in his heart is quite so cynical as a well-bred woman.

The usual result of a man's cohabitation with a woman, however sanctioned by society, is to make him a little more petty, a little meaner than he would otherwise have been.

Man's ideal of a woman is still the princess in the fairy-tale who could not sleep upon seven mattresses because a dried pea was beneath the undermost. He is always rather frightened of a woman who has no nerves.

An acquaintance with the rudiments of physiology will teach you more about feminine character than all the philosophy and wise-saws in the world.

It goes hard with a woman who fails to adapt herself to the prevalent masculine conception of her.

There is nothing like love to make a man alter his opinions. For new opinions are mostly new emotions. They are the result not of thought, but of passion.

Half the difficulties of man, half the uncertainties, lie in his desire to answer every question with *Yes* or *No*. *Yes* or *No* may neither of them be the answer; each side may have in it some *Yes* and some *No*.

I am never so happy as when a new thought occurs to me and a new horizon gradually discovers itself before my eyes. A fresh idea dawns upon me and I feel myself uplifted from the workaday world to the blue empyrean of the spirit. Detached for a moment from all earthly cares I seem to walk on air.

There are times when I look over the various parts of my character with perplexity. I recognize that I am made up of several persons and that the person which at the moment has the upper hand will inevitably give place to another. But which is the real me? All of them or none?

Life cannot fail to be amusing to me when there are so many errors and misconceptions in which I'm enmeshed and which I can tear away. To destroy the prejudices which from my youth have been instilled into me is in itself an occupation and an entertainment.

I wonder when Christianity will have sufficiently decayed for the fact to be driven out of men's heads that pleasure is not hurtful nor pain beneficial.

People continually ruin their lives by persisting in actions against which their sensations rebel.

It occurs to few people that a man who sits out in the rain for a noble object is just as likely to get rheumatism as the drunkard who lies out because he is too drunk to get home – even more so.

If you don't deny yourself for others they look upon you as detestably selfish; but they bear with astonishing fortitude the ills you may incur by the sacrifices you have made for their sakes. There are no feminine characteristics more marked than a passion for detail and an unerring memory. Women can give you an exact and circumstantial account of some quite insignificant conversation with a friend years before; and what is worse, they do.

Pain is hurtful and the notion that pain ennobles is absurd. Nietzsche with his glorification of suffering is like the fox in the fable who had lost his tail. His argument that pain strengthens the character resolves itself into the fact that a man who has suffered wants revenge. What he takes for strength is merely the pleasure he finds in inflicting upon others the anguish he has himself endured.

Our conduct towards our fellow-men is determined by the principle of self-preservation. The individual acts towards his fellows in such and such a manner so as to obtain advantages which otherwise he could not get or to avoid evils which they might inflict upon him. He has no debt towards society; he acts in a certain way to receive benefits, society accepts his useful action and pays for it. Society rewards him for the good he does it and punishes him for the harm.

It is not in a cathedral, or confronted with any mighty human work, that I feel the insignificance of man; then I am impressed rather with his power; his mind seems capable of every feat, and I forget that he is an insignificant creature crawling on a speck of mud, the planet of a minor sun. Nature and art, even against one's will, persuade one of the grandeur of man; and it is only science that reveals his utter insignificance.

Science is the consoler and the healer of troubles, for it teaches how little things matter and how unimportant is life with all its failures.

To eschew pleasures because they are fleeting or are followed by satiety is as stupid as to refuse to eat because one's appetite is soon appeased and after one has satisfied it one is not hungry.

It is quite as difficult to fit one's practice to one's precepts as to fit one's precepts to one's practice. Most people act in one way and preach in another. When the fact is brought to their notice, they assert that it is their weakness, and that their desire is to act up to their principles. That is pretence. People act according to their inclinations and adopt principles; because these are generally at variance with their inclinations they are ill-at-ease and unstable. But when they force themselves to act up to their principles and suppress their inclinations, there is no hope for them – but in heaven.

That generosity is almost always praised above justice shows that people assess qualities by their value to themselves. The just man who gives none more than his due is disliked rather than admired.

One of the most absurd statements imaginable is that because pleasures cannot be expressed in mathematical terms, they must be worthless.

The position of the individual towards society is the same as that of individual towards individual. When A helps B to build a house on the understanding that B will help A when occasion arises, B performs his part of the contract so that he may afterwards get the benefit he requires.

Because a man does not state in so many words the reason that leads him to some action, it does not follow that he is led by no reason. Because he does not even know the reason, it does not follow that there is none. And giving himself one, he may be again mistaken and give the wrong one.

One's relation to society is the same as that of the savage who is restrained from acting to the detriment of his fellows by fear of the vengeance they will take on him.

If morality has evolved with the evolution of society, as means to social self-preservation, it has not necessarily anything to do with the individual.

It is odd that in so many cases the individual conscience should judge according to the precepts of society.

Man's duty is to exercise all his functions, permitting none to overbear the others. When between man and man there are innumerable differences how can there be a common system of morality?

The difficulty is to find the common denominator that governs the actions of men.

Most people pay eighteenpence for every shilling they get. In putting aside an immediate advantage for one more remote, one has to be certain that the more remote is greater. Remoteness in itself is no advantage.

Altruism without pleasure, immediate or remote, is absurd. When one expects unselfishness from another and does not get it, one can only shrug one's shoulder and pass on. Certainly one has no right to be angry.

What if an individual does not care if his race survives? What if he is not prepared for the sacrifice entailed by propagation of his species?

Unselfish parents have selfish children. It is not the children's fault. It is natural that they should accept the sacrifices their parents make for them as their right; and how should they know that in this world you get nothing for nothing?

From the standpoint of pure reason, there are no good grounds to support the claim that one should sacrifice one's own happiness to that of others.

Even if it is held that pure unselfishness without after-thought gives most pleasure and brings the greatest rewards, that pleasure and those rewards are still its justification.

There would be very little altruism in the world if it were not a source of pleasure. In some way or other everyone expects a return for his unselfishness. There is no such thing as absolute altruism. Social altruism means no more than that there is often an advantage to the individual in sacrificing himself for others. The only self-sacrifice which is primordial is that which has to do with the production and rearing of young. But here the strongest of animal instincts is concerned, and extreme discomfort, real pain even, ensues if its exercise is thwarted. Parents are foolish when they accuse their children of ingratitude; they should remember that what they have done for them was for their own pleasure.

There can be nothing praiseworthy in sacrifice in itself, and before a man does a self-sacrificing thing, he may reasonably ask himself if it is worth while; but it proves how intense a pleasure there is in self-sacrifice that people are willing to sacrifice themselves for the most ignoble objects.

It is a great pleasure to confer favours upon another; and it is a pleasure which is increased by the praise of the world; but the giver seldom considers whether his favours will be welcome. Nor is he satisfied with the pleasure he has obtained: he demands gratitude into the bargain.

Pleasures are largely a matter of opinion. They change like women's fashions, and a pleasure that is fashionable is doubly desirable. Actions which are not in themselves pleasurable can be made by fashion the source of keen delight.

To-day persons pursue no pleasures so avidly as the luxury of pity and goodness. I think it was unjust to accuse the women in the Boer War of going to the Cape merely for a pleasant change and to flirt with soldiers: the pleasures that attracted them were more definite and less hackneyed.

Few misfortunes can befall a boy which bring worse consequences than to have a really affectionate mother.

The relations between the individual and society are like a roulette table. Society is the banker. Individuals sometimes win and sometimes lose; but the banker wins always.

They say that sympathy with pain, long continued, turns into callousness; but does not sympathy with pleasure do the same?

Ideal pleasure, that is pleasure imagined, cannot be so vivid as pleasure experienced.

However harmless a thing is, if the law forbids it most people will think it wrong.

We hear much of the nobility of labour; but there is nothing noble in work in itself. Looking at early societies, we see that when warfare was rampant, work was despised and soldiering honoured. Now that the vast majority are workmen, work is honoured. The fact is simply that men in their self-conceit look upon their particular activities as the noblest object of man.

Work is lauded because it takes men out of themselves. Stupid persons are bored when they have nothing to do. Work with the majority is their only refuge from ennui; but it is comic to call it noble for that reason. It requires many talents and much cultivation to be idle, or a peculiarly constituted mind.

It is notorious that persistence in any course, however immoral to the ordinary mind, robs it of any idea of immorality.

If you only tell people often enough that they must do such and such a thing, they will end by doing it, and never ask you why. And if you only tell people often enough that such and such a thing is right, they will end by believing you; and possibly they will believe you with greater readiness if you give no reason.

I would not disapprove the bloody wars of civilized nations against uncivilized; but it is as well to note that the only justification for them is that might is right. It is an unequal encounter, a contest without nobility or chivalry between good weapons and bad. To say that a vanquished barbaric people gain in happiness when the civilisation of their conquerors is forced upon them is hypocrisy. Is there any reason to suppose that they are less happy in their primitive state than when, compelled to accept a culture they do not want and reforms they see no need for, they are ruled by an alien law?

People starting with the idea that certain things are right and are the law, come to believe that others are right because they are the law.

The English, after the first defeats of the Boer War, were continually applauding themselves on their superior numbers. The end of war being to win, superior numbers are evidently essential; but to win by means of them appeals neither to chivalry, heroism nor sentiment. It is odd how quickly people who set store on these virtues forgot them when things began to look black. The moral to be drawn is: be as chivalrous as you like so long as you have the best of it; but if you haven't – well, see that you do and never mind about the chivalry.

My object is to find a rule of conduct for the average man under the normal conditions of the present day.

Can the perfect adaptation of man to society ever take place? It may be that the sheer struggle for existence will be put an end to, but will that effect the end desired? There will still be the fact that some are weak and some are strong. The physical needs of one are not the same as those of another. Some will always be more beautiful than others. The greater talents of some will bring them greater rewards. The unsuccessful will continue to envy the successful. Men will always grow old, and not feeling their age, insist on retaining the perquisites of youth till they are violently wrested from them. Even though every other reason for discord were removed, differences will arise in sexual matters. No man will give up the woman he cares for because another man wants her. Wherever there is love, there cannot fail to be hatred, malice, jealousy, rage. However willing people may be to surrender their own gratification to the common good, it is hard to believe that they will ever surrender their children's. Men do not change: passions are always likely to be awaked and the brutal instincts of the savage to reassert their domination.

It is seldom realized that youth and age must have their different codes. Laws are made by staid or old men who seek unreasonably to restrain the exuberance of youth. But youth has a right to its fling. The old can talk till they're blue in the face about the spiritual satisfaction to be found in art and literature, but when you're young there's a lot more fun to be got out of having a girl than by listening to a sonata.

The evils incident on peace might be shown by a study of those peoples whose circumstances have preserved them from war. The wood-veddahs and the Esquimaux are races unacquainted with war, but their immunity does not seem to have brought them to a high state of cultivation.

The altruistic activities of the individual arise from egoistic motives. A man will not agitate for the removal of an abuse till he himself has felt the harm of it. But he must have the power to make himself heard: the poor must endure in silence.

The moral ideas of the present day are so ingrained that the philosopher only feels perfectly sure of himself when his conclusions bring him in accordance with current opinion. If opinion were different he would be led to agree with it by arguments as keen and reasons as cogent.

There are few minds in a century that can look upon a new idea without terror. Fortunately for the rest of us, there are very few new ideas about.

If one pursuit has come to be considered nobler than another it is either because it was at one time more essential, as for example the pursuit of arms; or because, as in the arts, its practitioners in their vanity have never ceased to glorify it. A marvellous instance of the gullibility of man is that he has been willing to take the artists at their own valuation. It must often surprise the writer to see with what respect his opinions are received by men who in their own field are as competent as himself.

If the actions and ideas of men had any importance whatever there would certainly be no excuse for the human race. Men are mean, petty, muddle-headed, ignoble, bestial from their cradles to their death-beds; ignorant, slaves now of one superstition, now of another, and illiberal; selfish and cruel.

Tolerance is only another name for indifference.

Now after nearly two years in which I have occupied myself in looking for some rule, in which I have asked myself what is the reason, the aim, the object of life, I just begin to have a vague notion of what I take to be the truth. Answers to all these questions are slowly forming themselves in my mind; but at present everything is confused. I have collected a mass of facts, ideas, experience, but I cannot yet arrange them into any system or order them in a definite pattern.

It is the necessities of life which generate ideas of right and wrong.

The ideals with which youth is brought up, the fairy tales and phantasies upon which his mind is fed, unfit him for life; so that till his illusions are shattered, he is miserably unhappy. And for all this useless misery are responsible the half-educated persons, mother, nurse, masters, who surround him with their loving care.

The relations of the sexes are dependent upon external circumstances. War and the slaughter of men has induced polygamy; and infertile country has induced polyandry. Now that population is so vastly increased, and the difficulty of earning a living and supporting children is so great, prostitution will naturally increase. The young man cannot afford to marry and he must have sexual gratification. What will happen to the women?

Prostitution will have to be legally as well as tacitly recognized. The chastity of women before marriage will come to be considered of less moment.

I was wrong about prostitution, but right about chastity.

Why should not one cultivate sensations? Pleasure arises from sensations gratified; whether solicited or not. It is only their after-effects that must be considered. When Spencer says it is wrong to solicit sensations, he is influenced by his Wesleyan birth, the influence of which he has never escaped. He expressly approves the pursuit of aesthetic delights such as are found in travelling.

One can only rule men by dogmatic affirmations. That is why men of strong opinions, prejudices and enthusiasms, and not philosophers, are the leaders of the people. But the philosophers console themselves by thinking that they do not want to lead an ignoble rabble.

A moral code is only accepted by the weakminded; the strong form their own.

Capri. I wander about alone, forever asking myself the same questions: What is the meaning of life? Has it any object or end? Is there such a thing as morality? How ought one to conduct oneself in life? What guide is there? Is there one road better than another? And a hundred more of the same sort. The other afternoon I was scrambling among the rocks and boulders up the hill behind the villa. Above me was the blue sky and all around the sea. Hazy in the distance was Vesuvius. I remember the brown earth, the ragged olive trees, and here and there a pine. And I stopped suddenly, in confusion, my head buzzing with all the thoughts that seethed in it. I could make nothing out of it all; it seemed to me one big tangle. In desperation, I cried out: I can't understand it. I don't know, I don't know.

A rough day in the Bay of Naples. The Neapolitans vomited great platefuls of undigested macaroni. They vomited with a sudden rush, like water escaping from a burst main, and their gaping mouths gave them the stupid, agonised look of a fish out of water, but you can't bang them on the head and put them out of their misery as you do with a fish you've caught. Besides, you have nothing to bang them with.

I suppose it is to the Jews that we owe our idea of the sanctity of home life. They found in their home safety and peace from the turmoil and persecution of the world without. It was their only refuge and so they loved it, but they loved it because of their weakness. The Greeks seem to have had no home life. No one has accused them of domesticity. Full of energy, eager, abounding as perhaps no other people has been with the joy of living, they looked upon the world as a battle place; and the din of warfare, the shouts of triumph, even the groans of the vanquished were music in their ears. They flung themselves into the business of life as a fearless swimmer breasts the waves.

One of the commonest errors of the human intelligence is to insist that a rule should be universally applicable. Take an instance in Anatomy. Out of twenty cases the branch of an artery in eight will arise from the second part of the root, in six from the first, and in six from the third. Though the exceptions surpass it, the rule will be that it arises from the second part.

The great majority use quite ignobly the portion of intelligence they have over after providing for their self-preservation and the propagation of their species.

I think it possible that, having arrived at a certain high stage of civilization, men will wilfully revert to barbarism; or fall back from inability to maintain the high level they have reached.

Everything in life is meaningless, the pain and the suffering are fruitless and futile. There is no object in life. To nature nothing matters but the continuation of the species. And is not this last a hasty proposition based on over-brief periods of time, the observation of an eye that sees but a little way?

May death cover my years with night.

1897

The spirituality of man is most apparent when he is eating a hearty dinner.

T. was standing at a railway station; a woman came up to him and told him that he had prosecuted her in a criminal action, and he was so kind that she wanted to thank him. She wanted above all to assure him that she was innocent. He couldn't even remember her face. What to her was a tragic and dreadful ordeal to him was no more than a drab little incident which had slipped his memory.

A Thames waterman was in love with a girl and couldn't take her on the spree for lack of money. He saw a body in the water, a man who gave some last signs of life; but he got no money for saving a live man, so he put his hook in his clothes and dragged him in. The man was landed, and a bystander said he wasn't quite dead. The waterman turned upon him and blackguarded him. He laid the man on his face and effectually prevented him from recovering. So he got his five shillings and took his donah out.

Three women were charged at the police court. They were whores. Two were strong and healthy, but the third was dying of consumption. The first two had money and paid their fines, but the third had none. Fourteen days. In a little while the two came back, having pawned their jackets notwithstanding the cold, and paid the fine. They refused to let the girl go to the workhouse infirmary. 'We'll see the last of her,' they said, and all three went into a brothel. They looked after the dying girl for a month, and then she died. They paid for her funeral, to which they went, each with a wreath, in new black dresses, driving in a cab behind the hearse.

A woman sat looking at her husband. He was in bed drunk, and it was the twentieth anniversary of their wedding. When she married him she thought she was going to be happy. Married to an idler, a drunkard and a brute, her life had been one of hardship and of misery. She went into the next room and took poison. She was taken to St Thomas's and recovered, but then was charged at the police court with attempted suicide. She said nothing to excuse herself, but her daughter stood up and told the magistrate all her mother had had to suffer. She was given a separation order under which she was to receive fifteen shillings a week. The husband signed the deed of separation and, having done this, put down fifteen shillings, saying: 'Here's your first week's money.' She picked it up and flung it in his face. 'Take your money,' she screamed, 'give me back my twenty years.'

The other day I went into the theatre to see a Caesarian. Because it's rarely done it was full. Before starting Dr C. made a short discourse. I didn't listen very attentively, but I seem to remember his saying that the operation so far was seldom successful. He told us that the patient couldn't have a child naturally and had had to be twice aborted; but she'd set her heart on having one now that she was pregnant again and though he'd explained the danger to her and said that it was only an even chance that she'd come through, she'd told him that she was prepared to risk it. Her husband wanted it too, and that seemed to weigh with her. The operation appeared to go very well and Dr C's face beamed when he extracted the baby. This morning I was in the ward and asked one of the nurses how she was getting on. She told me she'd died in the night. I don't know why, it gave me a shock and I had to frown because I was afraid I was going to cry. It was silly, I didn't know her, I'd only seen her on the operating table. I suppose what affected me was the passion of that woman, just an ordinary hospital patient, to have a baby, a passion so intense that she was willing to incur the frightful risk; it seemed hard, dreadfully hard, that she had to die. The nurse told me the baby was doing well. That poor woman.

The *cri du cœur* is never without its effect, but the odd thing is that it need never come from the heart at all; it need only be perfectly simulated, and the trick is done.

A big dinner-party is merely an opportunity for the common indulgence of sensual appetites.

The Vicar expounded twice on Sunday the more obvious parts of the Scriptures, in twenty minutes or so, making for the benefit of the vulgar a number of trite reflections in a slovenly language compounded from the Authorised Version and the daily version. He had a great facility for explaining earnestly and at decorous lengths texts which were plain to the poorest intelligence. His offertories were devoted alternately to the poor of the parish and to the necessities of the church. He saw a connection between the need for coal to warm the vestry and for candles to light the altar and the dogmas of religion. So on these occasions he made it his practice to attack the scarlet weeds of heresy, expounding to an intelligent congregation of yokels and small boys, the difficulties of the Athanasian Creed. But he was at his best when he poured the withering vials of his contempt on the false crowd of Atheists, Romanists, Dissenters and Scientists. He could barely keep serious in his scorn for the theories of evolution; and would set up like a row of ninepins the hypotheses of philosophers and learned men and knock them down by the aid of his own fearless intellect. It might have been a dangerous experiment but that his congregation were convinced beyond the need of argument of the faith of their fathers, and not very attentive listeners.

1900

When a woman of forty tells a man that she's old enough to be his mother, his only safety is in immediate flight. She'll either marry him or drag him through the divorce court.

One should always cultivate one's prejudices.

Cornwall. The wind dragged up the sea by its roots and the water in heavy dark masses hurled itself against the rocks.

Overhead the sky was in frantic motion, the tormented clouds raced across the night and the wind whistled and hissed and screamed.

Fragments of cloud, tortured and rent, fled across the sky like the silent souls of anguish pursued by the vengeance of a jealous God.

There was a moaning of thunder in the distance and one by one fell the first rain-drops; they were like the tears of God.

The wind was like a charioteer in a chariot, and the horses, muscles straining, quivered in their traces; he lashed them furiously with his whip and they sprang forwards with a rush and a whirl, and the morning air was rent with a long, shrill scream as though women in panic fled a danger there was no escaping.

I wandered at random, and the soft ground, broken by the tortuous courses of a hundred streamlets, with its carpet of brown, dead leaves, exhaled an odour of moist soil, the voluptuous scents of our mother, the Earth, gravid with silent life. The long branches of the briar-rose entangled my feet. Here and there, in sheltered corners, blossomed the primrose and the violet. The delicate branches of the beech trees were black amid the young leaves, vivid and tender, that had but just burst their buds. It was an emerald paradise. The eye could not pierce that intricate greenery. It was a filagree finer upon the slender twigs than the summer rain and more subtle than the mists of sunset. It was as intangible as a beautiful thought. It was a scene that drove away all thought of the sadness and the bitterness of life. The verdure was so pure that my mind became pure also and I felt like a child. Here and there, far above the other trees, rose a fir, immensely tall, straight as a life without reproach; but cheerless, cold and silent. The only sound was the rustling of a rabbit among the dead leaves or the hasty springing of a squirrel.

After the rain, in the evening, the birds broke into such a joyous chant that it seemed impossible that it was a world of sorrow. Hidden among the leaves, aloft in the beeches, the starling sang with full-throated melody; and the bullfinch and the thrush. From a distant meadow a cuckoo called with endless repetition, and far away, like an echo, a second cuckoo called back.

The Green Park in Winter.

The snow fell lightly as the footsteps of children. The snow lay masking the trim pathways, shrouding the trodden grass, the snow as far as one could see, on the housetops, on the trees. The sky was low, heavy with the cruel cold, and the light was grey and dim. In a long line gleamed the round lamps, and entangled with the leafless trees was a violet mist, and it trailed along the ground like the train of the winter night. The piercing cold had killed the other colours, but the mist was violet, exquisitely soft, but cold, cold so that the weary heart could scarcely endure its anguish. The houses of Carlton House Terrace were dark menacing masses against the whiteness of the snow. The day dwindled away in a ghostly silence, and there was no glimpse even of the setting sun. The grey sky grew darker, and the lights gleamed more brightly, surrounded each one by a pale aureole.

London. The western clouds of the sunset were like the vast wing of an archangel, flying through the void on an errand of vengeance; and the fiery shadow cast a lurid light upon the city.

The buttercups were spread over the green meadow like a cloth of gold, a carpet for the king's son Fleur-de-Lys, and Jonquil the white-limbed shepherd's boy.

Over the trees, entangled in the naked branches, floated the thin black clouds like the rags of some ample sinuous garment.

The thin black clouds dragged themselves through the tree tops, tearing raggedly among the naked branches.

The aerial, oceanic petrel.

The dark immovable clouds were piled upon one another in giant masses, so distinct and sharply cut, so rounded, that one almost saw the impression of the fingers of a titanic sculptor.

There was a clump of tall fir trees, dark and ragged, their sombre green veiled in a silver mist, as though the hoar-frost of a hundred winters had endured into the summer as a chill vapour. In front of them, at the edge of the hill up which in serried hundreds climbed the pine trees, stood here and there an oak just bursting into leaf, clothed with its new-born verdure like the bride of a young god. And the everlasting youth of the oak trees contrasted, like day and night, with the undying age of the fir.

The fir trees were like the forest of life, that grey and sombre labyrinth where wandered the poet of Hell and Death.

The fields were fresh with the tall young grass of spring, the buttercups flaunted themselves gaily, careless of the pitiless night, and rejoiced in the sunshine as before they had rejoiced in the enlivening rain. The pleasant raindrops still lingered on the daisies. The feathery ball of the dandelion, carried away by the breeze, floated past, a symbol of the life of man, an aimless thing, yielding to every breath, useless and with no mission but to spread its seed upon the fertile earth, so that things like unto it should spring up in the succeeding summer and flower, uncared for, and reproduce themselves and die.

I didn't know then how succulent a salad can be made of this humble herb.

The hawthorn hedges, well-trimmed and flourishing, were putting out their tiny buds, and here and there, already in full flower, bloomed the wild rose.

At sunset over the slate-grey of the western clouds was spread a fiery vapour, a rain of infinitesimal tenuity, a great dust of gold that swept down upon the silent sea like the train of a goddess of fire; and presently, thrusting through the sombre wall of cloud like a titan bursting the walls of his prison, the sun shone forth, a giant ball of copper. With almost a material effort, it seemed, it pushed aside the obstructing clouds, filling the whole sky with brilliancy; and then over the placid sea was stretched a broad roadway of flame upon which might travel the passionate souls of men, endlessly, to the source of deathless light.

The clouds hung over the valley pregnant with rain; and it gave a singular feeling of discomfort to see them laden with water and yet still painfully holding it up.

The pine wood was cool and silent, fitting my humour. The tall trunks, straight and slender like the masts of sailing boats; the gentle aromatic odour; the light subdued; and the purple mist, so tenuous as to be scarcely discernible, a mere tinge of warmth in the atmosphere—it all gave me an exquisite sense of rest. My footfall on the brown needles was noiseless, and the tread was soft and easy. The odours filled me with a drowsy intoxication, like an Eastern drug. The tints were so soft that one could not believe it possible for paints and paint-brushes to reproduce them; the faintly-coloured air visibly surrounded things and softened their outlines. A pleasant reverie possessed me, unanalysable, a waking dream of half-voluptuous emotion.

How fortunate is his lot who can accept the charming emotions that Nature gives him without trying to analyse the charm!

The wind sighed through the pine trees with the pitifulness of a girl sighing for a love that was dead.

The field all yellow with countless buttercups, a spring carpet whereon might fitly walk the angels of Messer Perugino.

It was a concert of endless variety; in every hedgerow, in the branches of every tree, hidden among the leaves, sang the birds. Each one, as though trying to outsing the rest, sang as if his life depended on it, and as if life were irresponsible and joyous.

The country was undulating and afforded spacious views of verdant hills and fat Kentish fields. It was the most fertile part of the county and thickly wooded. Elms, oak trees and chestnuts. Each generation had done its best, and the country was tended like a garden.

It was a landscape as formal as Poussin's or Claude's. It had no abandon, no freedom; the hand of man was perpetually obvious in the trimness and in the careful arrangement.

Sometimes, from a hill a little higher than the rest, I could look down into the plain bathed in sunlight, golden and dazzling.

The fields of corn, the fields of clover, the roads and the rivulets, formed themselves, in that flood of light, into an harmonious pattern, glowing and ethereal.

A square white house of stucco, with two great bow windows and a veranda overgrown with honeysuckle and the monthly rose. Nature could do little to beautify the hideous structure, a bastard product of Georgian architecture and merciless common-sense. Yet it had an air of comfort and of solidity. It was surrounded by fine-grown trees, and the garden in summer was rich with a dozen varieties of rose. It was separated by a low hedge from the green where in the long evenings the village boys played cricket. Opposite, in convenient propinquity, stood the village church and the village public-house.

The sky was slate grey, and so drab and melancholy was its colour that it seemed a work of man. It was a colour of infinite sorrow.

St James's Park.

The sky was grey, even and low; and the sun, a narrow circle of white shining through uncertainly, cast a rippling gleam on the dark waters. The trees, in the dingy day, had lost their verdure; an infinitely subtle mist obscured their massive foliage. Beyond, half hidden by the poplars, in uneven outlines, were the Government offices and the heavy roofs of Trafalgar Square.

The water, reflecting the grey sky and the sombre trees, was dark and restful; and the moist, stagnant odour that arose from it made one faint and sick.

In the sun, the valley, all green and wooded, was pleasant and cool; but when the clouds rolled up from the west, heavy and grey, brushing the surrounding hills, the aspect was so circumscribed that I could have cried out as with physical pain. The primness of the scene was insufferable. The sombre, well-ordered elms, the meadows so carefully kept. When the massive clouds joined with the hills, I felt myself shut in. Then to get out of that little circle seemed a task impossible, and all power of flight seemed to abandon me. It was a scene so ordered and arranged that it made me feel that my life cast amid such surroundings could never escape its thraldom. The past centuries of people, living in a certain way, actuated by certain standards, influenced by certain emotions, were too strong for me. I felt myself like a foolish bird, a bird born in a cage without power to attain freedom. My lust for a free life was futile, for I knew myself devoid of the power it needed. I walked along the fields, by the neat iron railing with which they were enclosed. All about me was visible the care of man. Nature herself seemed under the power of the formal influence. and flourished with rigidity and decorum. Nothing was left wild. The trees were lopped into proper shape, cut down here where their presence seemed inelegant and planted there to complete the symmetry of a group.

The sky after the storm, swept clean by the howling wind, had the terrible inhumanity of justice.

Over the past swept a light mist, a painted haze which enveloped my memories, subduing their harshness so that they had something of an exotic charm; they were like a city or a harbour that you see from a distance through a veil of evening light, its contours indistinct and its flaming colours softened into a more delicate and subtler harmony. But the mist crept up from that deep sea of eternity, unrelenting and unrelieved, and the years at last hid my recollections in a grey, unfathomable night.

The passing years are like a mist sweeping up from the sea of time so that my memories acquire new aspects; their harshness seems less harsh and the brutal facts less brutal. But then, by chance, as a sudden wind on the coast will dispel the mist that has rolled up from the sullen waters, a word, a gesture, a tune will destroy the fancy that the treachery of time has occasioned so that I see again with a fresh, with a more piercing distinctness, the events of my youth in all their cruel reality. And I find myself unaffected by the sight. I am like the unconcerned spectator of a play, like an old actor watching a part which he had himself created, wondering, perhaps, at the old-fashioned shoddiness of it. I look at my past self with astonishment and with a certain contemptuous amusement.

The happy rain of April.

The patient night.

In the heat a heavy silence sank upon the country.

The rich death-colours of autumn were like an infinitely sad melody, like a sad song of unavailing regret; but in those passionate tints, in the red and the gold of the apples, in the varied hue of the fallen leaves, there was still something which forbade one to forget that in the death and decay of nature there is always the beginning of other life.

The ardent, starlit night.

The changing, rosy light of dawn.

The wind, sinister and ghostly, rustled like a sightless animal through the topmost, leafless branches.

To the lover waiting for his love no sound is sadder than the tardy striking of the hours.

The lamp flickered like the last wandering glance of a man at the point of death.

A dawn would follow the long and weary night, but no light would come to his wretched heart; his soul must wander for ever in darkness, for ever in darkness, for ever.

In the country the darkness of night is friendly and familiar, but in a city, with its blaze of lights, it is unnatural, hostile and menacing. It is like a monstrous vulture that hovers, biding its time.

The morning crept out of a dark cloud like an unbidden guest uncertain of his welcome.

C. G. and I looked at the sunset and he remarked that he considered sunsets rather vulgar. I, who was impressed with what I saw, felt humiliated. He told me contemptuously that I was very English. I had thought the fact rather praiseworthy. He informed me that his spirit was French; I thought it a pity in that case that he spoke it with such a British accent.

C. G. He has all the graces and all the virtues (figuratively speaking only, since his morals are none too good) and he prides himself on his sense of humour. To his mind the best argument you can bring in favour of a cause is that it is unpopular. He takes a singular pride in running down his country and this he takes to be an example of his breadth of mind. Ten days in Paris with Cook's coupons have sufficed to convince him of the superiority of the French. He talks of ideal love, of Hope with a rippling laugh, and buys a harlot off the Strand for ten shillings. He explains his failures by bemoaning the age. What is there to be said for an age and country which refuses to take him at his own estimate? He wishes he had been born in ancient Greece, but he's the son of a country doctor and there and then he would have been a slave. He despises me because I take a cold bath. He is plucked in all his exams; but he turns every humiliation into a new reason for self-esteem. He writes poetry which lacks only originality to be quite passable. He has no physical courage, and when bathing is terrified at the idea of being out of his depth. But he is proud of being a coward; he says anyone can be brave, it merely shows lack of imagination.

God goes through all the ways of the earth, ploughing the land and sowing pain and anguish, sowing from East to West.

The sumptuous gold of a summer evening.

Like the sword whose fire dried the tears in the desolate eyes of Eve.

The hothouse beauties of Pater's style, oppressive with a perfume of tropical decay: a bunch of orchids in a heated room.

The sun was a roaring furnace, melting the massive clouds into a golden, ardent rain; and the glow was so tremendous that one thought of some giant cataclysm in which might be forged a new and mighty world; and the Eastern clouds were the trailing volumes of smoke from the vast combustion. One could imagine the titan creators of a new world, throwing into the seething cauldron the false gods, the pomps and vanities, the thousand metals, the innumerable works of man; and with an awful silence all living things were sundered and dissipated and resolved into new, invisible, ethereal, mystical substances.

The young leaves shivering a little, voluptuously, under the quick pressure of the breeze.

My soul seemed a stringed instrument upon which the Gods were playing a melody of despair.

My heart was sad for her sake, and though I had ceased to love her, I found no consolation. A painful sense of emptiness had replaced the bitter anguish of before; and it was perhaps even harder to bear. Love may go and memory yet remain, memory may go and relief even then may not come.

The bitter waves of the sea.

The clouds sped across the sky, copper and red against the milky blue.

The heather rich with the subdued and decorous richness of the amethyst.

Under the low grey sky the colours of the landscape stood out with singular distinctness; there was a richness in the fields, brown or green, in the sombre tones of the hedges and the trees, unlike the brilliancy of an Italian landscape, but as intense and as opulent, as though composed of elemental colours. It reminded one of those early pictures in which the same luminous quality is obtained by a ground of solid gold.

When you are in love what use is it to you if all you get in return is kindness, friendship, affection? It is Dead Sea fruit that sticks in your throat.

In the old days it had been enough to be with ——, to walk with her in silence, to talk of the most insignificant things; but now when silence fell upon us, I racked my brain for something to say, and when we talked, our conversation sounded forced and unnatural; I felt it embarrassing to be alone with her.

What a strange idea is this that change must always be progress! Europeans complain that Chinese workmen use the same implements as they have used for centuries; but if with these rude tools they have been able to work with a delicacy and a sureness unsurpassable by Western artificers, why on earth should they change?

The three duties of woman. The first is to be pretty, the second is to be well-dressed, and the third is never to contradict.

The vague low song of London, like the distant hum of a mighty engine.

As one grows older one becomes more silent. In one's youth one is ready to pour oneself out to the world; one feels an intense fellowship with other people, one wants to throw oneself in their arms and one feels that they will receive one; one wants to open oneself to them so that they may take one, one wants to penetrate into them; one's life seems to overflow into the lives of others and become one with theirs as the waters of rivers become one in the sea. But gradually the power one felt of doing all this leaves one; a barrier rises up between oneself and one's fellows, and one realizes that they are strangers to one. Then perhaps one places all one's love, all one's faculty of expansion on one person, making, as it were, a final effort to join one's soul to his; with all one's might one draws him to one trying to know him and be known by him right down to the bottom of one's heart. But little by little one finds that it is all impossible, and however ardently one loves him, however intimately one is connected with him, he is always a stranger to one. Not even the most devoted husband and wife know one another. Then one retires into oneself and in one's silence builds a world of one's own which one keeps from the eyes of every living soul, even from the person one loves best, knowing he would not understand it.

Sometimes one feels rage and despair that one should know so little the people one loves. One is heart-broken at the impossibility of understanding them, of getting right down into their hearts of hearts. Sometimes, accidentally or under the influence of some emotion, one gets a glimpse of those inner selves of theirs, and one despairs on seeing how ignorant one is of that inner self and how far away from one it is.

When two people have been talking of some subject and a silence suddenly rises between them, the thoughts of each travel in their own direction, and in a little while, on speaking again, they will find how intensely they have diverged.

They say that life is short; to those who look back it may seem short enough; but to those who look forward, it is horribly long, endless. Sometimes one feels one cannot endure it. Why cannot one fall asleep and never, never again wake? How happy must be the lives of those who can look forward to eternity! The thought of living for ever is horrible.

There are so many people in the world that the action of an individual can be of no importance.

How sententious you are! One feels your observations should be punctuated with pinches of snuff.

It is terrible to have no means of expressing oneself, always to have to keep one's feelings a secret.

Am I a minor poet that I should expose my bleeding vitals to the vulgar crowd?

If it were possible decently to dissolve marriage during the first year not one in fifty couples would remain united.

Readers do not know that the passage which they read in half an hour, in five minutes, has been evolved out of the heart's blood of the author. The emotion which strikes them as 'so true' he has lived through with nights of bitter tears.

Human sorrow is as great as human heart.

There are people who say: quite well, thank you, when you say, how d'you do, to them. How vain they must be to think you can possibly care!

One of the most difficult things for a man to do is to realize that he does not stand at the centre of things, but at the circumference.

Scotchmen seem to think it's a credit to them to be Scotch.

1901

End of a life. It is like reading a book at close of day; one reads on, not seeing that the light is failing, and then suddenly as one pauses for a moment, one finds the light has gone; it is quite dark and looking down again at the book one cannot see, and the page is meaningless.

Carbis Water. The furze was saffron and green. Someone had gathered a bunch of heather and then let it fall; and it lay on the grass dying, a faded purple, like a symbol of the decay of an imperial power.

The Monument. It was on a hill overlooking the valley and the sea; and Hale, with its placid river, was like an old Italian town, coloured and gay even under the sombre heaven. Around the monument lay the dead ferns, brown as the earth, and they deadened the footfall; they, the first of the summer plants to go, chilled to death by the mild wind of September.

Joannes Knill, 1782. Who was he? One can imagine some splenetic, melancholy character such as the eighteenth century produced in reaction from the formalism of the age. It was an age that was withering for lack of fresh air. It drank of that cup in which the Elizabethans had found a multi-coloured joy of life, and a later generation a passion which fired the soul to freedom; but the wine in the cup had gone thin, and in its dregs was nothing but weariness.

The dead trees had seemed incongruous in the summer, a patch of darkness that had no business with the joyous colours of the Cornish June; but now the whole of Nature was drawing into harmony with them, and they stood, gnarled and leafless, with a placid silence as though they felt a contented sense of the eternity of things: the green leaves and the flowers were dainty, ephemeral as the butterflies and the light breeze of April, but *they* were changeless and constant. The silence was so great that one seemed to hear the wings of the rooks as they beat the air, flying overhead from field to field. And in the stillness, curiously, I thought I heard the song of London calling.

The sky was overcast, and the clouds, pregnant with rain, swept over the hilltops; and with the closing day the rain began to fall; it was very fine, a Cornish drizzle that hovered over the earth like a mist, and it was all-penetrating, like human sorrow.

The country sank into darkness.

The wind sang to himself like a strong-limbed plough-boy as he marches easily through the country.

The earth was enswathed in vapours, opalescent, and they had a curious impenetrable transparency.

Jeremy Taylor. Of no one, perhaps, can it be said with greater truth that the style is the very man himself. When you read *Holy Dying*, with its leisurely gait, its classical spirit, its fluent, facile poetry, you can imagine what sort of a man was Jeremy Taylor; and from a study of his life and circumstances you could hazard a guess that he would write exactly as he does. He was a Caroline prelate. His life was easy, moderately opulent and gently complacent. And such was his style. It reminds one, not, like Milton's, of a tumultuous torrent breaking its way through obstacles almost insurmountable, but of a rippling brook meandering happily through a fertile meadow carpeted with the sweet-smelling flowers of spring. Jeremy Taylor is no juggler with words, but well content to use them in their ordinary sense. His epithets are seldom subtle, and seldom discover in the object a new or striking quality; he uses them purely as decoration, and he repeats them over and over again, as if they were not living, necessary things, but merely conventional adjuncts of a noun. Consequently, notwithstanding his extreme floridity, he gives an impression of simplicity. He seems to use the words that come most naturally to the mouth, and his phrases, however nicely turned, have a colloquial air. Perhaps, also, the constant repetition of *and* adds to this sensation of naïveté. The long clauses, tacked on to one another in a string that appears interminable, make you feel that the thing has been written without effort. It seems like the conversation of a good-natured, rather long-winded, elderly cleric. Often, it is true, the endless phrases, clause after clause joined together with little regard to the meaning, with none at all to the construction of the sentence, depend merely upon looseness of punctuation, and by a rearrangement of this can be made into compact and well composed periods. Jeremy Taylor, when he likes, can put together his words as neatly as anyone, and then writes a sentence of perfect music. 'He that desires to die well and happily above all things must be careful that he do not live a soft, a delicate, and voluptuous life; but a life severe, holy and under the discipline of the Cross, under the conduct of prudence and observation, a life of warfare and sober counsels, labour and watchfulness.' On the other hand, sometimes his phrases run away with him, then *and* is heaped upon *and*, idea upon idea, till one cannot make head or tail of the meaning; and the sentence at last tails off obscurely, unfinished, incomplete and ungrammatical. On occasion, however, these tremendous sentences are managed with astonishing skill; and in a long string of clauses the arrangement of epithets, the form and order of the details, will be varied with skill and elegance.

But the great charm of *Holy Dying* lies in the general atmosphere of the book, scented and formal, calm and urbane like an old-world garden; and still more in the beautiful poetry of stray phrases. One cannot turn a page without finding some felicitous expression, some new order of simple words which seems to give them a new value; and often enough some picturesque passage, overladen, like that earliest charming rococo in which decoration was exuberant, but notwithstanding kept within the bounds of perfect taste.

Nowadays in looking for an epithet the conscientious writer searches (generally in vain!) for one which shall put the thing to be described in a new light, disclosing some characteristic which has never before been revealed; but Jeremy Taylor never even tries to do anything of the kind. The adjective which comes first to his mind is the one he uses. There are a thousand epithets with which you may describe the sea, the only one which, if you fancy yourself as a stylist, you will scrupulously avoid is *blue*; yet it is that which most satisfies Jeremy Taylor. He has not the incisive phrase of Milton, the poetic power of putting together nouns and adjectives, adverbs and verbs, in a conjunction which has never been used before. He never surprises. His imagination is without violence or daring. He is content to walk the old road, using phrases and expressions as he finds them; and the chief peculiarity of his style in his mild, bucolic outlook upon life. He sees the world amiably and transcribes it exactly, without great art; but with a pleasing desire to put things as picturesquely as he can.

The rising sun coloured the mist variously, till it was iridescent as the chalcedony, purple and rosy and green.

Terracotta Statuettes. I was enchanted by the facile motion of the little figures, by their bold gestures and nonchalant attitudes. In the folds of their drapery, in their arrested movements, there was all the spirit of that civilization of the fresh air which was perhaps the chief part of Hellenic existence. A row of figurines from Tanagra fills the imaginative mind with an ardent longing for that freer, simple life of ancient times.

The sad, stormy night of eternal damnation.

And occasionally, in a break of the rapid clouds, appeared a pale star shivering in the cold.

An azure more profound than the rich enamel of an old French jewel.

The ploughed fields gaining in the sunshine the manifold colours of the jasper.

The foliage of the elm trees more sombre than jade.

In the sun the wet leaves glistened like emeralds, meretricious stones which might fitly deck the pompous depravity of a royal courtesan.

Rich with an artificial, elaborate richness like those old gorgeous jewels incrusted with precious stones.

A green like that of the old enamelled jewels which is more translucent than emerald.

The rich profundity of the garnet.

It had the transparent, coloured richness of a scale of agate.

The sky more luminously blue than the lapis lazuli.

Under the dying sun, after the rain, the colours of the country assumed a new, an almost laboured richness, resembling for a moment the opulent hues of Limoges enamel.

Like a Limoges plate sparkling with opulent colours.

The water, in the deep translucent shadow, had the dark, heavy richness of jade.

The reader may well ask himself what these enamels, what these stones, precious and semi-precious, are doing here. I will tell him. At that time, still impressed by the exuberant prose that was fashionable in the nineties and aware that my own was flat, plain and pedestrian, I thought I should try to give it more colour and more ornament. That is why I read Milton and Jeremy Taylor with laborious zeal. One day, my mind upon a florid passage in Oscar Wilde's Salome, I took pencil and paper and went to the British Museum where, hoping they would come in handy, I made these notes.

Piccadilly before dawn. After the stir and ceaseless traffic of the day, the silence of Piccadilly early in the morning, in the small hours, seems barely credible. It is unnatural and rather ghostly. The great street in its emptiness has a sort of solemn broadness, descending in a majestic sweep with the assured and stately ease of a placid river. The air is pure and limpid, but resonant, so that a solitary cab suddenly sends the whole street ringing, and the emphatic trot of the horse resounds with long reverberations. Impressive by reason of their regularity, the electric lights, self-assertive and brazen, flood the surroundings with a harsh and snowy brilliance; with a kind of indifferent violence they cast their glare upon the huge silent houses, and lower down throw into distinctness the long evenness of the park railings and the nearer trees. And between, outshone, like an uneven string of discoloured gems, twinkles the yellow flicker of the gas jets.

There is silence everywhere, but the houses are quiet and still, with a different silence from the rest, standing very white but for the black gaping of the many windows. In their sleep, closed and bolted, they line the pavement, helplessly as it were, disordered and undignified, having lost all significance without the busy hum of human voices and the hurrying noise of persons passing in and out.

The autumn, too, has its flowers; but they are little loved and little praised.

This is such nonsense that I cannot believe it was meant literally, and I have wondered whether this conceit occurred to me because a woman somewhat advanced in years had made a pass on the shy young man I was then.

K. I think you can often get to know a good deal about a man by discovering what books he reads. In the quiet life which falls to the share of most of us, the spirit of adventure is with difficulty able to satisfy itself in any way other than by reading. In the perusal of books men are able to lead artificial lives which are often truer than those circumstances have forced upon them. If you asked K. which books had chiefly influenced him, he would have perhaps been at a loss for an answer; it is a question often asked, and it is not really so silly as at first sight it seems. The answer generally given is the Bible and Shakespeare, sometimes from mere hypocritical foolishness, but often for fear of being thought pretentious if the reply is more original than was expected. I do not think K. would name the books which have most occupied his mind, which have given him the most vivid sensations, without some complacency. The *Satyricon* of Petronius Arbiter would be on the list along with Newman's *Apologia*, Apuleius along with Walter Pater; George Meredith, the Judicious Hooker, Jeremy Taylor, Sir Thomas Browne and Gibbon. What takes his fancy most is gorgeousness of style. He likes the precious. Of course, he's rather an ass; an intelligent, well-read ass.

He felt like a man in a deep chasm who sees at midday the stars which those that live in daylight cannot perceive.

It seemed to himself that his burning thirst could be assuaged by nothing less than the collected force of all the currents which make up life.

A sound and well-advised judgement.

The Canon. He avoided all religious questions, almost as though they were improprieties; but when pressed, spoke in a tentative, deprecatory way. He was always saying that evolution must take place in religion as in everything else. He took his stand on the boundary line between knowledge and ignorance. 'Here human reason can go no further,' he said, and straightway proceeded to appropriate that dark and undiscovered country. But when science, like a tongue of the sea, forced its way in and showed that the reason of man was at home in yet another region, he fell back quickly. Like a defeated general who colours his despatches, he called his reverse a tactical move to the rear. He put his faith in the unknowable. He staked his all upon the limitations of reason, but, like a spendthrift watching the usurer gather his estate acre by acre, he watched the progress of science with difficultly concealed anxiety.

He read from his lectern, knowing that part of his congregation accepted them as literally true, while part took them as manifestly false, passages of the Bible which he himself knew were legends which no sensible man could believe. Sometimes doubts assailed him with regard to his justification for so doing, but mentally he shrugged his shoulders. 'After all,' he said, 'it's good that the ignorant should believe these things. It's always dangerous to tamper with people's beliefs.' Sometimes, however, he went so far as to arrange that his curate should read what he himself could scarcely bring himself to. He preferred his curates rather stupid.

When he flew into a passion he called it righteous anger; and when someone did a thing he didn't like he called his own state of mind virtuous indignation.

Matthew Arnold's style. It is an admirable instrument for the presentation of thought. It is clear, simple and precise.

It runs like a smooth, limpid river—with almost too tranquil a stream. If style resembles the clothes of a well-dressed man, which attract no attention, but when by chance examined are found seemly, then Arnold's style is perfect. It is never obtrusive, never by a vivid phrase or a picturesque epithet distracts attention from the matter; but when one scrutinizes it, one discovers how carefully balanced are the sentences, how harmonious, graceful and elegant is the rhythm. One perceives the felicity with which the words are put together and is a little astonished that so great an effect can be obtained by the use of words which are quite homely and in common use. Arnold gives distinction to everything he touches. His style reminds one of a very well-bred and cultured lady, somewhat advanced in years so that the passions of life are more than half forgotten, and of such exquisite manners as to suggest a bygone day, yet with humour and vivacity such that the thought never occurs to one that she belongs to an older generation. But this style, so well suited to irony and wit, to exposition, so apt for pointing out the weakness of an argument, makes tremendous demands upon the matter. It discovers weakness of reasoning or commonplace of thought without pity; it has then a sort of ghastly bareness which is disconcerting. It is a method rather than an art. No one more than I can realize what immense labour it must have needed to acquire that mellifluous cold brilliance. It is a platitude that simplicity is the latest acquired of all qualities, and one can see sometimes in passages of Matthew Arnold traces of the constant effort, of the constraint he must have put upon himself, before the fashion of writing he had adopted became a habit. I do not mean by this any disparagement; but I cannot help thinking that after the long toil necessary to attain it, Arnold's style was almost automatic. We know that Pater's never became so; and indeed it is obvious that the picturesqueness, the wealth of imagery, the varied metaphors by which he got his effects required constant invention. But in all these Arnold's style is lacking; his vocabulary is small and his turns of phrase constantly recur; the simplicity he aimed at allowed little scope to the imagination. Whatever he writes about, his style is the same.

And it is to this, perhaps, as much as to his classicism, that is due the frequent reproach of impersonality. But to me Arnold's style is just as personal as that of Pater or of Carlyle. Indeed it seems to express very clearly his character, slightly feminine, pettish, a little magisterial, cold, but redeemed by a wonderful grace, agility of thought and unfailing elegance.

I'm glad I don't believe in God. When I look at the misery of the world and its bitterness I think that no belief can be more ignoble.

An interesting question is whether more than a certain degree of civilization is not harmful to the race. In antiquity degeneration has invariably followed upon a high state of culture; and the history of ancient times is a history of the decline and fall of one great nation after another. The explanation appears to be that more than a certain amount of civilization renders the nation unfit for the struggle of life; and its people are conquered by others, hardier and more courageous, who have attained to no such exquisiteness of cultivation. Just as the Greeks were destroyed by the barbarous power of Rome, France, cultivated, highly civilized, refined and sensitive, was defeated by the rough and brutal might of Germany. The artist is overthrown by the philistine and the man of culture ousted by the boor. The conclusion appears to be that coarseness of taste and want of delicacy are advantageous rather than the reverse.

Canadians, Australians, New Zealanders have the same pre-eminence over the English that the Scotch have long been observed to have. Bred under harder conditions, so that natural selection has greater play, they are better adapted to the struggle for life than are the members of the older civilization. They look upon existence with a less analytic eye, their grosser instincts are more powerful; less civilized than we, less concerned with the graces of life, they are more robust. Their morality, their view of life is directed (unconsciously, of course) to the good of the race rather than to the benefit of the individual; they produce fewer men of mark, but on the other hand their race-character is stronger and more distinctive.

After all, the only means of improving the race is by natural selection; and this can only be done by elimination of the unfit. All methods which tend to their preservation – education of the blind and of deaf-mutes, care of the organically diseased, of the criminal and of the alcoholic – can only cause degeneration.

Reason must act eventually on the side of Natural Selection. Admitting the conflict between selfishness supported by reason and altruism supported by religion, it is, after all, as the history of Evolution shows, the individual advantage which has occasioned progress; and it seems illogical to suppose that in human society it should be different.

Goodness originated in human instincts, and those characteristics which have been peculiar to a tribe have always been dignified as virtues. Just as the ideal of beauty in any tribe has always been its average appearance carried to a rather higher degree, so the instincts which it has found in itself it has called good.

All this effort of natural selection, wherefore? What is the good of all this social activity beyond helping unessential creatures to feed and propagate?

The ethical standard is as ephemeral as all else in the world. Good is nothing more than the conduct which is fittest to the circumstances of the moment; and the result of further evolution may be to dethrone the present ethical ideal and overthrow all that we now regard as virtue. Failure or success in the struggle for existence is the sole moral standard. Good is what survives.

Morality is the weapon which society in the struggle for existence uses in its dealings with the individual. Society rewards those actions and praises those qualities which are necessary to its survival. The office of morality is to persuade the individual that what is of benefit to society is of benefit to him.

There are men whose sense of humour is so ill developed that they still bear a grudge against Copernicus because he dethroned them from the central position in the universe. They feel it a

personal affront that they can no longer consider themselves
the pivot upon which turns the whole of created things.

Put, for the sake of argument, the End in Itself of Kant in Truth,
Beauty, Goodness; what answer will you make to the simple
observation that Truth, Beauty and Goodness are scarcely less
ephemeral than the flowers of the field? Even in the short period
of recorded history the connotation of these three concepts has
radically changed. Why should you presumptuously assume that
the ideas of the present day on these subjects are absolute? How
then can you take as the End in Itself what is purely relative?
Before you talk to us of the End in Itself tell us what is the
Absolute.

It is the fashion to despise the palate and its pleasures; but in
point of fact the sense of taste is more important than the aesthetic
instinct. A man can get through life more easily without an
aesthetic sense than without a sense of taste. If, as seems reasonable, the various faculties of man are ranked according to their
necessity for his preservation, the digestive apparatus, with the
sexual, is the highest and the most important.

It is obvious that the hedonic element is very present to the mind
of the religious man, and influences his action as profoundly
as it influences that of the hedonist pure and simple—only he
puts a future happiness as the reward of his deed rather than an
immediate one. In fact, hedonism is nowhere more conspicuous
than in those who choose a certain course because they will enjoy
eternal bliss; and if their idea of this future happy state be examined, it will generally be found so grossly material that many
a professed hedonist would be ashamed to acknowledge it.

But by a curious refinement of emotion some deeply religious
persons persuade themselves that they act with no hope of
reward, but merely for the love of God. Yet here too, if the
feeling is analysed, a hedonic element will be discovered; the
reward is in the intimate self-satisfaction of virtuous action, in
the pleasant consciousness of having done right; and this for
emotional natures can be more satisfying than any grosser,
more obvious benefits.

What mean and cruel things men can do for the love of God.

Human beauty is determined by sexual attractiveness. It is an intensification of traits common to a certain people at a certain time, but a slight one, for too great a departure from the normal excites aversion rather than admiration. Sexually the aim both of men and of women is to distinguish themselves from others and thus call attention to themselves. This they do by accentuating the characteristics of their race. So the Chinese compress their naturally small feet and the Europeans constrict their naturally slim waists. And when the characteristics of a people change, their ideal of beauty changes too. English women have added to their stature during the last hundred years; the heroines of the older novels were far from tall, and literature had to wait for Tennyson to learn that inches added to beauty.

They talk about art as though they knew all about it and what they don't know weren't worth knowing. But art isn't as simple as all that. How can it be when so many diverse things enter into its origins: sex, imitation, play, habit, boredom and the wish for change, emotional desire for enhancement of pleasure or diminution of pain.

It is the irreparableness of every action which makes life so difficult. Nothing occurs again precisely as it came about before, and in the most important things there has been no previous experience to guide one. It is once for all that one takes each action, and every mistake is irremediable. Sometimes, looking back, one is appalled at one's errors, one seems to have wasted so much time in idle byways, and often to have mistaken the road so completely that whole years appear frustrate.

In most biographies it is the subject's death which is most interesting. That last inevitable step has a fascination and even a practical interest which no previous event can equal. I cannot understand why a biographer, having undertaken to give the world details of a famous man's life, should hesitate, as so often happens, to give details of his death also. It is the man's character which is the chief interest, his strength and weakness, his courage and despondency; and these are nowhere more apparent than on a death-bed. It imports us as much to know how great men die as to know how they live. Our lives are conditioned by outer circumstances, but our death is our own. To see how others have taken that final journey is the only help we have when ourselves we enter upon it.

Sometimes I ask myself at night what I have done that day, what new thought or idea I have had, what particular emotion I have felt, what there has been to mark it off from its fellows; and too often it appears to me insignificant and useless.

Moralists say that the performance of duty brings happiness. Duty is dictated by law, by public opinion, and by conscience. Each by itself may have no great power, but the three together are probably irresistible. But public opinion and law are sometimes antagonistic – as in duelling on the continent; and public opinion is variable; what one section reprobates another approves; and different professions, army, church and commerce, have their different standards.

There are occasions when to do one's duty obviously is not a pleasure; then often enough it is not done, and for its performance new sanctions must be found. In the Boer War officers placed in dangerous positions surrendered very easily, preferring that dishonour to the chance of death; and it was not till some were shot and more cashiered that the majority nerved themselves to a stouter courage.

After all, the distinctive element of Christianity as it is taught by the divines is the consciousness of sin. It is this which looms in the outlook on life of believers, intimidating them, and renders them unable and unwilling to take existence frankly. The theory of man is imperfect, they say, unless the fact of sin is recognized. But what is sin? Sin is an action which troubles the conscience. And what is conscience? It is the feeling you have that you have done something of which others (and maybe God) would disapprove. It would be interesting to attempt an analysis of conscience. It would be necessary to examine how it arose, the estimation in which it has been held, its psychological ground and the affairs upon which it exercises sway. The Pathan who has killed his man is not conscience-stricken, nor is the Corsican who has murdered his enemy in vendetta. The scrupulous Englishman will hesitate to lie; the Spaniard, no less scrupulous, will not think twice about it.

Cesare Borgia may well be taken as an example of almost perfect self-realization. The only morality, so far as the individual is concerned, is to give his instincts, mental and bodily, free play. In this lies the aesthetic beauty of a career, and in this respect the lives of Cesare Borgia and of Francis of Assisi are parallel. Each fulfilled his character and nothing more can be demanded of any man. The world, judging only of the effect of action upon itself, has called one infamous and the other saintly. How would the world judge such a man as Torquemada, the most pious creature of his age, who perfected an instrument of persecution which has cost more deaths and greater misery than many a long and bloody war?

On the individual in relation to himself there is neither obligation nor duty: to the individual the words are meaningless, and it is only in his relation to others that they acquire significance. With regard to himself the individual has perfect freedom, for there is no power with authority to give him orders.

Society makes rules for its own preservation, but the individual can have no duty towards society: there is nothing to restrain him but prudence. He can go his own way, freely, doing what he wills, but he must not complain if society punishes him when he does not act in accordance with its dictates. More efficacious than all the laws society has made for its self-preservation is the institution of conscience, setting thereby a policeman in every man's bosom to see that its laws are obeyed; and it is singular that even in a man's most private affairs, where one might imagine society has no concern, conscience leads him to act according to the good of this organism outside himself.

One of the great differences between Christianity and Science is that the first gives a high and important value to the individual, while to the other, to Science, he is of no account.

Relativity applies to conscience necessarily from the transitoriness of human ideas of good and evil. A man in one age will be conscience-stricken for neglecting to do an act the performance of which in another will be followed by remorse.

Common-sense is often taken as the rule of ethics. But if it is analysed, if its dictates are taken one by one, the student will be astounded at the contradictions he finds. He will not be able to understand how common-sense orders diametrically opposite things in different countries and among different classes and sections in the same country. He will even find that the dictates of common-sense in the same country, in the same class and section, are often mutually incompatible.

Common-sense appears to be only another name for the thoughtlessness of the unthinking. It is made up of the prejudices of childhood, the idiosyncrasies of individual character and the opinion of the newspapers.

Common-sense makes a great show of disinterestedness in regard to our dealings with others, but it is only a show. Take the question whether it is proper to refrain from indulgence till the surrounding want and misery have been removed; common-sense gives an unhesitating negative.

If sensual indulgence is condemned the condemnation should be thorough. If you condemn the appetites of the palate or of sex, you should condemn also the other appetites for warmth, comfort, exercise and the beauties of art and nature. Otherwise it is not sensual indulgence that you condemn, but some other frailty which rests only in the pleasures of eating or of sex.

The success of religious systems is proof of the absorbing egoism of men and of their lack of mental balance.

No egoism is so insufferable as that of the Christian with regard to his soul.

Wisdom can hardly be termed a virtue for it is made up of

intellectual qualities which one man has and another not. If wisdom is necessary to right action, this can only be possible to the minority of mankind.

Intuitionism rests on the principle of an absolute in morals, and its insecurity appears in the fact that the intuitions which tell men how to act differ from country to country, from age to age, and from man to man. Intuition will tell a man to commit a murder in one age and in another will cause him to revolt from the idea. The judgements which seem to come from no discernible source can very simply be shown to arise from the teaching of childhood and the practice of neighbours. The explanation of intuition is the same as that of advertisement: tell a man ten thousand times that Pears Soap is good for the complexion and eventually he will have an intuitive certainty of the fact.

It is curious to find a father of the church, St Chrysostum, hinting at the relativeness of morality in the words: 'Do not ask how these (Old Testament precepts) can be good, now when the need for them has passed: ask how they were good when the period required them.'

The hedonist must remember that self-consciousness is incompatible with happiness. Happiness will escape him if he fixes his mind on his own pursuit of pleasure.

Desire is pleasurable in its early stages, but, becoming intense, is painful. Then the result of desire is the same as that of pain, and we seek to get rid of the desire rather than to obtain the object desired. Sometimes love is so violent that the desire becomes no longer a pleasure but a pain, and then men will kill the woman they love so as to rid themselves of the desire.

Hunger is a desire which is on the boundary line between pain and pleasure. It shows better than any other state that pain and pleasure arise from the degree of desire. When hunger is moderate the sensation is agreeable, and the idea of food gives pleasure; but when it is excessive there is only pain, and then one's thoughts are engaged not with the satisfactoriness of eating a good dinner, but merely with the getting rid of an unpleasant feeling.

No more stupid apology for pain has ever been devised than that it elevates. It is an explanation due to the necessity of justifying pain from the Christian point of view. Pain is nothing more than the signal given by the nerves that the organism is in circumstances hurtful to it; it would be as reasonable to assert that a danger signal elevates a train. But one would have thought that the ordinary observation of life was enough to show that in the great majority of cases, pain, far from refining, has an effect which is merely brutalizing. An example in point is the case of hospital in-patients: physical pain makes them self-absorbed, selfish, querulous, impatient, unjust and greedy; I could name a score of petty vices that it generates, but not one virtue. Poverty also is pain. I have known well men who suffered from that grinding agony of poverty which befalls persons who have to live among those richer than themselves; it makes them grasping and mean, dishonest and untruthful. It teaches them all sorts of detestable tricks. With moderate means they would have been honourable men, but ground down by poverty they have lost all sense of decency.

For the average man a sufficient rule of life is to follow his instincts controlled by the moral standard of the society in which he lives.

He raged, a twopenny-halfpenny Prometheus, as unquiet thoughts gnawed at his heart, while he strove to pierce the mystery of life.

I am willing to take life as a game of chess in which the first rules are not open to discussion. No one asks why the knight is allowed his eccentric hop, why the castle may only go straight and the bishop obliquely. These things are to be accepted, and with these rules the game must be played: it is foolish to complain of them.

The study of Ethics is part and parcel of the study of Nature; for man must learn his place in the world before he can act rightly and reasonably.

There is as little justification for ascribing any end or object to the existence of man as for that pre-supposition accepted by the whole of antiquity and by the Middle Ages, that the heavenly bodies must move in circles because the circle is the most perfect figure.

With regard to the end of human existence compare that old objection of the Aristotelians to the Copernican system. What use, they asked, could be the immeasurable space between the outermost planets and the fixed stars?

That which is universal in mankind cannot be evil: it is a fault with many ethical systems that, more or less arbitrarily, they fix upon certain tendencies of man and call them good; and upon others and call them evil. How much greater would human happiness have been if the gratification of the sexual instinct had never been looked upon as wicked. A true system of ethics must find out those qualities which are in all men and call *them* good.

The actions to which men accord their praise appear to be those by which themselves, in whole or in part, will benefit; but also they are capable of admiration for any striking, dramatic deeds which strike their fancy or excite their wonder.

That we do not often consciously make pleasure our aim is no argument against the idea that the attainment of pleasure is the object to which all actions tend.

Theoretically there are no bounds to the power of the state except the fear of revolution; the only limit to its action is its own capacity. Consequently the state will nationalise all industries which it can carry on better than individuals, leaving to these only the parts of commerce which individual greed is likely to perform in a more thorough and more economical way. The state must never forget how much truth lies in the axiom of Mandeville that private vices are public benefits.

The right to freedom: there is no such right, except when the state for its own ends favours it.

To the individual, morality can be nothing more than the expression of a personal satisfaction; it is only a matter of aesthetics.

Might is right. There is no such thing as duty or moral obligation. In itself one course of action is as justifiable as another; the well-being of the state is the only standard of ethics. The relation between the individual and the state is a tacit contract: the individual for certain advantages to himself behaves in a way advantageous to the state.

If forty million people say a foolish thing it does not become a wise one, but the wise man is foolish to give them the lie.

To the universe and to man no end is discoverable. Everything is relative. Nothing is certain. Morality depends on the state, which is omnipotent. Might is right.

What is the advantage of progress? How does it benefit the Japanese that they have assumed Western Civilization? Are not the Malays, on the borders of their forests, the Kanakas, on their fertile islands, as happy as the London slummer? What does it all end in? What is the use of it? I don't know the answer.

That pleasure is transitory is no proof that it is evil, for what can man find that endures to all eternity?

It is salutary to realise the fundamental isolation of the individual mind. We have no certain knowledge of any consciousness but our own. We can only know the world through our own personality. Because the behaviour of others is similar to our own, we surmise that they are like us; it is a shock to discover that they are not. As I grow older I am more and more amazed to discover how great are the differences between one man and another. I am not far from believing that everyone is unique.

I think it can be proved very fairly that pleasure is the end which men set to their endeavours. The word, in puritanical ears, has an unpleasant sound, and many have preferred to talk of happiness; but happiness can only be defined as a continued state of pleasure, and if one deserves blame so does the other: you cannot reasonably call a straight line good if the points that compose it are evil. Of course pleasure need not consist exclusively of sensual gratifications, though it is significant of human feeling that it is those especially to which the mind, in using the word, seems to refer. To the average man the aesthetic pleasures, the pleasures of effort, the pleasures of the imagination are so pale in comparison with the vivid delights of sense that they do not enter his mind when he hears the word.

Some, like Goethe, have taken harmony as that which gives life its justification; and some, like Walter Pater, have taken beauty. But when Goethe tells men to cultivate all their capacities, bidding them to see life whole, he is preaching unabashed hedonism; for surely men gain greater happiness the more completely they develop themselves. To make beauty the aim and end of life is, I think, a little foolish: it is a fair-weather doctrine which can be of small use in any unusual stress; Rachel weeping for her children refused to be comforted; yet the sun that day set no less splendidly than usual.

Conscience. The power of it is well indicated by the statement of John Henry Newman, in a note to the Apologia, that men 'would rather be in error with the sanction of their conscience, than be right with the mere judgement of their reason.'

Theologians say that science is met somewhere by a barrier at which it can only confess its helplessness. But is religion in a better case? Tertullian acknowledged that it wasn't when he made the statement: *credo quia absurdum est.*

If the use of religion is to make men moral, and so long as it does this dogma is unimportant, it seems to follow that men can't do better than to accept the religion of the country they happen to have been born in. Why then should missionaries go to India and China to convert people who have already a religion that performs very adequately the chief function of religion? Probably few Hindus in India, few Buddhists in China are as moral as Hinduism and Buddhism would have them be, but that is no reason why they should not be left alone:

we all know that few Christians act up to the principles of Christianity.

Or is it that the missionaries think that God will condemn to endless torment all who do not share their particular beliefs? No wonder they think you're cursing and swearing when you say, Good God!

It would be interesting if it could be shown that the fear of death is a European malady: observe the stolid composure with which the Oriental and African races look forward to it.

Perfection seems to be nothing more than a complete adaptation to the environment; but the environment is constantly changing, so perfection can never be more than transitory.

A deep-rooted feeling in man is that innovation is wicked: this is very noticeable in children and in savages. The interests of savages are few, their dress is costly, intended to bear long usage; their arts are scanty; and so conservatism is forced upon them. But there is in man also a love of change for its own sake, and in a civilized state it overpowers the old fear. Civilized man has many facilities for procuring it; in dress, for instance, from the cheapness and variety of manufacture; in scene, from the convenience of locomotion.

The same sentence can never produce exactly the same effect on two persons, and the first quick impressions that any given word in it may convey will in two minds widely differ.

No one has ever proved the non-existence of Apollo or of Aphrodite; belief in them merely declined when it corresponded no longer with general intellectual conditions.

The dignity of man. When man gives himself arbitrarily, and in his inexhaustible vanity, attributes beyond all praise, he is after all very like those oriental rulers of petty states each of whom describes himself officially as lord of the earth and brother of the sun.

It is wise to be sceptical with regard to the ideas of one's period.

77

Notions which to past centuries seemed so certain, so well proved, to us appear obviously and even ludicrously false. The grounds upon which we accept the prevalent theories of our own day seem so cogent and so reasonable that we cannot bring ourselves to imagine that they are possibly as insecure as those others which we know now to have been erroneous. There may be no more truth in them than in those hypotheses of the eighteenth century concerning the primitive perfection of man.

They were talking about V. F. whom they'd all known. She published a volume of passionate love poems, obviously not addressed to her husband. It made them laugh to think that she'd carried on a long affair under his nose, and they'd have given anything to know what he felt when at last he read them.

This note gave me the idea for a story which I wrote forty years later. It is called 'The Colonel's Lady'.

The virtues are ranked according to their usefulness to the social state: therefore courage is set higher than prudence; people will call the man who unnecessarily risks his life a fine fellow; he is only a foolhardy one. There is generosity in courage: there is something sly and rather shabby in prudence. Intemperance is a failing which does not so obviously affect the common welfare and so is regarded with mingled feelings. To a certain degree (in England at all events) it is not disapproved, and men will tell you with self-complacency that they have got as tight as a drum. It is only when it causes others inconvenience that it is condemned. People are tolerant of the frailties which in one way or another they may profit by: they call the ne'er-do-well who wastes his time and money in the senseless pursuit of pleasure a good chap and the worst they say of him is that he's his own worst enemy.

Every generation looks upon the generation that preceded it as more vigorous and more virtuous than itself. You will find the same wail that men are not what they were in the histories of Herodotus, in the writers of the late Roman republic, in Montaigne, and in the authors of our own day. The reason for this is that men hate change and are terrified of it. Habits change, not men.

One has to be especially wary of the ideas which seem the most self-evident and the most obvious: they are current, we have heard them accepted as truisms from our childhood, and everyone around us accepts them without demur, so that often it does not even occur to us to question them. Yet it is exactly these ideas which must be first put upon the scales to be most carefully weighed.

The suppositions of one generation are often the principles of the next, and then to doubt them is preposterous. But one generation more sees them cast aside as useless, antiquated and absurd.

1902

Men, commonplace and ordinary, do not seem to me fit for the tremendous fact of eternal life. With their little passions, their little virtues and their little vices, they are well enough suited to the workaday world; but the conception of immortality is much too vast for beings cast in so small a mould. I have more than once seen men die, peacefully or tragically, and never have I seen in their last moments anything to suggest that their spirit was everlasting. They die as a dog dies.

Titian's *The Burial of Christ*. I feel nothing of the tragedy of that event, nothing of death's horror nor of the survivors' pain, but rather the warm breath of life and the passionate beauty of Italy. Even in that moment of death and horror the glory of life overwhelms everything; and so perhaps it should be in all art, beauty transfiguring every sordid scene, and even out of death and woe bringing forth the joy of life.

The highest activities of consciousness have their origins in physical occurrences of the brain just as the loveliest melodies are not too sublime to be expressed by notes.

Directly or indirectly the conscious life is determined by the position of the individual in the universe, and by his need to make acquaintance with his surroundings, and either bring them into harmony with him, or himself with them.

On what curious foundations rests the moral sense may be seen by the indifference with which the pious throughout the ages have regarded the wickedness of the Bible. Do they condemn the deceit of Jacob or the cruelty of Joshua? Not a bit of it. Are they shocked at the callousness with which the children of Job were treated? Not in the least. Do they feel any sympathy for the unfortunate Vashti? I've never seen a sign of it.

I can imagine no more comfortable frame of mind for the conduct of life than a humorous resignation.

Sorrow is lessened by a conviction of its inevitableness. I suppose one can control many of one's distresses if one can discover a physical cause for them. Kant became master of the hypochondria which in his early years bordered on weariness of life through the knowledge that it resulted from his flat and narrow chest.

The origin of character refers back to the origin of the individual organism. After birth physical conditions and environment influence it. It is very hard that a person through no fault of his own should possess a character, perverse and difficult, which condemns him to an unhappy life.

Each youth is like a child born in the night who sees the sun rise and thinks that yesterday never existed.

One great folly of modern culture, typically English, is the veil which has been cast over the natural functions of man. The scroll *decency forbids* is placarded not only on stray walls and corners, but on the very soul of Englishmen, so that numbers of harmless, necessary acts have acquired a tone which is almost pornographic. It is well to compare with this the candid simplicity with which in other ages the most refined minds treated these matters.

Man's superiority of organization gives him a greater capacity for pain: by reason of his complex nervous system he suffers bodily anguish which is keener and more various, but also moral and imaginative woes from which the lower animals are immune.

Perhaps all the benefits of religion are counter-balanced by its fundamental idea that life is miserable and vain. To treat life as a pilgrimage to a future and better existence is to disown its present value.

Bed. No woman is worth more than a fiver unless you're in love with her. Then she's worth all she costs you.

1904

Paris. She had something of the florid colouring of Helena Fourment, the second wife of Rubens, that blonde radiancy, with eyes blue as the sea at midsummer and hair like corn under the August sun, but a greater delicacy withal. And she hadn't Helena's unhappy leaning to obesity.

She was a woman of ripe and abundant charms, rosy of cheek and fair of hair, with eyes as blue as the summer sea, with rounded lines and full breasts. She leaned somewhat to the overblown. She belonged to that type of woman that Rubens has set down for ever in the ravishing person of Helena Fourment.

A fit scene for a group by Watteau; and standing on the lawn one thought to see Gilles, habited in white, with pink bows on his dainty shoes, looking at one with tired and mocking eyes, his lips trembling. But whether with a sob repressed or with a gibe, who can tell?

The Blessed Virgin wore a long cloak of sammet, azure like the sky of a southern night; and on it were embroidered in thread of gold delicate flowers and leaves.

The placid lake reflecting the white clouds, and the trees russet already with approaching autumn; the green woodland distance, the sober opulence of elm and oak. It was a stately scene that told of care and long tending; and by the borders of that lake might well have sat the decadent ladies of Watteau, discussing preciously with swains gallant in multi-coloured silks the verses of Racine and the letters of Madame de Sévigné.

A breezy, flaunting affectation, a defiant pose which contemned the philistine, yet needed his indignant surprise for full entertainment, like that delightful creature, all arts and graces, tripping immortally on the canvas of Antoine Watteau, *L'Indifférent*, in doublet of blue satin, and hose and shoes of rose, ruffles at his wrists, and a light cloak flung negligently over one arm.

In the early morning, the sun scarce risen, the trees, the water, had a tender, delicate grey that reminded one charmingly of a picture by Corot: there was a subtle and luminous grace in the scene that cleansed the heart of every base emotion.

His features were rather large, his face rather square, but notwithstanding his beauty was striking. But there was in his countenance more than beauty; for the sombreness of his expression, almost surly in moments of repose, his large dark eyes, almond and shaped like those of an Oriental, his red lips exquisitely modelled and sensual, his dark chestnut hair, cut short and curling becomingly over his head, gave him an appearance of cruel haughtiness, of a supreme and disdainful indifference to the passion he might arouse. It was a vicious face, except that beauty can never be vicious, it was a cruel face, except that indifference can never be quite cruel. It was a face that remained in your mind, and your feeling was partly admiring, partly terrified. His skin was very clear, like ivory suffused with a delicate carmine; and he had long fashioning fingers, the nervous, adroit, active hands of that portrait of a sculptor by Bronzino. You felt that at their touch the clay must almost mould itself into lovely forms.

It was a curious face, heartless and indifferent, indolent and passionate, cold yet sensual.

Radiant with health, like the persons of Venetian pictures in which the glory of living seems so comfortable a fact.

He had the malicious laugh of the faun of Vienne, the roguish lips and the glittering inhuman eyes: he had the same small nose, the same oddly shaped head, which notwithstanding its human form recalls the fabled creature's animality.

Coldly beautiful, she has an exquisite, virginal grace, a perfectly unconscious composure, so that she makes you think (and you smile as you think) of that statue in the Louvre in which Diana, in the likeness of a young girl, with collected gesture fastens her cloak. Her ear is as delicate and as finely wrought, and her features have an exquisite precision.

The thin straight nose, the tight-closed, austere lips of the fanatic. In his close-set eyes and compressed jaw, in the tension with which he restlessly held himself there was a cold determination and a sullen obstinacy.

With his black curling beard, square cut and luxuriant, his low forehead, straight nose and high colour he looked like those statues of Bacchus in which the god is represented as no stripling, but as a man in the full prime of life.

Vladimir. He hadn't seen Vladimir for several days and wondered what had become of him. He was in none of the usual cafes. He knew where he lived and so went to his hotel, a cheap hotel off the Boulevard Raspail, frequented by students and a riff-raff of actors and musicians. Vladimir had a sordid little room on the fifth floor. He found him in bed.

'Are you ill?' he asked.

'No.'

'Then why haven't you been about?'

'I can't get up. My only boots have fallen to pieces and the weather's so bad I can't go out in slippers.'

He looked at the boots and it was true no one could wear them, so, though he could ill afford it, he gave Vladimir twenty francs to buy a new pair. Vladimir thanked him profusely and they arranged to meet at the Dôme at the usual hour before dinner.

But Vladimir never turned up. Neither that evening nor the next, so on the third day he went to the hotel again and climbed the five flights to Vladimir's room. He found it full of flowers and Vladimir still in bed.

'Why haven't you come to the Dôme?' he asked.

'I can't go out, I have no boots.'

'But I gave you twenty francs to buy a pair.'

'I spent them on buying all these flowers. Aren't they beautiful? *Qui fleurit sa maison fleurit son cœur.*'

His soul was like a prisoner in a tower who saw through the narrow windows of his cell the green grass and the growing trees of the free world, yet remained perforce within those dank cold walls in perpetual gloom.

Softly the green trees grew among the ruined towers, and with a curious tenderness the ivy covered the grey stones which had withstood a hundred sieges.

The poplars, so graceful and erect, lining the river, threw on the languid stream their long reflections.

A shallow French river, limpid, mirroring the stars, while by the light of the moon the little islands shine white and beautiful. Trees in lean profusion line the banks. The fertile and charming Touraine, with its suave airs and its recollections of the romantic past.

The country stretches before you widely, so that you feel space to take a long breath, undulating and rich of soil, all green and smiling with its poplar trees, its chestnuts and its larches. It gives you a comfortable sense of prosperity, of opulence even, but of an opulence dignified by grace and beauty and a staid sobriety.

1908

Success. I don't believe it has had any effect on me. For one thing I always expected it, and when it came I accepted it as so natural that I didn't see anything to make a fuss about. Its only net value to me is that it has freed me from financial uncertainties that were never quite absent from my thoughts. I hated poverty. I hated having to scrape and save so as to make both ends meet. I don't think I'm so conceited as I was ten years ago.

Athens. I was sitting in the theatre of Dionysus, and from where I sat I could see the blue Aegean. When I thought of the great plays that had been acted on the stage, I got cold shivers down my spine. It was really a moment of intense emotion. I was thrilled and awed. A number of young Greek students came and began chattering to me in bad French. After a while one of them asked me if I would like him to recite something from the stage. I jumped at the chance. I thought he would recite some great speech by Sophocles or Euripides, and though I knew I shouldn't understand a word I prepared myself for a wonderful experience. He clambered down and struck an attitude, then with an appalling accent he started: *C'est nous les cadets de Gascogne.*

He was a philanthropist. His work was important and its value is enduring. He was hard-working and disinterested. He was in his small way a great man. He looked upon drink as a curse and, busy as he was, yet found time to go up and down the country giving temperance lectures. He would not allow any member of his family to touch alcohol. There was one room in his house which he kept locked and would permit no one to enter. He died suddenly, and soon after the funeral his family broke into the room which had always excited their curiosity. They found it full of empty bottles, bottles of brandy, whisky, gin, bottles of chartreuse, benedictine and kummel. It was only too plain that he had brought the bottles in with him one by one, and having drunk their contents had not known how to get rid of them. I would give a great deal to know what passed through his mind when he came home after delivering a temperance lecture and behind locked doors sipped green chartreuse.

1914

I met a curious man while I was having breakfast. He was a hussar and had ridden ahead of his regiment. While he breakfasted an orderly held his horse under the trees in the square. He told me he was a Cossack, born in Siberia, and for eleven years had been fighting Chinese brigands on the frontier. He was thin, with strongly marked features and large, very prominent blue eyes. He had been in Switzerland for the summer and three days before war broke out received orders to go to France at once. On the declaration he found himself unable to get back to Russia and was given a commission in a French cavalry regiment. He was talkative, vivacious and boastful. He told me that, having taken a German officer prisoner, he took him to his quarters. There he said to him: 'Now I will show you how we treat prisoners and gentlemen,' and gave him a cup of chocolate; when he had drunk it he said: 'Now I will show you how you treat them.' And he smacked his face. 'What did he say?' I asked. 'Nothing, he knew that if he had opened his mouth I would have killed him.' He talked to me about the Senegalese. They insist on cutting off the Germans' heads: 'Then you're sure they're dead – *et ça fait une bonne soupe*.' He described the shells: 'They go *zzz*, and until they fall you don't know if you're going to be killed or not.'

Fighting is going on within twenty-five kilometres. While waiting for luncheon I talked to a sharp lad of thirteen. He told me that the other day two prisoners were brought through; the boy added that he had his cap full of hot chestnuts, and he threw them one by one in the wretched men's faces. When I told him that was very wrong he laughed and said: 'Why? Everybody else was hitting them.' Some Germans came in afterwards to get a car that they had requisitioned and drove with the major to the house where it was. The *gendarmes*, ten of them, heard of this and followed. When they arrived the officer was passing into the house with the mayor, and one of the Germans was under the car doing something to it. The officer stepped to one side to let the mayor precede him: 'It showed that he had good manners,' said the old lady with whom I am billeted; and as he did so the *gendarmes* shot him; then they shot the man who was under the car. The others held up their hands in surrender, but they shot them all.

I am billeted in a small, queer house with an elderly retired shopman and his wife; they have three sons mobilized; they are very cordial, glad to have an officer in their house, and anxious to do all they can for me. They offer me hot milk before I go to bed and say I shall be a son to them all the time I am there. It is a tiny room with a large wooden bed with a canopy, and looks out on a courtyard and a great sloping red roof.

All the morning I worked in a school turned into a hospital. There must have been between two and three hundred wounded. The whole place stank of pus, no windows were open, the floors were unswept, and it was incredibly dingy and melancholy. There seemed not to be more than two doctors in charge, and they were assisted by a couple of dressers and a number of women from the town who had no knowledge of nursing. There was one German prisoner with whom I talked a little. He had had his leg cut off and was under the impression that it would not have been amputated if he had been French. The dresser asked me to explain to him that it was necessary to save his life, and with graphic detail explained to me in what a state the leg was. The prisoner was sullen and silent. He was suffering from homesickness. He lay there, yellow, a straggly beard growing over his face, with wild, miserable eyes. In order to help him the doctor had put beside him a Frenchman whose leg had been amputated to show that this was done to the French too; and the Frenchman lay in his bed cheery and gay. I had done no work of this kind for many years and at first felt embarrassed and awkward, but soon I found I could do the little that it was possible to do – clean up the wounds, paint with iodine, and bandage. I have never seen such wounds. There are great wounds of the shoulder, the bone all shattered, running with pus, stinking; there are gaping wounds in the back; there are the wounds where a bullet has passed through the lungs; there are shattered feet so that you wonder if the limb can possibly be saved.

After luncheon we were asked to take a hundred wounded to the station because all efforts were being made to evacuate the temporary hospitals at Doullens in expectation of the large number of patients who must come when the great battle begins for which troops have been pouring along the road every day since we came here. Some could walk and some were carried out to the cars on stretchers. Just as the first stretchers were being brought out, there was a sound of chanting and the stretcher-bearers put down their burdens. A cracked bell began to tinkle with a melancholy sound. A priest, a big fat fellow, in a cassock and short surplice, came out preceded by a blind man, the beadle, I suppose, led by a little boy, and they chanted the beginning of the service for the dead. Then came, borne by four men, a coffin covered with poor black cloth, and lying on it was a little wooden cross of unstained deal tacked on to which was the indication tablet of the dead soldier. They were followed by four soldiers and a nurse. They went a few steps, then the priest stopped, looked round and peevishly shrugged his shoulders. They waited. At last another coffin came, then a third and a fourth; the procession started again, the cracked bell tinkled; they passed out of the courtyard into the road; the civilians took off their hats, the military saluted; and they went their way slowly to the cemetery. I wondered what the dying in the hospital felt each time they heard the ghastly tinkling of the little cracked bell.

It was in a château of white stone, a dignified building, with the date 1726 over the door, and it combined the solid grandeur of the age of Louis XIV with the beginnings of a lighter, daintier style. It had been hastily turned into a hospital. Wounded men were lying on straw mattresses on the floor in the hall and in the dining-room; the drawing-room had been made into a casualty ward – in the hurry the furniture had not been removed, but only pushed against the wall – and it was odd to see basins, dressings and drugs on the grand piano; the patient on his stretcher, waiting to be dressed, was placed on a Buhl writing-table. An attempt had been made the night before by the French to take the village of Andechy; the French had advanced before their artillery had properly prepared the way for them, one regiment had seized the enemy's trenches, but another regiment, territorials, had wavered and then fled, so that the regiment already in possession of the German trenches had to retreat, and in retreating was terribly cut up. There were three hundred dead and sixteen hundred wounded. We took our stretchers out of the ambulances and waited for them to be loaded with those whom it was possible to move. The circular bit of lawn in front of the house, which one could imagine under usual circumstances neat and trim, was muddy like a field after a football match in the rain, and cut up by the stretcher-bearers who had walked over it through the night, and the heavy wheels of motor ambulances. In an out-house by the side were piled the dead, those who were found to be dead when they reached the hospital and those who had died in the night. They were packed close together in every kind of grotesque attitude, their uniforms filthy with mud and blood, some were strangely contorted as though they had died in agony, one had his arms outstretched as though he were playing the harp, some were flung down shapelessly like clothes without a body in them; but in death their bloodless hands, the rough, dirty hands of private soldiers, had acquired an extraordinary delicacy and distinction. We made two or three journeys to this hospital and then went to the church of the village. It stood, a bare, weather-beaten village church, on the crest of a steep little hill. The chairs had been piled up in one of the chapels and the floor covered with straw. On this lay the wounded all round the wall and in long rows, so that there was scarcely room to thread one's way between

them. In the emergency there had been no time to take away
any of the emblems of religion, and from the high altar looked
down a Virgin in plaster, with staring eyes and painted cheeks:
on each side were candlesticks and gilded jars containing paper
flowers. Everyone who was not too ill smoked cigarettes. It was a
singular scene. Round the doorway was a group of soldiers,
smoking and chatting, while they glanced now and then gravely
at the wounded; here and there others wandered around, looking
for wounded comrades and stopping now and then to ask one
about his wounds; hospital orderlies passed among the stricken
with water or soup; stretcher-bearers stepped gingerly through
the crowd, bearing their load to the ambulance. Conversation
mingled with groans of pain and the cries of the dying; some,
less wounded than their fellows, joked and laughed because
they were glad to be alive. By a column a priest was giving the
last sacrament to one who was dying. He muttered his prayers
hurriedly in a low voice. Most of them seemed badly wounded,
and they lay already in the shapeless confusion which I had
seen in the dead. Propped up against the central door of the
church, by an accident apart from the others, lay a man with an
ashy face, bearded, thin and haggard; he made no sound or
movement, but stared sullenly in front of him as though, realizing
death was inevitable, he was filled only with anger. He had a
horrible wound in the belly, and nothing could be done for him;
he waited for death. I saw another, quite a boy, round-faced
and ugly, with a yellow skin and narrow eyes, so that he had
almost the look of a Japanese, who was desperately wounded;
he knew he was dying too, but he was horribly afraid. Three
soldiers were standing at his head, leaning over him, and he
clung to the hands of one of them, crying out: 'Oh God, I'm
going to die.' He sobbed heartrendingly and heavy tears rolled
over his dirty, ugly face, and he kept saying: 'I'm so unhappy,
oh God, I'm so unhappy.' The soldiers tried to comfort him,
and the one whose hand he held caressingly passed his other
hand over the boy's face. '*Mais non, mon vieux, ta guériras.*'
Another sat against the chancel steps smoking a cigarette and
coolly watched; his cheeks were rosy, he did not look ill; he

smiled gaily as I went up to him. I saw his arm was bandaged and I asked him if the wound was severe. He laughed a little. 'Oh, that's nothing, if I had no more than that! I've got a bullet in my spine, my legs are paralysed.'

A billet at Montdidier. I found my way into the library. The neighbouring gentry before the French Revolution had town houses at Montdidier, to which they used to come in winter for society, but their mansions have now been divided into two or three houses for the bourgeoisie who have taken their place; that in which I am billeted gives one the impression of having been part of a much larger one, and the library is a little room on the ground floor which you reach by what may once have been a back staircase. It is a panelled room and the whole of one side is taken up by a bookcase built into the wall, and the books are protected by a wire network; the doors are locked, and it is impossible to get a book, but I amused myself by looking at their titles. They seem for the most part to have been collected in the eighteenth century. They are bound in calf decorated with gold tooling. On the upper shelves are devotional works, but among them, tucked away modestly, I found the picaresque novel *Don Guzman de Alfarache* and immediately below the *Mémoires d'un Homme de Qualité*; then there are the complete works of Bossuet, the sermons of Massillon, and the works in a dozen volumes of a writer I have never heard of. I am curious to know who he was and how he deserved this splendid edition. I should like also to dip into the four quarto volumes which contain the *Histoire de Montdidier*. Rousseau is represented only by the *Confessions*. On a lower shelf I found the identical edition of Buffon's works which amused my own childhood. The collector of these books was of a serious turn of mind, for I found the works of Descartes and an imposing history of the world, a history of France in many volumes, and a translation of Hume's *History of England*. There was a large edition of Scott's novels, full octavo, bound in black leather and very depressing to look at; and there was an edition of the works of Lord Byron that looked most unsuitably solemn. Soon I did not want to read any of the books I saw; it seemed to me much more entertaining to look at their titles behind their prison of gilt wicker; they had a magic thus which was greater far than I should have found if I had been able to take hold of them and turn their musty pages.

Amiens. There are nearly as many English people here as in Boulogne, and great ladies drive about in huge motor-cars and visit the sick and conduct hospitals. I was told an agreeable story of one of them. A train-load of wounded had just come from the front and the wounded were placed temporarily in the hospital at the station. A lady went round giving them hot soup. Presently she came to a man who had been shot through the gullet and the lungs; she was just about to give him soup when the doctor in charge told her that if she did she would *drown* him. 'What do you mean?' she said. 'Of course he must have soup. It can't possibly do him any harm.' 'I've been in practice a great many years and through three campaigns,' answered the doctor, 'and my professional opinion is that if you give that man soup he'll die.' The lady grew very impatient. 'What nonsense,' she said. 'You give him soup on your own responsibility,' said the doctor. She held a cup to the man's mouth, who tried to swallow, and promptly died. The lady was furious with the doctor: 'You've killed that man,' she said. 'Pardon me,' he answered, 'you killed him. I told you what would happen.'

The landlord of the hotel at Steenvoorde. He is quite a character, a Fleming, cautious, slow, heavy and stout, with round eyes, a round nose, and a round face, a man of forty-five perhaps; he does not welcome the arriving guest, but puts obstacles in the way of his taking a room or having dinner and has to be persuaded to provide him with what he wants; when he has overcome his instinctive mistrust of the stranger, he is friendly. He has a childlike sense of humour, heavy and slow as himself, with a feeling for the practical joke; and he has a fat, tardy laugh. Now that he has come to know me, though still a little suspicious, he is pleasant and affable. When I said to him: '*Votre café est bien bon, patron,*' he answered elliptically: '*C'est lui qui le boit qui l'est.*' He speaks in a broad accent, mixing up chaotically the second person singular and the second person plural. He reminds one of those donors of altar pieces that you see in old Flemish pictures; and his wife might be the donor's wife; she is a large woman, with a stern, unsmiling, lined face, a rather alarming creature; but now and then you feel that there is the Flemish humour behind her severity, and sometimes I have heard her laugh heartily at the discomfiture of some offending person. The first day I arrived here, when I was persuading the patron to give me dinner, he went to ask his wife if it was possible. '*Il faut bien que je la demande,*' he said, '*puisque je couche avec.*'

I enjoyed myself at Steenvoorde. It was cold and uncomfortable. It was impossible to get a bath. The food was poor. The work was hard and tedious. But what a delight it was to have no responsibility! I had no decisions to make. I did what I was told, and having done it my time was my own. I could waste it with a clear conscience. Till then I had always thought it so precious that I could not afford uselessly to waste a minute. I was obsessed by the ideas that seethed in my head and the desire to express them. There was so much I wanted to learn, so many places I wanted to see, so many experiences I felt I couldn't afford to miss; ,but the years were passing and time was short. I was never without a sense of responsibility. To what? Well, I suppose to myself and to such gifts as I had, desiring to make the most both of them and of myself. And now I was free. I enjoyed my liberty. There was a sensual, almost voluptuous, quality in the pleasure of it. I could well understand it when I was told of certain men that they were having the time of their lives in the war. I don't know if there's such a word as hebetude in English, but if there is that's the state I so thoroughly enjoyed.

1915

We were sitting in a wine shop in Capri when Norman came in and told us that T. was about to shoot himself. We were startled. Norman said that when T. told him what he was going to do he could think of no reason to dissuade him. 'Are you going to do anything about it?' I asked. 'No.' He ordered a bottle of wine and sat down to await the sound of the shot.

1916

Liverpool to New York. Mrs Langtry was on board. We neither of us knew anybody so we spent much of our time together. I had never known her well before. She still had a fine figure and a noble carriage, and if you were walking behind her you might have taken her for a young woman. She told me she was sixty-six. Her eyes, which they say were so beautiful, were much smaller than one would have expected, and their blue, once intense, I believe, was pale. The only remains of her beauty were her short upper lip and her engaging smile. She used very little make-up. Her manner was easy, unaffected and well-bred; it was that of a woman of the world who has always lived in good society.

She made one remark which I think is the proudest thing I ever heard a woman say. The name of Freddy Gebhardt recurred frequently in her conversation one day, and I, to whom it was new, at last asked who he was. 'You mean to say you've never heard of Freddy Gebhardt?' she cried with real astonishment. 'Why, he was the most celebrated man in two hemispheres.' 'Why?' I inquired. 'Because I loved him,' she answered.

She told me that during her first season in London she had only two evening dresses, and one of these was a day dress which by the pulling out of a string could be arranged for wearing at night. She told me that in those days no woman made up, and her advantage was the brilliant colouring that she had by nature. The excitement she caused was so intense that when she went to the livery stable to mount her hired horse to ride in the park they had to shut the gates to keep out the crowd.

She told me that she had been very much in love with the Crown Prince Rudolf, and he had given her a magnificent emerald ring. One evening they had a quarrel, and in the course of it she snatched his ring off her finger and threw it on the fire. With a cry he flung himself down on his knees and scrabbled out (this was the word she used) the burning coals to save the valuable stone. Her short upper lip curled scornfully as she related the incident. 'I couldn't love him after that,' she said.

I saw her two or three times after we arrived in New York. She was mad about dancing and went nearly every night to a dance hall. She said the men danced beautifully and you only had to pay them fifty cents. It gave me a nasty turn to hear her say this so blandly. The notion of this woman who had had the world at her feet paying a man half a dollar to dance with her filled me with shame.

Honolulu. The Union Saloon. You get to it by a narrow passage from King Street, and in the passage are offices so that thirsty souls may be supposed bound for one of these just as well as for the bar. It is a large square room with three entrances, and opposite the bar two corners have been partitioned off into little cubicles. Legend states that they were built so that King Kalakaua might go and drink without being seen by his subjects. In one of these he may have sat over his bottle, a bronze potentate, with R.L.S., discussing the misdeeds of missionaries and the inhibitions of Americans. The saloon is wainscoted with dark brown wood to about five feet from the floor, and above, the wall is papered with a varied assortment of pictures. They are an odd collection. Prints of Queen Victoria, a portrait in oils, in a rich gold frame, of King Kalakaua, old line engravings of the eighteenth century (there is one after a theatrical picture by Dewilde, heaven knows how it got there), oleographs from the Christmas supplements of the *Graphic* and *Illustrated London News* of twenty years ago, advertisements of whisky, gin, champagne and beer, photographs of baseball teams and of native orchestras. Behind the bar serve two large half-castes, in white, fat, clean-shaven, dark-skinned, with thick curly hair and large, bright eyes.

Here gather American men of business, sailors, not able seamen, but captains, engineers and first mates, storekeepers and Kanakas. Business of all sorts is done here. The place has a vaguely mysterious air and you can imagine that it would be a fit scene for shady transactions. In the daytime the light is dim and at night the electric light is cold and sinister.

The Chinese quarter. Streets of frame houses, one, two, three storeys high, painted in various colours, but time and weather have made the colours dingy. They have a dilapidated look as though the leases were running out and it was worth no tenant's while to make repairs. In the stores is every imaginable article of Western and Eastern commerce. The Chinese clerks sit impassive within the shops and stare idly at the passers-by. Sometimes, at night, you see a pair, yellow, lined, with slanting eyes, intent on a mysterious game which might be the Chinese equivalent of chess. They are surrounded by onlookers as intense as they, and they take an immense time between each move, calculating deeply.

The Red Light District. You go down sidestreets by the harbour, in the darkness, across a rickety bridge, and you come to a road, all ruts and holes; a little farther, and there is parking room for motors on either side; there are saloons gaily lit and a barber's shop; there is a certain stir, an air of expectant agitation; you turn down a narrow alley, either to the right or to the left, and find yourself in the district. The street divides Iwelei into two parts, but each part is exactly like the other. Rows of little bungalows, painted green and very neat and tidy in appearance, even a trifle prim; and the road between them is broad and straight.

Iwelei is laid out like a garden city, and in its respectable regularity, its order and trimness, gives an impression of sardonic horror; for never can the search for love have been so planned and systematized. The pretty bungalows are divided into two lodgings; each is inhabited by a woman, and each consists of two rooms and a kitchenette. One is a bedroom in which there is a chest-of-drawers, a large bed with a canopy and curtains, and a chair or two. It has an overcrowded look. The parlour contains a large table, a gramophone, sometimes a piano, and half a dozen chairs. On the walls are pennants from the San Francisco exhibition and sometimes cheap prints, the favourite of which is *September Morn*, and photographs of San Francisco and Los Angeles. In the kitchenette is disorder. Here beer and gin are kept for visitors.

The women sit at their windows so that they may be clearly seen. Some are reading, some are sewing, and take no notice of the passer-by; others watch him approach and call out to him as he passes. They are of all ages and all nations. There are Japanese, Negro women, Germans, Americans, Spaniards. (It is strange and nostalgic as you pass to hear on a gramophone *coplas* or a *seguidilla*.) Most of them have no trace of youth or beauty, and you wonder how, looking as they do, they can earn a living. Their cheeks are heavily rouged and they are dressed in cheap finery. When you go in the blinds are drawn down and if someone knocks the answer is: Busy. You are at once invited to drink beer and the woman tells you how many glasses she has had that day. She asks you where you come from. The gramophone is turned on. The price is a dollar.

The streets between are lit by a rare street lamp, but chiefly by the light that comes from the open windows of the bungalows. Men wander about, for the most part silently, looking at the women; now and then one makes up his mind and slinks up the three steps that lead into the parlour, is let in, and then the door and window are shut and the blind is pulled down. Most of the men are only there to look. They are of all nationalities. Sailors from the ships in port, sailors from the American gunboats, mostly drunk, Hawaiians, soldiers from the regiments, white and black, quartered on the island, Chinese, Japanese. They wander about in the night, and desire seems to throb in the air.

For some time the local papers had been writing articles about the scandal of Iwelei, the missionaries had been clamorous, but the police refused to stir. Their argument was that with the great preponderance of men in Oahu prostitution was inevitable, and to localize it made it easy to control and rendered medical examination more reliable. The papers attacked the police and at last they were forced to act. A raid was made, and fourteen ponces were arrested; oddly enough on the charge sheet most of them claimed French nationality. It suggests that the profession is peculiarly attractive to the citizens of France. A few days later all the women were summoned and sentenced to be on their good behaviour for a year on pain of being sent to prison. Most of them went straight back to San Francisco. I went to Iwelei the night of the raid. Most of the houses were closed, and there was hardly anyone in the streets. Here and there little groups of three or four women discussed the news in undertones. The place was dark and silent. Iwelei had ceased to exist.

Haula. A little hotel on the windward side of Oahu kept by a German Swiss and his Belgian wife. It is a wooden bungalow with a wide veranda and the doors are protected from mosquitos by wire netting. In the garden bananas, papaias and coconut trees. The Swiss is a little man with a square German head, a head too large for his body, bald, with a long, untidy moustache. His wife is matronly, stout and red-faced, with brown hair severely brushed back. She gives you the impression of being competent and business-like. They like to talk of their homes which they haven't seen for seventeen years, he of Berne, she of the village near Namur where she was born. After dinner the hostess comes into the living-rooms and chats while she plays patience and presently the landlord, who is also the cook, comes in and sits down to gossip.

From here you visit the sacred waterfall, passing through fields of sugar-cane, and then along a narrow brook upwards towards the mountains. A track runs along it, now on one side, now on the other, so that every now and then you have to ford the stream. Wherever there is a large stone with a flattish top, you see numbers of leaves that have been placed on it and are held down by a pebble. They are offerings to propitiate the deity of the place. The water falls through a narrow gorge into a deep round pool, and you are surrounded by tangled scrub, green and immensely luxuriant. Beyond, above, is a valley which, it is said, no one has ever explored.

The Hawaiians. Their colour ranges from copper almost to black. They are tall and well-made, their nose is flattish, their eyes are large and their lips full and sensual. Their hair is dark and crisply curling. They incline to fat, and the women, graceful and slender in youth, with age become very stout. When they grow old both sexes become ugly, like monkeys; and it is strange after the beauty of their youth. Perhaps age is only beautiful when thought, activity, or violence of emotion has moulded the character. The Hawaiians, having lived a life purely animal, revert with age to the animal type.

Kanakas at Waikiki. Tough Bill: a tall, dark fellow, with protruding lips, boastful like a child or a Negro. Holstein: known as Bananas, a descendant of a shipwrecked sailor in a Danish boat lost on one of the islands in the eighteenth century, odd on account of his dark red hair. Fat Miller: a stout, very dark man with a round face and the manner of a buffoon oddly at variance with a kind of innate dignity.

The Hula-Hula. A small room with papered walls, decorated with Californian pennants and furnished with cheap wicker furniture. At one end sits an old man on the floor, with his legs tucked under him. He is thin and lined, with grey hair cut very short. He looks like a fisherman in some piece of realistic sculpture of the Hellenistic school. His dark face is impassive. He makes strange rhythmical sounds by beating a gourd with his hands and sings in a monotonous undertone. He seems never to stop to take breath. The dancers are two women, neither of them young, one fat, the other thin. They dance with little movement of the feet, but much of the body. Each dance is said to express in motion the words of the song the old man sings.

The Departure. At the entrance to the wharf women assail the passers-by with offers of *leis*, garlands of flowers or of yellow tissue paper. They are hung round the neck of the departing. The people on board throw coloured streamers to those standing below, and the side of the ship is gay with the thin lines of paper, yellow, green, blue and violet. The band plays 'Aloaha Oe', and amid shouted farewells the ship, breaking the streamers, moves slowly away.

Kilauea. The volcano is on Hawaii, the largest island of the group. You land at Hilo and drive up, first through fields of rice and sugar-cane and then, climbing all the time, through a forest of great tree-ferns. They are weird and strange like the imaginations of some draughtsman of the horrible. All manner of climbing plants wind around the trees in an impenetrable tangle. Gradually the vegetation stops and you come to the lava field, grey, dead, silent; here no plants grow and no birds sing; you see the smoke rising, here and there thickly, in other places ascending thin and straight like the smoke from a cottage chimney. You get out and walk. The lava crunches under your feet. Now and then you step over narrow fissures from which the sulphurous smoke rises, making you cough. You come to the jagged edge of the crater. Nothing has prepared you for the sight. It is stupendous and alarming. You look down upon a vast sea of lava. It is black and heavy. It is in perpetual movement. The lava is only a thin crust and it is broken at irregular intervals by gashes of red fire, and here and there again are geysers of flame rising into the air, thirty, or forty, or fifty feet. They spurt up, white hot, like artificial fountains. The two most impressive things are the roar: it is like the roar of surf on a gloomy day, as unceasing, or like the roar of a cataract, as formidable; and secondly the movement: the lava moves on, on, all the time, with a stealthy movement in which you may almost see the purpose of a living thing. There is something strangely determined about its quiet progress, it has a malign tenacity; and yet it transcends anything living, it has the inevitableness of fate and the ruthlessness of time. The lava is like some huge formless creature born of primeval slime crawling slowly in pursuit of some loathsome prey. The lava moves forward steadily towards a fiery gap and then seems to fall into a bottomless cavern of flame. You see vast holes of fire, great caves of flame. A man standing near said: 'Gosh, it's like hell,' but a priest beside him turned and said: 'No, it is like the face of God.'

The Pacific. On some days it offers all your fancy pictured. The sea is calm and under the blue sky brilliantly blue. On the horizon are fleecy clouds, and at sunset they take strange shapes so that it is almost impossible not to believe you see a range of mountains. The nights then are lovely, the stars very bright, and later, when the moon rises, it is dazzling in its brilliancy. But more often than you would have expected the sea is rough, capped with white crests, and sometimes it is as grey as the Atlantic. There is a heavy swell. The most wonderful thing about the Pacific is its solitariness. You pass day after day without seeing a ship. Now and then a few seagulls suggest that land is not far distant, one of those islands lost in a wilderness of waters; but not a tramp, not a sailing vessel, not a fishing-boat. It is an empty desert, and presently the emptiness fills you with a vague foreboding. There is something frightening about the vast, silent emptiness.

Passengers. Gray: A tall Jew, powerfully built and very strong, but ungraceful and clumsy of gesture; he has a sallow face, long and thin, a big nose and dark eyes. His voice is loud and strident. He is aggressive and a bully and he always wants to have his own way. He is irascible, sensitive and perpetually on the look-out for slights. He keeps vaguely threatening to give someone a hit on the nose. He's fond of poker. He's not above having a look at the cards of the person sitting next to him if he gets the chance. He constantly abuses his cards and curses his luck, but almost every time he plays, he rises a winner. When he loses, he loses his temper too and insults the table, then goes away and won't speak to anyone for the rest of the evening. He's very sharp in money matters and will cheat a friend out of sixpence if he can.

But a sentimental tune on the gramophone, the obvious beauties of the moon over the Pacific wonderfully affect him and his voice trembles as he says: 'Hell, isn't that swell.'

Elfenbein. He is travelling to Sydney for his firm. He is much younger than Gray, short, sturdy, with a big head covered with crisp dark hair receding very far over the temples; he is clean-shaven, and he has prominent brown eyes. He comes from Brooklyn. He is as noisy, vulgar and loud-voiced as Gray, but he is kindly, and notwithstanding a roughness of speech which is a sort of defensive armour, sensitive and emotional. He is self-conscious of his race and when the conversation touches it looks away, silent and embarrassed. He has tremendous vitality. He bellows unceasingly. He is sharp on money and will not be 'done'. At Pago-Pago he took some old shirts on shore and traded them with the natives for toy canoes, bananas and pineapples.

Marks is the opal king of Australia, a little man of nearly forty, with hair going grey and a much lined small face. He is a natural buffoon and loves to make himself ridiculous. He goes in for all the ship's sports with gusto. At the dress-parade he got himself up like a Hula girl and played the part with immense animation.

Melville. A tall man, with a saturnine countenance, long, dark, curling hair, turning grey, and strongly marked features. He is going to Australia to produce American farces and musical comedies. He has travelled all over the world and talks enthusiastically of Ceylon and Tahiti. He is very affable when spoken to, but naturally silent. He sits reading French novels all day long.

The engineer told me about Ah Fons. He started life in Hawaii as a coolie, became a cook, bought land, imported Chinese labour, and in the end became rich. He married a Portuguese half-caste and had a large family. They were brought up as Americans and he felt himself a stranger among them. He had a deep contempt for Western civilization. He thought of the wife of his youth in China and the life of the seaport in which he lived then. One day he called his family together and told them he was going to leave them. He disappeared into mystery.

*There is the making of a story here, but I never wrote it because
I discovered that Jack London had already done so.*

Pago-Pago. The ship makes her way along a beach rising quickly
to hills covered to the top with luxuriant vegetation; the coconuts
grow thickly along it and among them you see the grass houses
of the Samoans, and here and there, gleaming white, a little
church. Presently you come to the entrance of the harbour.
The ship steams slowly in and docks. It is a great landlocked
harbour big enough to hold a fleet of battleships, and all round
it rise, high and steep, the green hills. Near the entrance, getting
such breeze as comes from the sea, stands the Governor's
house in a garden. Near the quay are two or three trim bungalows
and a tennis court, then the quay with its warehouses. To receive
the ship come a little crowd of natives, a number of U.S. sailors,
and some officials. Ships come from the States once in three weeks
and their arrival is an event. To barter with the travellers on their
way to Sydney the natives bring pines and huge bunches of
bananas, tapa cloths, necklaces, some made from the backs of
beetles, others of brown seeds, kava bowls and models of war
canoes.

There is not a breath of air in Pago-Pago. It is terribly hot
and very rainy. From out of a blue sky you will see heavy grey
clouds come floating over the mouth of the harbour, and then
the rain falls in torrents.

The natives. They are brown, copper-coloured is the usual
epithet, and mostly they have dark hair, often curling, but often
straight. Many dye it white with lime, and then, with their
regular features, they have an appearance of extraordinary
distinction. They often dye it, men, women and children, various
shades of red, and then in the young it has an agreeably frivolous
air. Their eyes are rather far apart and they are not set deeply
in the head, which gives them a little the look of archaic bas-
reliefs. They are tall and finely-built, and often you see types
that remind you of the Aegina marbles. They walk with long
steps, with ease and dignity, slowly; and when they meet you
on the road they call a greeting, and their faces light up with

smiles. They are quick laughers. Most of the children and boys have *yaws*, disfiguring sores like torpid ulcers. You see many cases of elephantiasis, men going along with a huge heavy arm or a grossly-mis-shapen leg into which the foot has sunk away. The women wear lava-lavas and over them a loose gown shaped something like a chemise.

The men are tattooed with an elaborate pattern from the waist to the knees and round the wrists; the women on the arms and thighs with little crosses rather far apart. Men often wear a flower of the hibiscus attached to the ear; the scarlet looks like a red flame against their brown faces. Women put the white sweet-smelling *tiare* in their hair, and its fragrance scents the air as they walk.

The missionary. He was a tall thin man, with long limbs loosely jointed, hollow cheeks and high cheekbones; his fine, large dark eyes were deep in their sockets, and he had full sensual lips; he wore his hair rather long. He had a cadaverous look, and a look of suppressed fire. His hands were large, rather finely shaped, with long fingers, and his naturally pale skin was deeply burned by the Pacific sun.

Mrs W., his wife, was a little woman with her hair very elaborately done, with prominent blue eyes behind gold-rimmed *pince-nez*; her face was long, like a sheep's, but she gave no impression of foolishness, rather of extreme alertness. She had the quick movements of a bird. The most noticeable thing about her was her voice, high, metallic and without inflection; it fell on the ear with a hard monotony, irritating the nerves like the clamour of a pneumatic drill. She was dressed in black, and wore round her neck a thin gold chain from which hung a small cross. She was a New Englander.

Mrs W. told me that her husband was a medical missionary, and as his district (the Gilberts) consisted of widely separated islands, he frequently had to go long distances by canoe. The sea was often rough and his journeys were not without danger. During his absence she remained at their headquarters and managed the mission. She spoke of the depravity of the natives in a voice nothing could hush, but with a vehement, unctuous horror; she described their marriage customs as obscene beyond description. She said that when first they went to the Gilberts it was impossible to find a single 'good' girl in any of the villages. She was very bitter about the dancing.

Miss Thompson. Plump, pretty in a coarse fashion, perhaps not more than twenty-seven: she wore a white dress and a large white hat, and long white boots from which her calves, in white cotton stockings, bulged. She had left Iwelei after the raid and was on her way to Apia, where she hoped to get a job in the bar of a hotel. She was brought to the house by the quartermaster, a little, very wrinkled man, indescribably dirty.

The lodging house. It is a two-storey frame house with verandas on both floors, and it is about five minutes' walk from the dock, on the Broad Road, and faces the sea. Below is a store in which are sold canned goods, pork and beans, beef, hamburger steak, canned asparagus, peaches and apricots; and cotton goods, lava-lavas, hats, rain-coats and such like. The owner is a half-caste with a native wife surrounded by little brown children. The rooms are almost bare of furniture, a poor iron bed with a ragged mosquito-curtain, a rickety chair and a washstand. The rain rattles down on the corrugated iron roof. No meals are provided.

On these three notes I constructed a story called 'Rain'.

Red. He has been a sailor in the U.S. Navy and coming down to Pago had bought his discharge. He was by trade a butcher, but during the three years he had been at Pago had done little work. He was as near a beachcomber as I saw. He was a man of twenty-six, perhaps, of middle size, slender, with good features but a sullen look, a small red moustache and three days' growth of beard, and a fine head of curling red hair. He was dressed in a sleeveless singlet and a pair of dirty drill trousers. The proprietor of the eating-house being ill, Red was running it in return for his keep. He talked of going back to the States to get work, but you felt he could never summon up resolution to leave the island. He asked vaguely if any work was to be got at Apia. The eating-house consisted of a little green bungalow at the back of Pago, almost on the edge of the bush, among breadfruit trees, coconuts and mangoes. It had a modest room in which was a bar, but no drinks were served there, since Pago is dry, and two small tables covered with a red cloth. There were shelves behind the bar, and on these a few dusty tins of canned beef, tomato soup and preserved apricots. Next door was a small slovenly bedroom, and behind the bungalow, in the open, protected only by the veranda roof, were the stove on which Red did the cooking and a rough table to act as pantry, larder and whatnot. When the ship came in and brought eggs these were to be had, but otherwise nothing save hamburger steak, which he made every day, and coffee. For dinner Red made soup out of the remains of the joints from which he had made the hamburger steak. The clients were the very few strangers who dropped in at Pago on their way to Australia, a few sailors from the U.S. station, and a number of natives. Red was a man of few words. It was difficult to get him to speak. He refused the offer of cigarettes or cigars in a surly way. When at last he became more communicative it was to talk of women, of the place, to lament that it ruined one and made one fit for nothing, and to show one a collection of dirty postcards.

The *Manua*. A schooner of seventy tons, with paraffin auxiliary; she does, when there is no head wind, between four and five knots; she is a bedraggled craft, painted white long ago and now dirty, dingy and mottled. She was built for shallow waters and rolls terribly. 'One day,' the skipper told me, 'she'll turn turtle and we shall all go to the bottom of the Pacific.' The cabin, about eight foot by five, serves as a dining-room and sleeping quarters for passengers, and the supercargo makes out his accounts in it. It is lit at night by a paraffin lamp.

The crew consists of a captain, a supercargo, an engineer and his assistant, a Chinese cook and half a dozen Kanakas. The boat smells overpoweringly of the paraffin with which she is run. The Kanakas wear blue cotton trousers and nothing else;

the cook is dressed in dirty, ragged whites. The captain wears a
blue flannel shirt, open at the neck, an old grey felt hat, and a
very old pair of blue serge trousers. The engineer is dressed like
engineers all over the world, a very old tweed cap, old dark pants
and an old grey flannel shirt, the whole a mess of grime and dirt.

There are three tiny cabins, with a couple of berths in each,
quite dark when the door is shut and with hardly room to stand
in. The skipper has a rather larger cabin, with a single berth
and a porthole. It is airy and comparatively roomy. The native
passengers, in lava-lavas, are crowded aft and forwards; they
have baskets made of green coconut leaves in which are their
provisions and little bundles done up in large coloured handkerchiefs containing their personal belongings.

We left Pago at about half-past four. A number of natives
had come to see their friends off, and there was much weeping
among those who were going and those who were staying
behind. We went along the coast under our power, and the
schooner rolled heavily, but presently, the wind favouring, the
sail was hoisted and she rolled less. There were no waves, but
a long heavy swell.

Supper was served by the cook at half-past five. A soup made
of heaven knows what, balls of mince meat strongly flavoured
with garlic, and potatoes, and to finish, canned apricots. Tea
and canned milk. Our party consisted of a Scotch doctor and
his wife, going to Apia to take up an appointment at the hospital,
a missionary, an Australian storekeeper going to Burns Philip's
store at Apai, Gerald and myself. After supper we went on deck.
The night fell quickly and the rolling grew less. The land was now
only a darker mass against the sky. The Southern Cross was very
bright. After a while three or four members of the crew came up
and sat down smoking. One had a banjo, another a ukulele and a
concertina. They began to play and sing, and as they sang they
clapped their hands in time. A couple of them stood up and
danced. It was a strange, barbaric dance, in which there was
something savage and primeval, a rapid dance, with quick
movements of hands and feet and strange contortions of the
body; it was sensual, sexual even, but sexual without passion,

it was animal, naïve, weird without mystery, natural in short and one might almost say child-like.

It was a curious emotion to sail through this silent sea under the stars and the passionate sky, while the Kanakas played and sang and danced. At last they grew tired and stretched themselves out on the deck and slept, and all was silence.

The skipper. He is a little plump man, without angles, with a round face like the full moon, red and clean-shaven, a little fat button of a nose, very white teeth, fair hair close-cropped, with short fat legs and fat arms. His hands are plump too, dimpled on the knuckles. His eyes are round and blue and he wears gold-rimmed spectacles. He is not without charm. He never speaks without an oath, but a good-natured one. He is a jolly soul. He is American, of thirty perhaps, and he has spent all his life on the Pacific. He has been first officer and then captain in passenger ships plying along the coast of California, but he lost his ship and with it his certificate and has now come down to the command of this dirty little tramp. It has not interfered with his good humour. He takes life easily, he is fond of his whisky and fond of the Samoan girls, and he tells vivid, funny stories of his success with them.

The supercargo. He is a clerk in the charter's firm, R. & Co., of San Francisco, a little wiry man, quite young, from Portland, Oregon. His head is shaved, and he has large brown eyes and an amusing face. He seems to be on springs, always alert and merry, hard-drinking; and in the mornings he is torpid from the night before. 'Gee, I had a hell of a night,' he says, 'never again, I'm going on the wagon from now on.' But by noon he has recovered, his head aches less, and with a drink he is as bright and cheery as ever.

Apia. It lies along the beach amid coconut trees, a straggling little town of frame buildings with red roofs of corrugated iron. The Catholic cathedral, all white, stands out not without impressiveness; and beside it the Protestant chapels look like meeting-houses. It is hardly a harbour that you sail into, it is an open roadstead by the reef. There is little shipping, a few cutters, a number of whale-boats, a motor-boat or two, and some native canoes.

The Central Hotel. A frame building of three storeys, with verandas all round it, a paddock on one side in which feeds a grey pony, and behind, a couple of yards in one of which is a bungalow for the Chinese servants and in the other stalls for horses and spaces for the traps and buggies of men coming from other parts of the island. The principal room in the hotel is a bar divided into two parts; there is a long, low dining-room and a small hall with a round table and wickerwork chairs. On the first floor there is a larger veranda, overlooking the street, with big chairs in it. The bedrooms are on each side of a central passage at the end of which are two little chambers in which are showers.

The owner of the hotel. He is a dentist by profession, and comes from Newcastle. He is a little man, not fat, but not lean either, with black hair, thin on the top and turning grey, and a small untidy moustache, a very red face, partly due to sunshine, partly to alcohol, and a small red nose. He wears white ducks and a black tie. He is an excitable little man, more often than not tipsy, and he loves to tell you the scandal of the island. He is fifty but talks grandly of going to the front next February, and you are pretty sure that in February he will talk of going in March. He spends his time chatting with the guests and behind his own bar, where he can always be persuaded to take a drink with a customer. He has owned hotels in Sydney and is invariably ready to buy or sell anything from a hotel to a horse, from a motor-car to a camp bedstead. He is bellicose in his conversation and fond of telling you how he hit this person or the other on the nose. He never fails to come out of his contests victorious. He is a figurehead in the hotel, which is run by his wife, a tall gaunt woman of five and forty, with an imposing presence and a determined air, a large-featured woman with a firm mouth. He is terrified of her, and rumours run about the hotel of domestic quarrels in which she has used her fist and her foot as well as her tongue to keep him in subjection. She has been known after a night of drunkenness to keep him for a day in his own little bit of veranda, and on these occasions, afraid to leave his prison, he talks rather pathetically to people on the street below.

Banana leaves. They have a kind of battered beauty like a lovely woman in rags.

The frivolous elegance of palm trees.

The coconut trees came down to the water's edge, not in rows, but spaced out with a certain ordered formality. They had something of the air of a ballet of spinsters, elderly but flippant, who stood with a simpering grace in affected attitudes.

The administrator. He is in Apia because his wife is awaiting her confinement. She is a big untidy woman, in flowing draperies, who suggests Notting Hill Gate or West Kensington. She has languid movements and a drawling voice. She is not handsome, nor even pretty, but she has a pleasant, ingenuous face. He is a tall man, and his small thin face is tanned by years of exposure to the tropical sun. A small moustache barely conceals the weakness of his mouth. He has a foolish laugh, and when he laughs he displays long yellow teeth. He began life as a medical student and prides himself on his medical knowledge. He likes silly jokes, practical chiefly, and is fond of chaffing people. He has the utmost contempt for the whites of Apia. One can guess that he runs his island competently, but with an exaggerated insistence on insignificant details. He measures everything by the standards of the public schoolboy. He regards the natives as wilful children, unreasonable and only just human, who must be treated without any nonsense, but not unkindly. He boasts that he keeps his island like a new pin. There is something old-maidish about him. He looks forward to the time when he can retire and live in the dull London street which you feel he regards as his only real home. He is incredibly conceited.

When you come out of the Central and turn to the left, you pass stores, mostly kept by half-castes; then you come to the large buildings of the German Firm: this is the name by which are known the offices and headquarters of the great German company which had something close to a monopoly of the South

Pacific commerce; then you come to pleasant little friendly bungalows inhabited by residents, and farther still, straggling, a native village. When you turn to the right from the hotel, you pass more stores, Government buildings, the English club, and then you come to another native village. In the back part of Apia are stores and small frame houses in which live Chinese and half-castes, and farther back still, clusters of native huts. Coconut trees grow everywhere, mangoes, and here and there trees rich with clustered flowers.

L. He was an estate agent in London and came to Samoa originally for his health. He is a little, thin man, with a long face and a narrow, weak chin, a prominent nose, large and bony, and good, dark brown eyes. He is married to a half-caste and has a small son, but she lives with her parents and he at the hotel. He has rather a cunning, shifty look and does not impress you as honest or scrupulous; but he is anxious to be thought a good sport and is full of a surface jollity. He is quite intelligent. He drinks a great deal and is dead drunk three or four days a week, often by mid-afternoon. Then he is quarrelsome and wants to fight people. He is sullen and vindictive. He lies about stupefied, and when obliged to walk waddles on bent knees.

Gardner is a German American who has changed his name from Kärtner, a fat, bald-headed, big man, always in very clean white ducks; he has a round, clean-shaven face and he looks at you benignly through gold-rimmed spectacles. The *faux bon homme*. He is here to open a business for a San Francisco firm of jobbers in the goods sold on the island, calicos, machinery, everything that is saleable, which they exchange for copra. He drinks heavily, and though fifty is always willing to stay up all night with the 'boys', but he never gets drunk. He is jolly and affable, but very shrewd; nothing interferes with his business, and his good fellowship is part of his stock in trade. He plays cards with the young men and gradually takes all their money from them.

Dr T. A. Scot with an Aberdeen accent, who was in practice in New Zealand until the war took him to France as a surgeon. He had been invalided out and sent here 'on light duty'. He is a thin man, with a peaked face and thinning short red hair. He talks with a Scottish accent in a very low, quiet voice. He is a precise, rather pedantic little man.

Sharp. An engineer, formerly in the U.S. navy. He is married to a half-caste in Apia, by whom he has two children. He is a long thin man, with a scraggy neck, a small face with a hooked nose; he has a rather bird-like air, the air of a bird of prey. He is dressed in blue overalls and a sleeveless blue jersey; his arms are heavily tattooed with flags naked women and initials. On his naked feet he wears sand shoes which were white, but are now quite black, and on his head, indoors and out, a shapeless black cap.

The English Club. It is a simple little frame house facing the sea, with a billiard room on one side, and a small bar at the back of it, a lounge with wicker chairs on the other side, and above, a room in which are old papers and magazines. It is used merely for drinking and playing cards and billiards.

C. He trains horses for the local races. He is an Australian, a very tall athletic fellow so dark that you might take him for a half-caste; his features look a little too big for his face, but in his white riding breeches, spurs and gaiters, he is a trim, handsome and upstanding figure. He is very fond of his half-caste wife, who is plain and sallow, with several gold teeth, and he is proud of a sprawling, white-faced baby with black eyes. His house, in the middle of his plantation, is surrounded by a veranda, and has magnificent views over the fertile country, with Apia and the sea in the distance. It is untidy, poorly furnished, with mats on the floor, rockers and cheap wooden tables. There is a litter of papers and illustrated weeklies, guns, riding boots and diapers.

Swan. A tiny little old man, wrinkled, battered and bowed, who looks like a white monkey. He has pale blue eyes peering shrewdly from between red-rimmed lids. He is knotted and gnarled like a very old tree. He is a Swede and came out to the islands forty years ago as mate of a sailing vessel. Since then he has been skipper of a schooner engaged in the slave trade, a 'black-birder', a blacksmith, a trader, a planter. Men have sought to kill him, and he has a hernia in the chest which is the result of a wound got in a scrap with Solomon Islanders. At one time he was fairly rich, but he was ruined by the great hurricane which destroyed the stores he owned, and now he possesses nothing but the eighteen acres of coco plantation on the proceeds of which he lives. He has had four native wives and more children than he can count. He is to be seen every day in the Central bar, dressed in shabby blue linen clothes, drinking rum and water.

A trader. He looks as if he had been in the tropics all his life, he is burned dark brown, and he is thin as though all the flesh had been sweated off him; he is bald and clean-shaven; he pays no particular attention to anybody but goes quietly about his business.

Another. A dapper tallish man with his hair worn long, with the love-lock of the London tradesman. He talks with a Cockney accent and has mincing genteel ways; you feel he is just about to wash his hands, his backbone is always trembling to a bow, and you can imagine the words coming from his mouth: 'This way, Madam, second on the right, ladies' hosiery.' He might have come out of Swan & Edgar ten days ago; in point of fact he has been at Apia ten years.

Gus. He is a half-caste, son of a Danish father and a Samoan, and owns an important store dealing in copra, canned and dry goods; he has several white men in his service. He is fat and smooth and quietly smiling; he reminds you of the eunuchs you see in Constantinople; he has an ingratiating way and a suave, oily politeness.

Salologa. The schooner started from Apia about one, and towards six we arrived off Savaii. The reef was a white line of foam. We went along it, up and down, trying to find the opening, and then night came, so the skipper turned round, putting out to sea, and anchored. When the sail was furled, the boat rolled a good deal. We spent the evening playing poker. Early next morning we found the opening and entered the lagoon. It was shallow and clear so that the bottom could be seen distinctly. There was not a cloud in the sky, not a ripple on the water. The coast was heavily wooded. It was a scene of perfect tranquillity. Presently we lowered a dinghy and landed in a little cove. There was a small village. One hut, embowered by a great tree with red flowers and coconuts and surrounded by croton bushes, was one of the most beautiful things I ever saw. When we came ashore a young woman came out of the hut and invited us in. We sat down on the mats and were given slices of pine-apple to eat. The household consisted of two very old crones, bowed and wrinkled, with short grey hair; two younger women; and a man. Then we walked along the grassy road lined with coconuts, along the shore, three miles, till we came to the house of a trader called Lawrie. He lent me a pony and trap and I drove on down the road, past villages, past little bays, past bathing pools where boys were swimming and eventually came to the house of another trader called Benn. I went into his house and asked if he could give me dinner. He was a very thin man, with a small head and grey hair; he wore spectacles and was dressed in dirty pyjamas. He had a half-caste wife and three very fair, weedy children. He was just recovering from a prolonged bout of drunkenness and hardly knew what he was saying. He was intensely nervous and could not keep still. His hands, thin and bony, kept twitching, and every now and then he cast behind him quick, nervous glances. He had been on the island for more than twenty years, an Englishman, and traded in copra, cottons and canned goods. His wife prepared a dinner for us of pigeons and vegetables and cheese, and he tried to eat with us, but couldn't persuade himself to swallow a thing. As soon as we had finished he said: 'Well, you've got to get on, I won't keep you.' He was evidently eager to be rid of us. We went back to Lawrie. This was a different type of trader. He had been a blacksmith in Apia for many years and had fixed up a forge in a galvanized iron shed. He was a little man of fifty, with a dark beard. He gave me the impression of being at the same time sturdy and frail. He was very deaf and you had to shout to make him hear. He spoke in a low soft voice with an Australian accent. His wife was a large woman, strong and good-humoured, with pleasant features; her abundant hair was done with some elaboration. They had several children, two boys being at school in New Zealand, and the rest helping in the store and on the plantation. There were two bright, fair boys and two little girls. They wore nothing but shirt and breeches and went barefoot. They were obviously strong and healthy, and there was an attractive openness about them. They were Adventists, they kept Saturday as the day of rest instead of Sunday, teetotallers, and the man had never smoked. I got the impression of a hardworking, honest and united family. They were hospitable people and the tea which they set before me was plentiful, a well-cooked chicken, a good salad grown by themselves, and a couple of sweets. They neither drank tea nor coffee themselves, but gave them to their guests. They were just a little conscious of their difference from other people, but that, so far as I could tell, was the only fault you could find in them.

We had brought them cases of various goods in the dinghy and having landed these, we got in and rowed back to the schooner. It was a pull of two or three miles and the rowers sang as they rowed. They shouted witticisms to the girls in the native huts by the shore.

In the evening, going ashore again, with the crew this time, we went to the house of a chief. Kava was made and drunk, pineapple passed round, and then to the sound of a banjo and a ukulele the crew began to dance. The women of the house joined them. There was a Fijian, one of the sailors, almost coal black, with a mass of fuzzy hair, who was able to twist himself into all sorts of outrageous attitudes to the shrieking delight of the onlookers. The dancing grew more and more obscene. We went back to the schooner in the deep silence of the night.

Next day we set out for Apolima. We had arranged for a whale-boat to take us across the reef, and this, with its crew, we towed behind us in a rolling heavy sea. Several women, evidently prepared to make a picnic of it, came with the rowers. Apolima is a small island, almost circular, between Savaii and Manono. When we came to the reef we got into the whale-boat and rowed towards the shore. The opening of the reef is not more than twelve feet broad and on each side are great jagged rocks. The chief steered. We got to the opening and when a big wave came he shouted to the men, they pulled with all their might, their great muscles straining, and we were carried over into the lagoon. It was small and shallow.

The island is an extinct volcano, and when we got inside the lagoon, which covers the floor of the crater, it looked like the inside of a Stilton cheese all eaten away except the rind and one bit of this (the opening to the sea) gone too. There was a village at the edge of the lagoon, almost the only flat part of the island, and from there the land, covered with coconuts, bananas and breadfruit, rose rapidly. We climbed up to the edge of the crater and looked out to sea; below us two turtles were sunning themselves on the beach. When we came down the chief asked us into his house for kava. By this time the wind was blowing hard and the whale-boat men looked doubtfully at the grey and stormy sea; they weren't sure whether it would be possible to get out against the waves that dashed furiously through the opening. But we got into the boat, and the chief, a fine-looking old man with white hair, came to help us. The women who had landed with us took their places at the oars. We pushed through the shallow water to the opening and watched the waves. After waiting a little they made the attempt, but the boat got jammed against the rock, and it looked as though the next wave must inevitably swamp us. I took off my shoes in case I had to swim. The old chief jumped out and pushed the boat off. Then, with a tremendous effort, the rowers, shouting their heads off, rowing like mad, the sea beating over the boat and soaking us to the skin, we got out. The chief swam out to us, and it was a fine sight to see the old man fighting against the great waves. He was hauled in and sat there panting. The schooner was far out and showed no signs of seeing us. We rowed towards her slowly, for an hour, and at last she bore down on us. She was rolling heavily, so that it was not easy to get on board. I jumped into the rigging as she swayed towards the boat, and the Chinese cook seized my wrist and helped me on.

Kava. It is made by a girl and she is supposed to be a virgin. A young man or another girl pounds the root on a stone, then gives it to her; she pours a little water in a bowl and puts in the powdered root, then mixes it with her hands. Then she draws a bundle of coconut fibre through the mixture to act as a sieve, squeezes it out, and hands it to the young man who shakes it out on the air. This is done several times till all the root is melted. Then more water is added and the kava is ready. The virgin utters the prescribed words and the rest of the company clap their hands. The young man hands her a coconut bowl which she fills; the headman mentions a name and the bowl is taken to the most distinguished guest. He pours a little on the ground, says 'health to the company', drinks what he wants and then throws the rest away. He hands back the bowl and the next guest in order of age or honour is served.

The Lagoon. It is crossed by a bridge made of coconut trees laid end to end and supported by a forked branch driven into the bottom. There is a native hut here and there on the bank, surrounded by bananas, and all along coconut trees. You walk through the bush for a quarter of a mile and come to a shallow river surrounded by trees, where the natives bathe. The water is sweet except at high tide, when it is brackish from the lagoon into which it empties itself, very cold by contrast with the temperature, and clear. A lovely spot.

Wms. An Irishman. When he was a boy of fifteen he took on the paternity of a child got from some girl by the son of the local clergyman. This young man, after promising to pay for the child's keep, did not do so, and Wms had to pay half a crown a week till the child was fourteen. Twenty years later, on going back to Ireland, he sought the man out, then married and the father of children, and fought him till he made him ask his pardon.

For some time he was in New Zealand. One day he was shooting with a friend, a bank clerk, who had no gun licence: suddenly they saw a policeman, the clerk was in dismay, thinking he would be arrested, so Wms told him to keep on calmly and himself started running. The policeman pursued and they ran back to Auckland. Once there Wms stopped, the policeman came up, asked for his licence, which Wms immediately produced. The policeman asked him why he had run away, whereupon he answered: 'Well, you're an Irishman same as I am, if you promise to hold your tongue about it I'll tell you; the other fellow hadn't a licence.' The policeman burst out laughing and said: 'You're a sport, come and have a drink."

He is a gross, sensual man, and he loves to tell you about the women he's lived with. He's had ten children by Samoan women; one a girl of fifteen, he keeps at school in New Zealand, but the rest he's handed over to the Mormon mission with a sum of money. He came out to the islands when he was twenty-six as a planter. He was one of the few white men settled in Savaii at the time of the German occupation and had already a certain influence with the natives. He loves them as much as it is in his selfish nature to love anybody. The Germans made him Amtmann, a position he occupied for sixteen years. On one occasion, having to call on Solf, the German minister for foreign affairs, Solf said to him: 'Being governor of a German colony I suppose you speak German fluently.' 'No,' he answered, 'I only know one word, *prosit*, and I haven't heard that since my arrival in Berlin.' The minister laughed heartily and sent for a bottle of beer.

R. He is a thin, weedy youth, with the look of a clerk in a London stockbroker's office, and he has decayed teeth, crowned with gold, and a small peevish mouth. He is vulgar, illiterate and h-less. He has been on the islands for some years and is tattooed like a native. I wonder why he exposed himself to the torture of the operation. Perhaps the beauty of the place, the charm of those friendly people stirred his vulgar soul to what he thought was a romantic gesture. Perhaps he merely thought it made him more attractive to the women he slept with.

Savaii. After the rain, when the sun is shining and you walk through the bush it is like a hot-house, seething, humid, sultry, breathless, and you have a feeling that everything about you, trees, shrubs, climbing plants, is growing with an impetuous violence.

I travelled back to Apia in the *Marstal*. It is a cutter about thirty feet long and belongs to a kanaka. A ten-hour trip. It was loaded with sacks of copra and smelt rankly of coconut. There was no cabin, and I lay on deck over the engine, with a rug over me, and rested my head on the knobbly copra sacks. The crew consisted of the skipper at the tiller, a handsome, swarthy fellow, with somewhat the look of a later Roman emperor, inclined to corpulence, but with a fine strong face; another kanaka, stretched at full length and covered with sacking, who slept; and a Chinese, who sat looking idly at the moon and smoked cigarettes.

The moon shone brightly, dimming the stars, and the sea was very calm except for that long, uncanny swell of the Pacific. When we entered the harbour at Apia, its coconuts dark against the sky, with the dim whiteness of the Cathedral, lights here and there on boats, it was like entering an enchantment of stillness and silence. I looked for words to describe it, but could find none. Two stray lines came into my mind, and I couldn't imagine what they were doing there: 'Shall shine the traffic of Jacob's ladder Pitched between heaven and Charing Cross.'

Suva. The bay is fine and spacious, surrounded by grey hills that stretch away mysteriously into a blue distance. You feel that in that farther country, thickly wooded, there is a strange and secret life. It suggests something aboriginal and darkly cruel. The town stretches along the borders of the harbour. Here are many frame buildings, more shops than at Apia, but there is still the air of the trading station which the place must once have been. The natives walk about in lava-lavas and singlets or shirts, tall strapping men for the most part, as dark as Negroes, with their curly hair, often bleached with lime, cut into a curious shape. There are numbers of Hindus, walking softly, dressed in white; and the women wear nose-rings, gold chains round their necks and bangles on their arms. When you go out into the country you pass crowded villages of Hindus and everywhere you see them working in the fields. They wear nothing but a loin-cloth and their bodies are frighteningly thin. The country is subtropical, palm trees grow poorly, but there are great groves of mangoes; it has not the blitheness of Samoa, it is more sombre and the green is heavy and dark. The air is hot and oppressive, heavy too, and the rain beats down incessantly.

The Grand Pacific Hotel. It is a large, two-storeyed building, faced with stucco and surrounded by a veranda. It is cool and empty. It has a large hall, with comfortable chairs in it, and electric fans constantly turning. The servants are Hindus, silent and vaguely hostile, who go about with bare feet, in clean white suits and turbans. The food is very bad, but the rooms are pleasant, fresh and cool. Few people stay there; the agent of the company with his family, a few people waiting for ships, and some officials from the other islands brought to Suva on business or holiday.

The Blue. He came out straight from Oxford, where he got his football blue, and he has been here five years. He is now a magistrate on one of the islands and is the only white man on it. When he has a vacation he comes to Suva and drinks steadily. He drinks all day long and by noon is drunk. He is a man of under thirty, little, well made, with the appearance still of an athlete, and he has an agreeable face and a breezy, rather charming manner. His hair is cut short and is pleasantly untidy. He has blue eyes and attractive, irregular features. You surmise a charming, good-natured fellow, with not an atom of harm in him. He is still a schoolboy.

The Schoolmaster. An Irishman who has been to the front, where he was badly wounded; and on his recovery the Government sent him to Fiji. He had read of it in his boyhood and the place had always had a romantic fascination for him. When the offer came he accepted it eagerly, and now he is bored, lonely and disillusioned. His school is about seven miles from Suva, but he drives in whenever he can; during the holidays he lives at the Grand Pacific, and he drinks, whisky and soda, all the time. He is not more than twenty-eight, short, with laughing blue eyes and a flashing smile.

The Insurance Agent. A tall elderly man, with white hair very thin but carefully brushed; he is neatly dressed and holds himself squarely and well notwithstanding an increasing obesity. He went out to Australia thirty years ago in a theatrical company, married a woman with money, and since then has followed many occupations; he has been a planter, and in the Government service, and a trader. Now he is under a cloud. He went to Apia on behalf of the insurance company he was representing and pocketed the premiums. The company made them good for its own reputation's sake, and he escaped a prosecution only because it desired to avoid scandal. He spends most of his time in the bar of the Grand Pacific and is able to drink steadily without showing signs of it. From his training as an actor he has something of the grand manner and it is amusing when you remember how narrowly he escaped a long imprisonment.

Rewa. The river is wide, with flat banks, along which are native villages and banana plantations. Beyond are the grey, misty mountains. There are great broad reaches which I know not why are vaguely mysterious and threatening. Now and then you see a native paddling along in a dug-out. There are sugar refineries at Rewa and a bedraggled hotel, a bungalow kept by a fat Englishman and his fat wife. They have precisely the look of the proprietors of a riverside hotel on the Thames, and the woman spends most of her day in a hammock on the veranda reading novels.

The Priest. He was a little old Frenchman of seventy, very active; and he wore a short shabby cassock, black top boots and a grey topee. He was all shrivelled up, with a wrinkled clean-shaven face, long, straight grey hair and red-rimmed, watery eyes. There was something extraordinarily grotesque in his appearance. He talked a great deal, in fluent English, but with a strong accent. His hands were knotted and gnarled, with broken nails. He was a schoolmaster; he had taught for seventeen years in France, for seventeen in Australia, and now for seventeen more in Fiji. He knew many languages. He was probably an Alsatian. He talked of his nephews, most of them priests, all fighting in the French Army, and was proud of the decorations they had received. He was proud of his school in Fiji and his pupils, almost all of them natives, and carried on a correspondence still with his old pupils in Australia. It was strange in that funny little hotel to hear him talk of Shakespeare and Milton to the two men with whom he found himself sitting at table. They listened, uncomprehending, with open mouths. He was enthusiastic for all things Fijian and was a mine of information for everything about the natives. Notwithstanding his years he gave you the impression of an indefatigable energy.

Two men are living together in Fiji, loathing the sight of one another, not speaking and yet bound together by their work. Every evening the two men get stupid and sodden with drink. One night there drops in an old priest, a Frenchman, who has been on the island for years; and they give him dinner and the night's lodging. He talks to them of Shakespeare and Wordsworth. They listen to him amazed. They ask him what made him come out to these parts. He tells them that he was sensual and pleasure-loving and almost regretted having become a priest; he felt himself made for a normal life, and because he loved so well all its good things he cut himself off from them. Now he is old and everything is over. They ask him if he thinks it was worth it. They see in him dimly a nobility of life which had never dawned on them. Their eyes meet and one holds out his hand to the other.

My meeting with the old priest suggested this sketch for a story. But I never wrote it.

Bau. It is a tiny island at the mouth of the river and within the reef, so small that in half an hour you can walk right round it, and separated from other land only by about half a mile of water. It was formerly the capital of Fiji, and the chief I stayed with told me that then the houses were so crowded together that one had to sidle through the streets. The men have land on the other shores and go to work on them every day, coming back in the evening. The children play about in the water all day long. The houses are made of grass, square or oblong, without windows and with wooden doors. Most of them are separated off by curtains of tapa into two compartments. The chief who received me was a nephew of the last king and a member of the legislature, a fine old fellow, tall and strong; and he bore himself with dignity. He was dressed in a pair of short white pants and a net singlet.

The sitting dance in Fiji. Girls, four of them, sit in a row on the ground, dressed in white, with green wreaths round their necks and the flowers of the frangipanni in their hair. The leader starts a weird song which is taken up by the rest and by men sitting behind them, and they sway their bodies and make rhythmical movements of the hands and arms. The dance is joyless and sombre.

The *Talune*. It is a ship belonging to the Union S.S. line, and does the trip from Auckland to Apia via Fiji and Tonga. It is thirty-six years old, twelve hundred tons, and very dirty, overrun with rats and cockroaches, but steady and a wonderful sea boat, with one very primitive bathroom, no smoking-room, and dingy cabins. It was laden with bananas when I took it from Suva to Auckland, and there were crates of them packed close, high up, on deck, aft; and it was crowded with passengers, children returning to school in New Zealand from Apia and Suva, soldiers on furlough, and the nondescript crowd that travels on the Pacific. The second class was reserved for natives, so that all manner of strange folk went first; the strangest was a tall, very thin man with a red face and large features. He wore a long black frock-coat and was remarkably clean. He went about by himself, talking to no one, smoking incessantly and spitting; he had two large parrots in cages. He was an enigmatic figure and it was impossible to guess whence he came or whither he was going, what his occupation was or his antecedents. He gave one vaguely the impression of an unfrocked priest.

Tonga. The Adventist. He is a little deaf old man who has lived on the island for thirty years. He lives alone, in poverty, scarcely known by his neighbours, whom he despises as outcasts. He looks upon himself as specially favoured of God. Everything has gone wrong with him. His wife has died, his children have gone to the bad, his coconuts have failed. He regards his misfortunes as a cross that God has given him to bear as a sign of his special grace, and yet it is obvious that most of them are his own fault.

Papeete. Sharks surrounded the ship as she entered the passage in the reef and followed her into the lagoon. The lagoon was very quiet and still and the water clear. A number of white schooners lay along the wharf. A crowd had assembled to see the ship come in, the women in bright colours, the men in white or khaki or blue. On the bright sunny quay the crowd, so brilliantly coloured, was a sight charmingly gay.

There are stores and office buildings along the beach and a long line of old trees, with heavy green foliage, and here and there, making the green more vivid, the rich scarlet of the *flamboyant*. The buildings, the post office, the offices of the Compagnie Navale de l'Océanie, haven't the severe, business-like dullness of most such buildings in the Pacific; they have a florid tawdriness which is not altogether unpleasing. The beach with its fine trees has something French about it and reminds you of the ramparts of a provincial town in Touraine. And Papeete as a whole, notwithstanding its English and American stores, its Chinese shops, has a subtly French character. It has an engaging trimness, and it is leisurely. You feel that people *live* there, and the desire for gain is not quite so much in evidence as in the English islands. The roads are good, as good and as carefully kept as many roads in France, and trees, giving a grateful shade, have been planted along them. By the beach, shaded by a huge mango tree, with a vast bamboo by the side of it, is a brick washing-place of exactly the same pattern as those I saw near Arras in which soldiers, resting, were washing their shirts. The market place might be in any village of some size in France. And yet the whole has an exotic note which gives it character peculiar to itself.

Besides Tahitian, English and French are spoken indifferently. The natives speak French trailingly, with an accent that reminds you of that of the Russian students in Paris. Round each little house there is a garden, wild and uncared for; a tangled mass of trees and gaudy flowers.

The Tahitians wear trousers for the most part, shirts and huge straw hats. They seem lighter than most Polynesians. The women wear the Mother Hubbard, but great numbers wear black.

The Hotel Tiare. It is about five minutes walk from the Custom House at the end of the town, and when you step out of the gate you walk straight into the country. In front is a little garden full of flowers and surrounded by a hedge of coffee shrubs. At the back is a compound in which grow a breadfruit tree, an avocado pear, oleander and taro. When you want a pear for lunch you pick one off the tree. The hotel is a bungalow surrounded by a terrace, part of which serves as a dining-room. There is a small sitting-room with a waxed parquet floor, a piano and bentwood furniture covered with velvet. The bedrooms are small and dark. The kitchen is a little house by itself and here, all day long, sits Madame Lovaina superintending the Chinese cook. She is a very good cook herself and very hospitable. Everyone in the neighbourhood in want of a meal comes to the hotel and gets one. Lovaina is a half-caste, very white, a woman of fifty, perhaps, and of enormous proportions. She is not merely fat, she is huge and shapeless; and she wears a pink Mother Hubbard and a small straw hat. Her face has kept its small features, but she has a vast expanse of chin. Her brown eyes are large and liquid; her expression pleasant and candid. She has a ready smile and a hearty, fat laugh. She takes a motherly interest in all young people, and when the boyish purser of the *Moana* got very drunk I saw her stir her immense bulk and take the glass out of his hand to prevent him from drinking more, and she sent her son to see him safely back to his ship.

The tiare is the national flower of Tahiti, a little star-shaped white flower which grows on a bush of rich green leaves, and it has a peculiarly sweet and sensual perfume. It is used for making wreaths, for putting in the hair and behind the ear, and when placed in the black hair of native women it shines with a dazzling brightness.

Johnny. At first glance no one would suspect that he had native blood in him. He is twenty-five. He is a rather stout young man, with black crinkly hair beginning to recede and a clean-shaven fleshy face. He is excitable and gesticulates a great deal. He speaks very quickly, his voice continually breaking into falsetto, English and French, fluently but not very correctly and with a curious accent, and his natural tongue is Tahitian. When he strips to bathe and puts on a pareo the native appears at once, and then only his colour betrays his white blood. At heart he is a native. He loves the native food and the native ways. He is proud of his native blood and has none of the false shame of the half-caste.

Johnny's house. It is about five miles from Papeete, perched on a little hill overlooking the sea on three sides, with Murea straight ahead. The shore is crowded thick with coconuts, and behind are the mysterious hills. The house is the most ramshackle affair imaginable. There is a large lower room, something like a barn, raised from the ground and reached by steps; the frame walls are broken away here and there; and at the back are a couple of small sheds. One of them serves as a kitchen; fire is made in a hole in the ground and the cooking is done on it. Above are two attics. There is a table in each one and a mattress on the floor and nothing else. The barn is the living-room. The furniture consists of a deal table covered with a green oilcloth, a couple of deck-chairs and two or three very old and battered bentwood chairs. It is decorated with coconut leaves, split at the top and nailed to the walls or woven round the supporting beams. Half a dozen Japanese lanterns hang from the ceiling, and a bunch of yellow hibiscus gives a note of bright colour.

The Chiefess. She lives in a two-storeyed frame house about thirty-five miles from Papeete. She is the widow of a chief who received the Legion of Honour for his services in the troubles at the time the French protectorate was changed into occupation; and on the walls of the parlour, filled with cheap French furniture, are the documents relating to this, signed photographs of various political celebrities, and the usual photographs of dusky marriage groups. The bedrooms are crowded with enormous beds. She is a large stout old woman, with grey hair, and one eye shut, which yet now and then opens and fixes you with a mysterious stare. She wears spectacles, a shabby black Mother Hubbard, and sits most comfortably on the floor smoking native cigarettes.

She told me there were pictures by Gauguin in a house not far from hers, and when I said I would like to see them called for a boy to show me the way. We drove along the road for a couple of miles and then,. turning off it, went down a swampy grass path till we came to a very shabby frame house, grey and dilapidated. There was no furniture in it beyond a few mats, and the veranda was swarming with dirty children. A young man was lying on the veranda smoking cigarettes and a young woman was seated idly. The master of the house, a flat-nosed, smiling dark native came and talked to us. He asked us to go in, and the first thing I saw was the Gauguin painted on the door. It appears that Gauguin was ill for some time in that house and was looked after by the parents of the present owner, then a boy of ten. He was pleased with the way they treated him and when he grew better desired to leave some recollection of himself. In one of the two rooms of which the bungalow consisted there were three doors, the upper part of which was of glass divided into panels, and on each of them he painted a picture. The children had picked away two of them; on one hardly anything was left but a faint head in one corner, while on the other could still be seen the traces of a woman's torso thrown backwards in an attitude of passionate grace. The third was in tolerable preservation, but it was plain that in a very few years it would be in the same state as the other two. The man took no interest in the pictures as such, but merely as remembrances of the dead guest, and when I pointed out to him that he could still keep the other two he was not unwilling to sell the third. 'But,' he said, 'I shall have to buy a new door.' 'How much will it cost?' I asked. 'A hundred francs.' 'All right,' I said, 'I'll give you two hundred.'

I thought I had better take the picture before he changed his mind, so we got the tools from the car in which I had come, unscrewed the hinges and carried the door away. When we arrived back at the chiefess's we sawed off the lower part of it in order to make it more portable, and so took it back to Papeete.

I went to Murea in a little open boat crowded with natives and Chinese. The skipper was a fair, red-faced native with blue eyes, tall and stout; he spoke a little English and perhaps his father was an English sailor. As soon as we got out of the reef it was clear that we were in for a bad passage. The sea was high and, sweeping over the boat, drenched us all. She rolled and pitched and tossed. Great squalls came suddenly and blinding sheets of rain. The waves seemed mountainous. It was an exciting (and to me alarming) experience to plunge through them. Through it all one old native woman sat on the deck, smoking the big native cigarettes one after the other. A Chinese boy was constantly and horribly sick. It was a relief to see Murea grow nearer, to discern the coconuts, and finally to enter the lagoon. The rain swept down in torrents. We were all soaked to the skin. We got into a whale-boat that came out from the shore and had to wade to land. Then followed a four-mile walk along a muddy road, through streams, the rain beating down continually, till we reached the house at which we were to stay. We took off our clothes and got into pareos.

It was a small frame house, consisting of a veranda and two rooms, in each of which was an enormous bed. Behind was a kitchen. It belonged to a New Zealander, then away, who lived there with a native woman. There was a little garden in front, filled with tiare, hibiscus and oleander. At the side rushed a stream, and a small pool in this served as a bathroom. The water was fresh and sparkling.

By the steps of the veranda was a large tin bowl of water with a small tin basin, so that one could wash one's feet before entering the house.

Murea. The native houses are oblong, covered with a rough thatch of great leaves, and made of thin bamboos placed close together which let in light and air. There are no windows, but generally two or three doors. Many of them have an iron bed and in almost all you see a sewing machine.

The meeting-house is built on the same plan, but is very large, and everyone sits on the floor. I went to a choir practice, led by a blind girl, in which hour after hour they sang long hymns. The voices were loud and raucous near-by, but when you listened from a distance, sitting in the soft night, the effect was beautiful.

Fish spearing. I walked along the road for a bit and then, guided by the sound of voices and laughter, struck through a swamp of reeds taller than a man, wading here and there through muddy water up to the waist, and presently came to a small rushing stream. Here were about a dozen men and women, clad only in pareos, with long spears, and on the ground beside them heaps of great silver fish, each one gory from the spear wound which had killed it. I waited for a time and then someone uttered a word of warning, everyone sprang to attention with poised spear, and all at once a shoal rushed down the stream towards the sea. There was an excitement and a shouting, a clashing of spears, a plunge into the water, and then the catch, a dozen big fish, was taken out and flung on the ground. The fish quivered and leapt and beat the earth with their tails.

Within the Reef. The water has all sorts of colours, from the deepest blue to pale emerald green. The reef is wide and the coral many-tinted. You can walk on the reef, and it is strange to see the great breakers so near at hand and the tumultuous sea, while inside, the water is as calm as a pond. All sorts of strange animals lurk among the coral, brightly coloured fish, sea snails, *bêches de mer*, urchins and wriggling things faintly pink.

The nets. The whole village turns out when the great net is cast; the owners of the net go out in a canoe and one or two of them plunge into the water; long strings of women, boys and men, seize each end of the rope and pull. Others sit on the beach to watch the fun. Gradually the net is drawn in and a boy leaps on to a silvery fish, putting it into his pareo, and the catch is landed. A hole is made in the sand and the fish are poured in. Then they are divided up among the assistants.

Christianity. A French admiral came to one of the islands in his flag-ship, and the native queen gave a formal luncheon in his honour. She proposed to put him on her right, but the missionary's wife insisted that he should sit on *her* right. As the wife of Christ's representative she ranked higher than the queen. The missionary agreed with her. When the natives protested they both flew into a rage; they threatened to get even with them if such a slight were put upon them, and the natives, frightened, at length yielded. The missionaries had their way.

Tetiaroa. We went over in a small cutter with a gasolene engine. We started at one in the morning so as to arrive at daybreak when the sea is supposed to be at its calmest and the passage over the reef less difficult. It was very lovely in the silence of the night. The air was balmy. The stars were reflected in the waters within the reef. There was not a breath of wind. We put a rug down on the deck and made ourselves comfortable. Outside the reef there was the inevitable swell of the Pacific. When dawn came we were still in the open sea, but presently we saw the island, a low line of coconut trees, some miles off. Then we came to the reef and got into a boat. The owner of the cutter was a man named Levy. He said he came from Paris, but he spoke French with a strong accent which suggested to me the Algerian Jew. He cast his anchor on the reef, we got into the dinghy and rowed to the opening. This is not an opening at all, but merely a slight dip in the reef and when something of a wave beats in there is just enough water for a boat to scrape over. Once over it is impossible to row, for the coral is thick, and the natives get out, up to their waists in water, and pull the boat through a narrow, tortuous passage to the shore. The beach is white sand, fragments of coral and the shells of innumerable crustacea; then there are the coconuts and you come upon the half-dozen huts which make up the tiny settlement. One is the hut of the headman; there are two huts for copra, and another for the workmen; then two pleasant grass huts, one serving as a parlour, the other as a bedroom, used by the owner of the island. There is a grove of old, enormous trees and it is among these the huts are built; they give coolness and shade. We unloaded our stores and bedding and proceeded to make ourselves at home. There were swarms of mosquitoes, more than I have ever seen anywhere, and it was impossible to sit down without being surrounded by them. We rigged up a mosquito-curtain on the veranda of the living hut and set a table and a couple of chairs beneath it. But the mosquitoes were ingenious to enter and before it was possible to settle down in anything like peace twenty at least had to be killed under the curtain. There was a little shed at the side which served as a kitchen, and here the Chinaman I had brought with me with a few sticks made a fire on which he did the cooking.

The island had evidently been raised from the sea at a comparatively recent date and much of the interior is barren, caked, almost swampy, so that you sink several inches as you walk, and it may be supposed that it was a brackish lake, now dried up; and in one part there is still a small lake which not so very long ago must have been much larger. Besides the coconuts nothing much seems to grow except rank grass and a shrub something like broom. In all these islands the mynah bird is seen everywhere; but here there are no more than two or three that have recently been brought. Bird life consists only in great sea-birds, black in colour, with long sharp bills, which make a piercing sort of whistle.

The sand on the beach has really the silver whiteness that you read of in descriptions of South Sea islands, and when you walk along in the sunshine it is so dazzling that you can hardly bear to look at it. Here and there you see the white shells of dead crabs or the skeleton of a sea-bird. At night the beach seems to be all moving; it is at first quite strange, this perpetual, slight movement, weird and uncanny; but when you light your torch you see that it comes from the incessant activity of innumerable shelled things; they move hither and thither on the beach slowly, stealthily, but there are such vast numbers of them that the whole beach seems alive.

The Reef. It is a broad causeway along which you can walk all round the island, but it is so rough and uneven that it tears your feet to pieces. In the pools fish dart about and now and then an eel raises a vicious head. Lobster-catching: you go along the reef at night with hurricane lamps and walk, peering right and left, into every nook and cranny; fish slither away frightened by the light; and you have to walk carefully, since everywhere are great sea-hedgehogs capable of causing nasty wounds on the feet. There are great numbers of lobsters and you do not walk far before you see one. You put your foot on it and then a native comes, takes it up quickly and throws it in the old kerosene can which he has strapped on his shoulder. Walking thus in the night one loses all sense of direction, and on the way back it was not easy to find the boat. For a few minutes it looked as though we should have to stay on the reef till dawn. There was no moon, but the sky was unclouded and the stars were bright.

Fishing on the Reef. At one point, near the passage, the reef is abrupt, like a precipice, and you look down directly into I know not how many fathoms of water. The natives had spread a net among the coral rocks of the lagoon and we had a number of fish to use as bait. It was rather horrid to see the natives killing them. They hit them with their fists on the belly or banged them with a piece of coral. When we reached the fishing-place, the canoe was attached to a coral rock, and the headman proceeded to pound up a couple of fish and threw the fragments in the water. This soon attracted a lot of small fry, thin, worm-like, active little things, and then a number of large black fish. In a few minutes a couple of sharks' fins showed themselves on the surface and we saw the brown sharks circling round with a kind of horrible stealth. The rod was merely a bamboo, and to this a line was attached. The big black fish circled round the bait and took it voraciously, so that one pulled them out of the water one after the other. The sharks were greedy too and we had to snatch the bait away from them since the line was too thin to hold them. Once I got a shark on my hook and he snapped the line in a twinkling. We put down a couple of lines with the innards of fish on them and caught a tunny that must have weighed the best part of forty pounds.

Catching sharks. Towards evening you attach the lights of a large fish to a hook and then tie the line to a tree. Not long elapses before you hear a great splashing, and going down to the beach you find that a shark is caught. You drag him in and when you get him on the beach he struggles and beats about. The native takes his large knife, a descendant of the cutlass brought by the first discoverers of the islands, and strikes at the head to get to the brain. It is an ugly, malicious-looking beast with hideous jaws. When it is dead the hook is cut out. Then the Chinaman cuts off the fins to dry them in the sun and a kanaka hacks out the jaw with its terrible teeth. The dead fish is cast back into the sea.

The natives often tie the line to one of their legs before they go to sleep and are awakened by the tugging.

Fish. Their variety is indescribable. Bright yellow fish, fish black and yellow, fish black and white, fish striped, fish curiously patterned. One day the natives went fishing and when they raised their net I saw their catch in all its brilliance. I had a sudden thrill, for it reminded me of the casting of a net in one of the stories in the Arabian Nights and among that astonishing confusion of colour and strange shapes I half expected to find a bottle sealed with the seal of Suleyman, the prison of a powerful djin.

The colour of the sea. It is deep blue in the open sea, wine-coloured under the setting sun; but in the lagoon of an infinite variety, ranging from pale turquoise to the brightest, clearest green; and there the setting sun will turn it for a short moment to liquid gold. Then there is the colour of the coral, brown, white, pink, red, purple; and the shapes it takes are marvellous; it is like a magic garden, and the hurrying fish are like butterflies. It strangely lacks reality; it has the fantastic air of the product of some extravagant imagination. Among the coral are pools with a floor of white sand, and here the water is dazzling clear.

Varo. In the Pacific they call it the sea-centipede. It is like a small lobster, but pale cream in colour. Two of them live in each hole. The female is larger and stronger than the male and somewhat more brightly coloured. They are found only in very fine sand and to catch them we went over the lagoon, about a mile, I should think, to one of the islands of which the group of Tetiaroa is composed. The natives had prepared a singular instrument. It consisted of the strong fibre from the central stem of the coconut leaf, about two feet long, and pliable; to this was tied a circle of hooks, turned upwards, so that it had a sort of umbrella effect; and about this was tied a piece of fish as bait. We walked along looking into the shallow water of the beach for the small round holes which marked the varo's dwelling, and then let down the hooks. The native said an incantation, asking the varo to come up out of his hole, then flipped the water with his fingers; mostly nothing happened, but sometimes the fibre was pulled down and then we knew a varo had seized the bait and was entangled in the hooks. Very cautiously he was hauled up, and it was quite exciting to see the little beast emerge on the surface clinging to the fibre. He was released and put into a basket which the headman rapidly made from a coconut leaf. However, it was not quick work and in three hours we only caught eight.

Evening on the Lagoon. At sunset the sea turns to a bright purple; the sky is cloudless and the sun, burning red, sinks into the sea, rapidly, but not so rapidly as writers lead one to believe, and Venus shines. When evening comes, clear and silent, an ardent, frenzied life seems to break out. Countless shelled animals begin to crawl about at the edge of the water, and in the water every living thing seems to be in action. Fish leap, there are mysterious splashings, and a sudden swift turmoil as a shark frightens everything within sight of its cruel stealthiness. Small fry leap by hundreds into the air and sometimes a large coloured fish gleams above the surface with a momentary glitter. But the most impressive thing is that feeling of urgent, remorseless life. In the quiet of the lovely evening there is something mysterious about it and vaguely alarming.

The night is wonderfully silent. The stars shine with a fierce brilliancy, the Southern Cross and Canopus; there is not a breath of wind, but a wonderful balminess in the air. The coconut trees, silhouetted against the sky, seem to be listening. Now and then a sea-bird gives a mournful cry.

1917

In this year I was sent to Russia on a secret mission. That is how I came to make the following notes.

Russia. I have been led to an interest in Russia for pretty well the same reasons as most of my contemporaries. The obvious one was Russian fiction. Tolstoi and Turgenev, but chiefly Dostoievsky, offered an emotion that was different from any offered by the novels of other countries. They made the greatest novels of Western Europe look artificial. Their novelty made me unfair to Thackeray, Dickens and Trollope, with their conventional morality; and even the great writers of France, Balzac, Stendhal and Flaubert, in comparison seemed formal and a little frigid. The life they portrayed, these English and French novelists, was familiar; and I, like others of my generation, was tired of it. They described a society that was policed. Its thoughts had been thought too often. Its emotions, even when extravagant, were extravagant within ordered limits. It was fiction fit for a middle-class civilization, well-fed, well-clothed, well-housed, and its readers were resolute to bear in mind that all they read was make-believe.

The fantastic nineties stirred the intelligent from their apathy, making them restless and discontented, but gave them nothing satisfying. Old idols were shattered, but those set up in their place were papier mâché. The nineties talked a great deal about art and literature, but their works were like toy rabbits that hop about for a while when you have wound them up and then suddenly with a click stop dead.

Modern Poets. I should be content with less cleverness if only they had more feeling. They make little songs not from great sorrows but from the sober pleasures of a good education.

The Secret Agent. He was a man of scarcely middle height, but very broad and sturdy; he walked on noiseless feet with quick steps; he had a curious gait, somewhat like a gorilla's, and his arms hung from his sides a little away from his body; he gave you the impression of an almost simian creature prepared at any moment to spring; and the feeling of enormous strength was disquieting. He had a large square head on a short thick neck. He was clean-shaven, with small shrewd eyes, and his face was strangely flattened as though it had been bashed in by a blow. He had a large, fleshy, flat nose and a big mouth, with small discoloured teeth. His thick pale hair was plastered down on his head. He never laughed, but he chuckled often, and then his eyes gleamed with a humour that was ferocious. He was decently dressed in American reach-me-downs, and at first sight you would have taken him for an immigrant of the middle class who had established himself comfortably in a small way of business in some thriving city of the Middle West. He spoke English fluently, but without correctness. It was impossible to be with him long without being impressed by his determination. His physical strength corresponded to his strength of character. He was ruthless, wise, prudent, and absolutely indifferent to the means by which he reached his ends. There was in the end something terrifying about him. His fertile brain teemed with ideas, and they were subtle and bold. He took an artist's delight in the tortuous ways of his service; when he told you a scheme he contemplated or a dodge that had succeeded his little blue eyes glistened and his face lit up with a satanic mirth. He had an heroic disregard for human life, and you felt that for the cause he would not have hesitated to sacrifice his friend or his son. None could doubt his courage, and with an equal mind he was capable of facing not only danger – that is not so difficult – but discomfort and boredom. He was a man of frugal habit and could go for an incredible time without food or sleep. Never sparing himself, he never thought of sparing others; his energy was amazing. Though ruthless, he was good-humoured, and he was capable of killing a fellow-creature without a trace of ill-feeling. He seemed to have but one passion in life, if you omit an extreme desire for good cigars, and that was patriotism. He had a great sense of discipline and obeyed as unquestioningly his leader as he exacted obedience from his subordinates.

The patriotism of the Russians is a singular thing; there is a great deal of conceit in it; they feel themselves different from other people and flatter themselves on their difference; they speak with self-satisfaction of the ignorance of their peasants; they vaunt their mysteriousness and complexity; they repeat that with one face they look to the west and with the other to the east; they are proud of their faults – like a boorish man who tells you he is as God made him – and will admit with complacency that they are besotted and ignorant, incoherent of purpose and vacillating in action; but in that complex feeling which is the patriotism one knows in other countries, they seem deficient. I have tried to analyse what this particular emotion in myself consists of. To me the very shape of England on the map is significant, and it brings to my mind pell-mell a hundred impressions, the white cliffs of Dover and the tawny sea, the pleasant winding roads of Kent and the Sussex downs, St Paul's and the Pool of London; scraps of poetry, the noble ode of Collins and Matthew Arnold's *Scholar Gipsy* and Keats' *Nightingale*, stray lines of Shakespeare's and the pages out of English history, Drake with his ships, and Henry VIII and Queen Elizabeth; Tom Jones and Dr Johnson; and all my friends and the posters at Victoria Station; then some vague feeling of majesty and power and continuity; and then, heaven knows why, the thought of a barque in full sail going down the Channel – *Whither, O splendid ship, thy white sails crowding* – while the setting sun hangs redly on the edge of the horizon. These feelings and a hundred others make up an emotion which makes sacrifice easy, it is an emotion compact of pride and longing and love, but it is humble rather than conceited, and it does not preclude a sense of humour. Perhaps Russia is too large for sentiments so intimate, its past too barren of chivalry and high romance, its character too indefinite, its literature too poor, for the imagination to embrace the country, its history and culture, in a single emotion. Russians will tell you that the peasant loves his village. His outlook goes no further. And when you read histories of Russia you are amazed to find how little the feeling of nationality has meant to one age after another. It is a startling incident when a wave of patriotism has arisen to drive out an invader. The general attitude has been one of indifference to his presence on the part of those not actually afflicted by it. It is not by chance that Holy Russia bore so long and so submissively the yoke of the Tartar. Now it causes no indignation that the Central Powers may seize portions of Russian soil: the possibility is dismissed with a shrug and the words: 'Russia is large enough anyway.'

But my work throws me in close contact with the Czechs, and here I see a patriotism that fills me with amazement. It is a passion so single and so devouring that it leaves room for no others. I feel that awe rather than admiration is due to these men who have sacrificed everything for the cause, and not in twos and threes, fanatics among an apathetic herd, but in tens of thousands; they have given everything they had, their peace, their home, their fortune, their lives, to gain independence for their country. They are organized like a department store, disciplined like a Prussian regiment. Most of the patriots I have come across – among my own countrymen, alas! too often – have been eager to serve their country, but determined it should not be without profit to themselves (who will ever tell of the hunting for jobs, the intrigues, the exertion of influence, the personal jealousies, that have distracted the nation when its very existence was in peril?), but the Czechs are completely disinterested. They think as little of payment as does a mother of reward for the care of her child. With alacrity they accept drudgery when others are given the opportunity of adventure, mean offices when others are awarded posts of responsibility. Like all men of political mind, they have parties and programmes, but they submit them all to the common good. Is it not a marvellous thing that in the great Czech organization which has been formed in Russia, all, from the rich banker to the artisan, have given a tenth part of their income to the cause throughout the war? Even the prisoners of war – and heaven knows how precious to these were their few poor kopecks – found they could spare enough to amount to some thousands of roubles.

The nineties appealed only to the mind, and that is a running stream that purifies what passes through it, but the literature of to-day appeals to the heart, and that is a well that grows foul. They wore their heart on their sleeve, a fantastic orchid in Solomon's window, but our contemporaries carry it about in a slop basin. It may have been absurd to burn with a hard gem-like flame, but it is tedious to be bread-sauce.

I read *Anna Karenina* when I was a boy in a blue-bound translation published by Walter Scott, long before I began to write myself, but my recollection of it was vague, and when I read it again many years afterwards, interested then from a professional standpoint in the art of fiction, it seemed to me powerful and strange, but a little hard and dry. Then I read *Fathers and Sons*, in French; I was too ignorant of Russian things to appreciate its value; the strange names, the originality of the characters, opened a window on romance, but it was a novel like another, related to the French fiction of its day, and for me at all events, it had no great significance. Later still, when I found myself definitely interested in Russia, I read other books by Turgenev; but they left me cold. Their idealism was too sentimental for my taste, and unable in a translation to see the beauty of manner and style which Russians value, I found them ineffectual. It was not till I came to Dostoievsky (I read *Crime and Punishment* in a German version) that I received a bewildering and arresting emotion. Here was something that really had significance for me, and I read greedily one after the other the great novels of Russia's greatest writer. Finally I read Chekov and Gorki. Gorki left me indifferent. His subject matter was curious and remote, but his talent seemed mediocre: he was readable enough when he set down unaffectedly the lives of the lowest orders of the population, but my interest in the slums of Petrograd was soon exhausted; and when he began to reflect or philosophize I found him trivial. His talent sprang from his origins. He wrote of the proletariat as a proletarian, not as do most authors who have dealt with the subject, as a bourgeois. In Chekov on the other hand I discovered a spirit vastly to my liking. Here was a writer of real character, not a wild force like Dostoievsky, who amazes, inspires, terrifies and perplexes; but one with whom you could get on terms of intimacy. I felt that from him as from no other could be learned the secret of Russia. His range was great and his knowledge of life direct. He has been compared with Guy de Maupassant, but one would presume only by persons who have read neither. Guy de Maupassant is a clever story-teller, effective at his best – by which, of course, every writer has the right to be judged – but without much real relation to life. His better known stories interest you while you read them, but they are artificial so that they do not bear thinking of. The people are figures of the stage, and their tragedy exists only because they behave like puppets rather than like human beings. The outlook upon life which is their background is dull and vulgar. Guy de Maupassant had the soul of a well-fed bagman; his tears and his laughter smack of the commercial room in a provincial hotel. He is the son of Monsieur Homais. But with Chekov you do not seem to be reading stories at all. There is no obvious cleverness in them and you might think that anyone could write them, but for the fact that nobody does. The author has had an emotion and he is able so to put it into words that you receive it in your turn. You become his collaborator. You cannot use of Chekov's stories the hackneyed expression of the slice of life, for a slice is a piece cut off and that is exactly the impression you do not get when you read them; it is a scene seen through the fingers which you know continues this way and that though you only see a part of it.

In the above I was grossly unfair to Maupassant. 'La Maison Tellier' is enough to prove it.

Russian writers have been so much the fashion that soberminded people have greatly exaggerated the merit of certain writers merely because they write in Russian, so that Kuprin, for instance, Korolenko and Sologub have received an attention which they hardly deserve. Sologub seems worthless to me, but his combination of sensuality and mysticism is evidently one that was bound to attract readers of a certain class. On the other hand I can't look on Artzibachev with the contempt some affect. *Sanine*, to my mind, is a book of some value; it has the merit, rare in Russian fiction, of sunshine. The characters do not pass their lives in the freezing drizzle which we are accustomed to: the sky is blue and the pleasant breezes of summer rustle through the birches.

What must surprise anyone who enters upon the study of Russian literature is its extraordinary poverty. The most enthusiastic critics claim no more than an historical interest for the works written before the nineteenth century, and Russian literature begins with Pushkin; then you have Gogol, Lermontov, Turgenev, Tolstoi, Dostoievsky; then Chekov; and that is all. Students mention a number of names, but they do not attach any importance to them, and the stranger has only to read works here and there of other writers to realize that he will lose little by ignoring them. I have tried to imagine what English literature would be if it began with Byron and Shelley (it would scarcely be unfair to put Tom Moore in Shelley's place) and Walter Scott; proceeded with Dickens, Thackeray and George Eliot; and finished with George Meredith. The first effect would be to give a far greater importance to these writers.

Because the Russians have so small a literature they know it with great thoroughness. Everyone who reads at all has read everything and read it so often that it is as familiar to him as to us the authorized version of the Bible. And because literature in Russia consists for the most part of novels, fiction has a much higher place in the opinion of the cultivated man than in other countries.

The *Revisor* has an extraordinary reputation in Russia. In itself it makes up the whole of Russian classical drama. It is read by every schoolboy as *Hamlet* is read by us, and acted on high days and holidays as *Le Cid* is acted at the Comédie Française. For the Russians this one trivial little play is like Shakespeare and the

Elizabethan dramatists, Congreve and Wycherley, Goldsmith and the *School for Scandal*. The characters have become labels to attach to people and a hundred different lines have grown into proverbs. Yet it is an extremely insignificant farce, neither better nor worse than Kotzebue's *Kleinstädter*, which possibly suggested it. It is about on a level with *She Stoops to Conquer*. The intrigue is unimportant and the persons of the play are drawn from the standpoint of caricature rather than character. Whatever your goodwill you cannot suspend your disbelief in them. Gogol, however, had the good sense not to distort his picture by the introduction of any person of intelligence or decency. There is a certain artistic completeness in his collection of rogues and fools which would have been ruined by the introduction of an honest man or a man of parts. Congreve had the same wisdom and took care not to bring a virtuous person into the company of his rips. It is not very strange that Gogol and his contemporaries should have attached importance to this merry little farce, but it is surely surprising that critics acquainted with the literature of Western Europe should have done the same. For the most part the interpreters of Russia to the world have known little of other countries; they have praised various traits as typically Russian because they were not English, and have not known that, being due to physical conditions, they could be found in all countries where the physical conditions were similar. To know a foreign country at all you must not only have lived in it and in your own, but also lived in at least one other. Arnold Bennett has never ceased to believe it a peculiar distinction of the French that they make their breakfast off coffee and rolls.

My native gifts are not remarkable, but I have a certain force of character which has enabled me in a measure to supplement my deficiencies. I have common-sense. Most people cannot see anything, but I can see what is in front of my nose with extreme clearness; the greatest writers can see through a brick wall. My vision is not so penetrating. For many years I have been described as a cynic; I told the truth. I wish no one to take me for other than I am, and on the other hand I see no need to accept others' pretences.

The student of a country other than his own can hope to know comparatively few of its inhabitants, nor with the difference of language and of culture will he even after many years become intimate with them. Even with the English and American, between whom the differences of language are very small, there can be no real understanding. Probably people are best able to know one another when their early years and their education have been similar. It is the impressions of a man's first twenty years which form him. Between the English and the Russians the abyss is wide and deep. The difficulty of the language must always keep them apart. Even if you know it well you will not know it well enough for people to forget that you are an alien, and they will never be quite the same with you as when they are with one another. It is by reading that the foreigner will gain most insight into a strange people, and here writers of the second class will be of more service to him than those of the first. Great writers create; writers of smaller gifts copy. Chekov will tell you more about the Russians than Dostoievsky. By comparing then the people you have known with the people you have read of an impression may be formed which if not coincident with the truth is at all events self-contained, reasonable and coherent.

I have my own views about learning a language. I think it waste of time to acquire a greater knowledge than suffices me to read fluently and talk enough for the ordinary affairs of life. The labour required to acquire a real familiarity with a foreign tongue is profitless.

God has of late years been very much the fashion among men of letters, and they have used the Almighty with picturesque effect to balance a phrase or give emotion to a paragraph. And now G. B. Shaw and H. G. Wells have taken him up, though only just in time, and they have hurried along to set themselves at the head of the movement. It must be hard work to be a leader of thought when you are no longer so active as you were, and it is not astonishing if they both seem a little out of breath.

I wish some thoughtful person would write an essay on the reason for which even before the war there was in English letters a revival of religious belief. The curious thing about it was that it left the masses untouched and the churches remained empty; nor had it any great effect on the more intelligent and highly educated sections of the population. Men of law and science, merchants and business men were on the whole sceptical; the movement was purely literary. It certainly had something to do with a similar movement in France, where its origin was largely political and where the ground was prepared for it by the defeats of 1870: the generation that grew up after this was of diminished vitality, and so naturally inclined to faith; the Third Republic was anti-Catholic, and all who were malcontent with it ranged themselves on the side of Catholicism; to many religion became identified with patriotism and the greatness of France; finally science had not fulfilled the promises which the unwise expected, and, dissatisfied at not receiving answers to questions that science never pretended to answer, many threw themselves into the arms of the Church.

Every literary movement in France has found imitators in England, and there have always been men of letters in our country who have acquired a reputation for originality by the simple process of reading attentively the French reviews. In England likewise many were dissatisfied with science. The universities had remained religious. They instilled into the young the notion that it was good form to believe in God. It is not hard to see why it should be chiefly among men of letters that this rebirth of religion showed itself: for one thing men with the religious instinct, who in former days would have taken orders, now that the Church is a profession little in favour, gave all or part of their time to writing; and for another, writers seek constantly after change, they are a volatile, inconstant race, and the upholding of a moribund belief not only gave them new themes, picturesque and telling, but appealed to their passion for romance. And the desire for romance, as we know, was a steadily growing passion among us during the last twenty years. We all sought Ruritania in the Bayswater Road. Then came the war, and grief, fear and perplexity brought many to religion. Many consoled themselves for the loss of persons they did not care very much about by their faith in an all-powerful, all-merciful and all-knowing Creator. Once, at sea, I thought I was in imminent danger of death, and words of appeal rose quite involuntarily to my lips, remains of the forgotten faith of my childhood, and it required a certain effort of will to suppress them and look forward to what might come with an equal mind. I was at that moment within an ace of believing in God, and it required an outraged sense of the ridiculous to save me from surrender to my fear. I tried in *Of Human Bondage* to set down why I had lost the very ardent faith of my childhood, but it is difficult to describe such things accurately and I have never been satisfied with the result. Though the turn of my mind is concrete and my intelligence moves inactively amongst abstractions, I have a passion for metaphysics and I find a keen delight in the acrobatics of philosophers on the tight-rope of the incomprehensible. I have read much philosophy, and though I do not see how it is possible to refuse intellectual assent to certain theories of the Absolute, I can find nothing in them to induce me to depart from my instinctive disbelief in what is usually meant by the word religion. I have little patience with the writers who try to reconcile in one conception the Absolute of the metaphysician with the God of the Christian. But if I had had any doubts, the war would have effectually silenced them.

No one can make excursions into Russian life or Russian fiction without noticing how great a place is taken by an acute sense of sin. Not only is the Russian constantly telling you that he is a sinner, but apparently he feels it, and he suffers from very lively pangs of remorse. It is a curious trait and I have tried to account for it. Of course we say that we are miserable sinners in church, but we do not believe it; we have the good sense to know that we are nothing of the kind; we have our faults and we have all done things that we regret, but we know quite well that our actions have not been such as to need any beating of our breasts and gnashing of our teeth. The majority of us are fairly decent, doing our best in that state of life in which chance has placed us; and if we believe in a judgement we feel that God has too much wisdom and good sense to bother much about failings which we mortals have no difficulty in forgiving in our neighbours. It is not that we are satisfied with ourselves, on the whole we are sufficiently humble, but we do the work which is next to our hand and do not trouble much about our souls. The Russians seem different. They are more introspective than we and their sense of sin is urgent. They are really overwhelmed by the burden and they will repent in sackcloth and ashes, with weeping and lamentation, for peccadillos which would leave our less sensitive consciences untroubled. Dmitri Karamazov looked upon himself as a great sinner, and Dostoievsky saw in him a violent, passionate man on whose soul Satan had laid his hold; but a calmer judgement can only look upon Dmitri as a very gentle transgressor: he played cards and drank more than he could decently carry, and when drunk was boisterous and noisy; he had strong sexual passions and a quick temper which he could not always control; he was hasty and impetuous; but that is about the extent of his wickedness. Monsieur de Valmont and Lord George Hell, before love made him a happy hypocrite, would both have looked upon his delinquencies with good-humoured contempt. As a matter of fact the Russian is not a great sinner. He is lazy and infirm of purpose; he talks too much; he has no great control over himself so that the expression of his passions is more lively than their intensity warrants; but he is kindly on the whole and good-humoured; he does not bear malice; he is generous, tolerant of others' failings; he is probably less engrossed in sexual affairs than the Spaniard or the Frenchman; he is sociable; his temper is quick, but he is easily appeased. If he is weighed down by a conviction of sin, it is evidently not on account of his acts of omission or commission (and in point of fact it is chiefly for the first that he loves to reproach himself) but on account of some physiological peculiarity. Few persons can have gone to a convivial gathering of Russians without noticing that they take their liquor sadly. They weep when they are drunk. They are very often drunk. The nation suffers from *Katzenjammer*. It would be an amusing thing if the prohibition of vodka took away from Russia the trait which sentimentalists in Western Europe have found such an engaging subject for their meditation.

I have nothing but horror for the literary cultivation of suffering which has been so fashionable of late. I have no sympathy with Dostoievsky's attitude towards it. I have seen a good deal of suffering in my time and endured a good deal myself. When I was a medical student I had occasion in the wards of St Thomas's Hospital to see the effects of suffering on patients of all sorts. During the war I had the same experience, and I have seen also the effects of mental suffering. I have looked into my own heart. I have never found that suffering improves the character. Its influence to refine and ennoble is a myth. The first effect of suffering is to make people narrow. They grow self-centred. Their bodies, their immediate surroundings, acquire an importance which is unreasonable. They become peevish and querulous. They attach consequence to trifles. I have suffered from poverty and the anguish of unrequited love, disappointment, disillusion, lack of opportunity and recognition, want of freedom; and I know that they made me envious and uncharitable, irritable, selfish, unjust; prosperity, success, happiness, have made me a better man. The healthy man exercises all his faculties, he is happy in himself and the cause of happiness in others; his abundant vitality enables him to use and improve the gifts that nature has endowed him with; his ripening intelligence enriches him with complicated thought; his imagination gives him sway over time and space; his educated senses enlarge the beauty of the world. He grows ever more complete a man. But suffering depresses the vitality. It coarsens the moral fibre rather than refines it; it does not increase a man, but lessens him. It is true that sometimes it teaches patience, and patience edifies. But patience is not a virtue. It is a means to an end and no more. Patience is essential to those who would do great things, but the patience exercised in doing small ones calls for no more respect than is due to small things. Waterloo Bridge is nothing in itself: it is merely a means of communication between two banks of the Thames, and it is London stretching on either side that gives it importance. You do not admire a man who uses infinite patience to collect postage stamps; the exercise of this quality does not save it from being a trivial pursuit.

It is said that suffering results in resignation, and resignation is looked upon as a solution to the perplexities of life. But resignation is a surrender to the hostile whims of chance. Resignation accepts the slings and arrows of outrageous fortune and calls them good. It kisses the rod that chastens it. It is the virtue of the vanquished. A braver spirit will have no dealings with resignation: it will struggle unceasingly against circumstances, and though conscious that the struggle is unequal, fight on. Defeat may be inevitable, but it is doubly defeat if it is accepted. To some, Prometheus, chained to his rock and strong in his unconquerable courage, is a more inspiriting example than that other, hanging on a shameful cross, who besought His Father to forgive His enemies because they knew not what they did. Resignation is too close to apathy for the spirited mind. It submits sometimes to what neither need nor should be borne. It is the final attempt of slaves to make their lack of mettle a reason for self-complacency. And even though the fetters that bind a man cannot be broken, let him remain a rebel still: though he suffers from cold and hunger, illness and poverty and lack of friends, though he knows that the road *is* uphill all the way and that the night has no morning. let him refuse ever to acknowledge that cold and hunger, illness and poverty are good; though he has not the strength to continue the hopeless battle, let him keep that one last spark of freedom in his heart which enables him to say that pain is bad.

Where the Russian has the advantage over us is that he is much less than we the slave of convention. It never occurs to him that he should do anything he does not want to because it is expected of him. Why he bore with a certain equanimity the oppression of centuries (and he surely bore it with equanimity, for it is inconceivable that a whole people could long endure a tyranny which they found intolerable) is that though politically coerced he was personally free. The Russian's personal freedom is much greater than the Englishman's. He is bound by no rules. He eats what he likes at the hours that suit him, he dresses as he chooses without regard to common usage (the artist will wear a bowler hat and a stiff collar as unconcernedly as the lawyer a sombrero); his habits seem to him so natural that everyone else accepts them as natural too; though often he talks for effect he never seeks to appear other than he is, he is only inclined to exaggerate himself a little; he is not shocked by a position he does not share; he can accept anything and he is perfectly tolerant of other people's eccentricities in thought or behaviour.

There is a deep streak of masochism in Russians. Sacher Masoch was himself a Slav and first drew notice to the malady in a volume of short stories which are not otherwise remarkable. According to the reminiscences of his wife he was himself a victim of the state he described. Briefly, it is a sexual desire in a man to be subjected to ill treatment, physical and mental, by the woman he loves. For example, Sacher Masoch himself insisted on his wife going for a trip with a lover while he, disguised as a footman, suffering agonies of jealousy, performed for the couple a variety of menial services. In Sacher Masoch's stories the women are described as large and strong, energetic, audacious and cruel. They use men with every sort of indignity. Russian fiction is full of characters of this sort. Dostoievsky's heroines are of this overbearing type; tenderness, sweetness, gentleness, charm do not appeal to the men who love them; on the contrary they find a horrible delight in the outrages to which they are exposed. They want to abase themselves. Turgenev's heroines are intelligent, alert, active and enterprising, while the men are weak of will, dreamers incapable of action. It is a characteristic of Russian fiction, and I imagine it corresponds to a deep-rooted instinct in the Russian character. No one can have lived among Russians without being struck by the aggressive way in which women treat men. They seem to take a sensual pleasure in humiliating them before others; they are contentious and brutal in their conversation; the men will endure things said to them that few Englishmen would tolerate; you will see them flush at a gibe, but make no attempt to retaliate; they are femininely passive, they cry easily.

The Russian sets store on self-abasement because it comes easily to him; he can accept humiliation because to humiliate himself gives him a singular sensual gratification.

The poverty of types in Russian fiction is rather surprising. You meet the same people, under a variety of names, not only in the works of the same author but in the works of others. Alyosha and Stavrogin are the two prominent and marked types. They seem to haunt the imagination of Russian writers, and it may be supposed that they represent the two sides of Russian character, the two persons whom every Russian feels more or less in himself. And it may be that it is the presence in him of these two irreconcilable selves which makes the Russian so unbalanced and so contradictory.

It is humour which discerns the infinite diversity of human beings, and if Russian novels offer only a restricted variety of types it is perhaps because they are singularly lacking in humour. In Russian fiction you will look in vain for wit and repartee, badinage, the rapier thrust of sarcasm, the intellectual refreshment of the epigram, or the lighthearted jest. Its irony is coarse and obvious. When a Russian laughs he laughs at people and not with them; and so the objects of his humour are the vapours of hysterical women, the outrageous clothes of the provincial, the antics of the inebriated. You cannot laugh with him, for his laughter is a little ill-mannered. The humour of Dostoievsky is the humour of a bar-loafer who ties a kettle to a dog's tail.

I can't think of a single Russian novel in which one of the characters goes to a picture gallery.

The message that Russia has given to the world seems to be the simple one that in love lies the secret of the universe. In opposition to it she places will, a rival but baneful force, and her novelists are never weary of showing to what catastrophe it may bring its bondsmen. They are fascinated by it, as women are fascinated by Don Juan, but it is with horror that they contemplate its satanic power; withal they look upon it with compassion and pursue it as Christ in *The Hound of Heaven* pursues the hurrying soul. They do not credit it with singleness of purpose. They believe that it is divided against itself and are sure that deep down in its essence lies a spark of that love which consumes their own breasts. They rejoice, as choirs of angels singing, when it abdicates its power and comes suppliant to their waiting bosoms, and if peradventure it refuses in the end to throw itself into their outstretched arms, like good Christians they consign it to outer darkness and to gnashing of teeth.

But in making this contrast between will and love Russia is merely placing one romantic figment of the imagination in face of another. They are both appearances, and if they have been thought to be something more it is presumably because they give us so intense a feeling of reality. But they begin and end in feeling. Love, so far as it is active, partakes of the nature of the will, and so cannot reasonably be set up against it as a rival answer to the riddle of existence; but it is its passive side, its self-abnegation, its humility which have attracted the Russian temperament; it is there they find the answer they seek to the mystery which torments them. Obviously this has nothing to do with thought, it is a surrender of thought to emotion; when they say that in love is the secret of the universe they confess that they have given up the search for it. It is singular that the Russians who occupy themselves so much with questions of man's destiny and the meaning of the world should have so little talent for metaphysical discussion. They have produced no philosopher even of the second rank. They seem to have no capacity for accurate and profound thought. Intellectually they all suffer from the malady of Oblomovism. It is interesting to inquire why this Russian message has had so great a success in Europe. The supremacy of love has had a good press. All manner of writers have been taken with it, and consciously or otherwise it has influenced their attitude. It came at a happy time. The world was disappointed with science. France, where most intellectual movements have their origin for the western world, was humbled and weary. The naturalistic school had grown dry and mechanical; Schopenhauer and Nietzsche had lost their novelty. There was a large class of educated persons interested in metaphysical questions, but with neither the education nor the patience to study metaphysical works; mysticism was in the air; and when they were told that love offered a solution of all their doubts they were more than willing to accept the statement. They thought they knew what it meant, for love is a word of many meanings and each one could give it that which was agreeable to his own experience; and the idea that this familiar feeling in some way rendered clear everything that had puzzled them gave. them an emotion which they were quite ready to take for an explanation. It never occurred to them that they were trying to explain a leg of mutton in the terms of a top hat. With some the message agreed with a faith which they had never surrendered, with others it re-established one which they had given up with their heads but not with their hearts. Nor must it be forgotten that love is a grateful theme for rhetoric.

I read a work on Dostoievsky by X. It might have been written at the menopause by the virgin daughter of a clergyman. There is no reason why one should not keep one's head about Dostoievsky. It is not necessary to read a novel with the ecstatic unction of a nun in contemplation of the Blessed Sacrament. To gush is not only tiresome to others, but unprofitable to oneself. And I think one pays a better compliment to the object of one's admiration when one considers him with sense than when one surrenders oneself to him like a drunkard to his glass of gin. I should have thought that if an author could enthral the minds of his readers he would be willing to let who would captivate their hearts. M. Arouet de Voltaire surely holds a more distinguished place among the dead than Mr Moody or even Mr Sankey.

I wish someone would analyse Dostoievsky's technique. I have an idea that, though his readers do not know it, the effect he has on them is largely due to his peculiar method. People speak sometimes as though he were negligible as a novelist, but this is not so, he is a very good novelist indeed, and he uses certain stratagems with great skill. A favourite one, which he employs constantly, is to bring together the chief persons in his story to discuss some action so outrageous that it is incomprehensible. He leads you along to an understanding of it with all the skill of Gaboriau unravelling a mystery of crime. These long conversations have a thrilling interest, and he heightens the thrill by an ingenious device: his characters are agitated quite out of proportion to the speeches they make; he describes them as trembling with excitement, green in the face or frightfully pallid, terror-stricken, so that a significance the reader cannot account for is given to the most ordinary words; and presently the reader is so wrought up by these extravagant gestures that his own nerves are set on edge and he is prepared to receive a real shock when something happens which otherwise would hardly have stirred his blood. An unexpected person comes in, a piece of news is announced. Dostoievsky is too good a novelist to baulk at the coincidence and his characters invariably find themselves at the necessary place at the dramatic moment. It is the method of Eugène Sue. That is not condemnation. All methods are good if you have talent. Racine found it possible to express all the variety of human passion within the iron convention of the Alexandrine, and Dostoievsky with the material of melodrama has created an enduring work of art. But he is a master hard to follow, and the amiable writers who fancy for themselves the role of an English Dostoievsky may find that they have succeeded only in becoming a shadow of Eugène Sue.

Sometimes he used this method in a purely mechanical way, and then his characters are agitated for no reason at all, and the thunderclap with which the scene ends in merely a ball rolled over a piece of tin. His people then are distorted like the figures of the School of Bologna. It is empty gesture.

I do not think there is great subtlety of characterization in

Dostoievsky. His people are all of a piece. The greatest novelists have at least indicated the diversity that is in every human breast. But his men are always themselves. They are like the 'characters' which were fashionable exercises of the seventeenth century: there is the man of iron, all iron, the flipperty-gibbet, all flightiness, the saint, all saintliness; they are passions, qualities, defects personified and seen with extraordinary vividness, but they are seldom human beings. The world of Western Europe has naïvely accepted them as Russians, but the Russians I have met are not very different after all from the rest of mankind. The man of iron has his weakness, the flipperty-gibbet has a kind heart, the saint has his faults. You do not get in Dostoievsky the supreme delight the novelist can give of showing you in one person the heroism and abjectness, the infinite contrariety and the disordered richness of man. Dostoievsky has never drawn a character of so intricate a complexity as Julien Sorel.

Man is so complex, he is a fit symbol of that Absolute which we are told contains all pain and pleasure, change, time and space, in its infinite incomprehensibility. But Dostoievsky's characters are like the persons in a morality play. They give you the impression that they are complicated because they do things that you do not understand, but a closer acquaintance shows you that in fact they are excessively simple and they always act really according to standard.

Dostoievsky reminds me of El Greco, and if El Greco seems the greater artist it is perhaps only because the time at which he lived and his environment were more favourable to the full flowering of the peculiar genius which was common to both. Both had the same faculty for making the unseen visible; both had the same violence of emotion, the same passion. Both give the effect of having walked in unknown ways of the spirit in countries where men do not breathe the air of common day. Both are tortured by the desire to express some tremendous secret, which they divine with some sense other than our five senses and which they struggle in vain to convey by use of them. Both are in anguish as they try to remember a dream which it imports tremendously for them to remember and yet which lingers always just at the rim of consciousness so that they cannot reach it. With Dostoievsky too the persons who people his vast canvases are more than life-size, and they too express themselves with strange and beautiful gestures which seem pregnant of a meaning which constantly escapes you. Both are masters of that great art, the art of significant gesture. Leonardo da Vinci, who knew somewhat of the matter, vowed it was the portrait-painter's greatest gift.

Resurrection is a book which owes its reputation to its authors'. The moral purpose has obscured the art, and it is a tract rather than a novel. The scenes in prison, the account of the convicts' journey to Siberia, give the unfortunate impression of having been mugged up for the occasion; but Tolstoi had great gifts and even here they are not missing. Effects of nature are described with a happy touch, at once realistic and poetic, and he can give as no one else in Russian literature the scents of the country night, the heat of midday and the mystery of dawn. His power of characterization is extraordinary, and in Achludof, though perhaps he has not drawn quite the character he intended, with his sensuality and mysticism, his ineffectualness, his sentimentality, his muddle-headedness, his timidity and obstinacy, he has created a type in which most Russians can recognize themselves. But perhaps from a technical point of view the most remarkable thing about the book is the immense gallery of subordinate characters, some of whom appear but on a single page, who are drawn, often in three or four lines, with a distinctness and individuality which any writer must find amazing. Most of the small characters in Shakespeare's plays are not characterized at all: they are merely names with a certain number of lines to say, and actors, who have often an accurate instinct in this matter, will tell you how great an effort it requires to put individuality into such puppets; but Tolstoi gives each man his own life and character. An ingenious commentator might devise the past and suggest the future of the most summarily sketched.

I have been reading Turgenev. I think it would be hard to find another writer who has achieved a greater reputation on such slender qualities. No other writer is so beholden for his celebrity to the exaggerated estimation in which Russian literature is held. He is a writer of the school of Octave Feuillet or Cherbuliez, and his chief merits are theirs, a well-bred sentimentality and the facile optimism of a contented mind. It would be interesting to know what was the opinion held of him in those literary circles in Paris where his size and origin seem to have made him a remarkable object. He knew Flaubert and Maupassant, the Goncourts, Huysmans, and the circle that gathered in the drawing-room of the Princesse Mathilde. He makes soothing reading. Curiosity will never impel you to look at the last page of one of his books, and you reach it without regret. To read him is like travelling by river, a calm and steady transit, without adventure or emotion. It is said that he indicated themes which the perils of Russian politics forbade him to touch (though he wrote from the safe distance of Paris and he need not have lagged so far behind the boldness of Herzen or Bakunin) and it appears that when he talked of one of his heroes cultivating the land his Russian readers, seeing in this a veiled way of indicating revolutionary movement, were vastly thrilled; but that of course is neither here nor there, and the political situation can no more make a poor book a good one than the needs of a wife and family make a pot-boiler a work of art. The merits of Turgenev consist chiefly in his love of nature, and he should not be blamed because he describes it in the manner of his generation, by means of cataloguing the various sounds and scents and sights rather than by giving the emotion which nature has given him; and his descriptions are graceful and charming. His descriptions also of provincial life in a noble family in the reign of Alexander II have a pleasing flavour, and changing times have given it a humorous grace and an historical interest. His character-drawing is stereotyped and the gallery of his creatures is small. There is in every book the same young girl, serious, dignified and energetic, the same vapid mother, the same talkative, ineffectual hero; and his subsidiary characters are vague and colourless. In all his books the only person who lives with a life of his own after you have turned the last page is that ponderous mass of flesh, Uvar Ivanovitch Stahov, who snaps his fingers and is plethorically inarticulate in the novel called *On the Eve*. But what must chiefly amaze the reader of Turgenev is the extreme triviality of his stories. *A House of Gentlefolk* is the story of an unhappily-married man who falls in love with a girl, and hearing that his wife is dead proposes to her. His wife turns up and the lovers separate. *On the Eve* is the story of a girl who falls in love with a young Bulgarian. He falls ill, they are married; he develops consumption and dies. In the one case if the hero had taken the elementary precaution of writing to his solicitor to find out if his wife was really dead, in the other if he had taken that of putting on a greatcoat when he went to get his passport, there would have been no story. An instructive parallel might be drawn between Turgenev and Anthony Trollope; in every point but style the comparison would be in favour of the English writer. He had more knowledge of the world, a greater variety, more humour, his range was wider and his characters were more diverse. Turgenev never wrote a scene that remains in the memory as that in which Bishop Proudie kneels at the bedside of his dead wife and prays God that he may not be thankful for her death.

This shows very poor judgement. It is true that Turgenev has neither the tortured passion of Dostoievsky nor the scope and the broad humanity of Tolstoi; but he has other qualities, charm and grace and tenderness. He has elegance and distinction – admirable qualities both – reasonableness, and a lovely feeling for the country-side. Even in a translation you can tell how beautifully he wrote. He is never excessive, never false, never boring. He is neither a preacher nor a prophet; he is content to be a novelist pure and simple. It may well be that a future generation will come to the conclusion that he was the greatest of the three.

The grave of Dostoievsky. It is surrounded by a neat iron railing and the plot of ground is neatly laid with sand. In one corner stands a huge round case with a glass front, containing an enormous wreath of artificial flowers, prim white roses and lilies of the valley larger than life; it is tied with a great bow and there is a long silk streamer on which is an inscription in gold letters. I wish the grave were as neglected, covered with fallen leaves, as are those which surround it. Its tidiness is distressingly vulgar. The bust is placed against a granite stele, a shapeless thing carved with meaningless emblems, and it gives you an uncomfortable feeling that it is on the point of toppling over.

It is a face devastated by passion. The dome of the head is stupendous and evokes irresistibly the thought of a world great enough to contain the terrible throng of his creatures. The ears are large, protruding, with the heavy lobes of the sensualist; the mouth is sensual too, with a cruel pout, but a pout like that of a sorrowful child; the cheeks are hollow, the temples deeply sunken; beard and moustache are long, bedraggled and unkempt; the long hair is lank; there is a great mole on the forehead and another on the cheek. There is agony in that face, something terrible that makes you want to turn away and that yet holds you fascinated. His aspect is more terrifying than all his works. He has the look of a man who has been in hell and seen there, not a hopeless suffering, but meanness and frippery.

Nevsky Prospekt. Bond Street has the narrow tortuousness of the medieval city, and it reminds one always of the town to which great ladies came for the season; it was in Bond Street that the last Duchess of Cleveland boxed her footman's ears. The Rue de la Paix has the flamboyance of the Second Empire; it is wide, handsome, coldly stately and gay withal, as though the shadows of Cora Pearl and Hortense Schneider still smiled brightly at the gathered gems. Fifth Avenue is gay too, but with a different gaiety, of high spirits, and it is splendid with the rich, unimaginative splendour of youth in its buoyancy. Though each has its character and could belong only to the city in which it is, these great streets have in common a civilized opulence; they represent fitly a society which is established and confident. But none of them has more character than the Nevsky. It is dingy and sordid and dilapidated. It is very wide and very straight. The houses on either side are low, drab, with tarnished paint, and their architecture is commonplace. There is something haphazard about the street, even though we know that it was built according to plan, and it has an unfinished air; it reminds you of some street in a town of the Western States of America which has been built in the hurry of a boom, and, prosperity having departed from it, has run to seed. The shop windows are crowded with vulgar wares. They look like bankrupt stock from the suburbs of Vienna or Berlin. The dense crowd flows ceaselessly to and fro. Perhaps it is the crowd that gives the Nevsky its character. It does not, as in those other streets, consist chiefly of one class of the population, but of all; and the loiterer may there observe a great variety of his fellow creatures, soldiers, sailors and students, workmen and bourgeoisie, peasants; they talk incessantly; in eager throngs they surround the men who sell the latest edition of a paper. It looks a good-natured crowd, easy-going and patient; I shouldn't imagine that they had the quick temper of the crowd in Paris which may so easily grow ugly and violent, and I can't believe that they would ever behave like the crowd of the French Revolution. They give the impression of peaceable folk who want to be amused and excited, but who look upon the events of life chiefly as pleasant topics of conversation. Outside butchers' and grocers' these days are the long food lines, women with kerchiefs over their heads, boys and girls, grey-bearded men and pale youths, waiting hour after hour, waiting patiently.

I think that the most astonishing thing in these crowds is the diversity of appearance; these people have not the uniformity of look which you find commonly in the crowds of other countries; it is as though the passions of the soul were written more plainly on their faces, and the faces were not a mask but an index, and walking along the Nevsky you saw the whole gallery of the characters of the great Russian novels so that you could put a name to one after the other. You see the thick-lipped, broad-faced merchant with his exuberant beard, sensual, loud-voiced and coarse; the pale-faced dreamer, with his pinched cheeks and sallow skin; you see the stolid woman of the people with a face so expressionless that it is like an instrument of music for wilful hands to play on, and you divine the cruelty of her sex's tenderness. Lust walks abroad like the personified abstraction of an old morality, and virtue and anger and meekness and gluttony. The Russians say constantly that the world can as little understand them as they understand themselves. There is a little vanity in the mysteriousness upon which they dwell. I have no idea of explaining what so many have claimed to be inexplicable, but I ask myself whether the mystery does not lie in simplicity rather than in complexity. They are strangely primitive in the completeness with which they surrender themselves to emotion. With English people, for instance, there is a solid background of character which emotion modifies, but which in turn reacts on emotion; with the Russians it looks as though each emotion took complete possession of the individual and swayed him wholly. They are like Aeolian harps upon which a hundred winds play a hundred melodies, and so it seems as though the instrument were of unimaginable complexity.

I often see brooding over the crowd on the Nevsky an extraordinary, a horrifying figure. It seems hardly human. It is a little misshapen dwarf, perched strangely on a tiny seat at the top of a stout pole high enough to bring him above the heads of the passers-by; and the pole is upheld by a sturdy peasant who collects the alms of the charitable. The dwarf sits on his perch like a monstrous bird and the effect is increased by something birdlike in his head, but the strange thing is that the head is finely shaped, the head of a young man, with a great hooked nose and a bold mouth. The eyes are large, rather close together, and they stare with an unwinking fixity. The temples are hollow, the cheeks wan and sunk. The strange beauty of the features is more than commonly striking because in Russia as a rule features are indistinct and flat. It is the head of a Roman of the Empire in a sculpture gallery. There is something sinister in the immobility of the creature, watching the crowd with the intentness of a bird of prey and yet seeing nothing, and that fierce bold mouth is curved into the shadow of a sardonic smile. There is something terrifying in the aloofness of the creature, contemptuous and yet indifferent, malicious and yet tolerant. It is like the spirit of irony watching the human race. The people pass to and fro and they put into the peasant's box kopecks and stamps and notes.

The Lavra of Alexander Nevsky. As you reach the end of the Nevsky Prospekt it grows shabbier and more dingy. The houses have the bedraggled look of those on the outskirts of a town, they suggest a sordid mystery, until the street ends abruptly in an oddly unfinished way and you come to the gateway of the monastery. You enter. There is a cemetery on each side of you and then you cross a narrow canal and come to the most unexpected scene in the world. It is a great quadrangle. Grass grows fresh and green as though you were in the country. On one side is a chapel and the cathedral and then, all around, the low white buildings of the monastery. There is something exquisitely strange in their architecture; the decoration is very simple and yet gives a sensation of being ornate; they remind you of a Dutch lady of the seventeenth century, soberly but affluently dressed in black. There is something prim about them, but not at all demure. In the birch tree rooks were cawing, and my recollection was carried back to the precincts of Canterbury; for there the rooks cawed too; it is a sound that never fails to excite my melancholy. I think of my boyhood, unhappy through the shyness which made me lonely among a crowd of boys, and yet rich with vague dreams of the future. The same grey clouds hung overhead. I felt homesick. I stood on the steps of the Greek church, looking at the long line of the monastery buildings, the leafless birches, but I saw the long nave of Canterbury cathedral with its flying buttresses and the central tower more imposing and lovely to my moved eyes than any tower in Europe.

With the revolution came a movement to abolish tips. Waiters in restaurants, servants in hotels, claimed instead a percentage of the bills. They looked upon tips as an insult to their manhood. People out of habit continued to offer them but they were invariably refused. I had an experience which I found peculiar.

I had given the boots in my hotel unusual trouble over something or other and so offered him five roubles. He refused it, and though I pressed it on him he would have none of it. Now, with a waiter in a restaurant who might be seen by his fellows, this would not have been astonishing, but here we were by ourselves in my room and no one could have known that the boots – member of a race born with an itching palm – had accepted a gratuity. There was no denying it, there was a change of heart; in some dim way these people, crushed by centuries of brutal oppression, had found a new sense of human dignity. It is foolish to abuse them because they have subjected themselves to the influence of demagogues; they see in these gestures of theirs the promise of a new life. I asked the waiter who generally served me whether the change was to his advantage or not. 'No,' said he, 'we all made more money when we took tips.' 'Would you like to go back to the old days then?' 'No,' he smiled. 'It's better as it is.' The spirit is worthy of praise.

Unfortunately the common experience is that all these people have grown very uncivil. Service is rendered badly and ungraciously. It is a hard conclusion that man is naturally a boorish fellow who resents service to his like and will be amiable only if he is going to be paid for it.

Savinkov. Before the revolution he was the leader of the terrorists. He planned and executed the assassinations of Plehve and of the Grand Duke Sergius. Hunted by the police, he lived for two years under a British passport. He was at last run to earth at an hotel. He was taken into the dining-room while a *compte rendu* was being made. He was told he could have anything he wanted. He asked for soda water and cigarettes. Soda water was brought and the officer in charge of the soldiers who had effected the arrest took a cigarette out of his case and flung it to him. Savinkov lost his temper. He took the cigarette and threw it in the officer's face. He laughed a little as he told me his words: 'You forget, sir, that I am no less a gentleman than you.' It bore out my theory that men in moments of great emotion express themselves in terms of melodrama. That is why the best writers are often so untrue to life.

I asked him what he felt when he was arrested, whether he was not horribly frightened. 'No,' he said, 'after all, I knew it was inevitable sooner or later, and when it came, strangely enough I felt relieved. You must remember that I had been leading a terribly strenuous life and I was tired out. I think my first thought was: now I shall be able to rest.'

He was sentenced to death, and while waiting for his execution was imprisoned at Sebastopol. I had heard a story that by his eloquence he had persuaded his jailers to join the revolutionary ranks and allow him to escape; and I asked him if it was true. He laughed. The real story was less romantic. The lieutenant in charge of the guard at the prison was already a revolutionary and was induced by others to effect Savinkov's escape. It was done in the simplest way. The lieutenant went boldly to the cell, ordered Savinkov to be taken out, and telling the prisoner to follow, marched out. The various sentries seeing an officer pass made no comment and presently they found themselves in the street. They went down to the harbour and got into an open boat which had been prepared for them and set sail over the Black Sea. They encountered fearful storms but in four days reached the coast of Rumania. From there Savinkov reached France and lived in Paris and on the Riviera till the revolution allowed him to return to Russia.

I said that it must have required enormous courage to plan and commit his assassinations. He shrugged his shoulders. 'Not at all, believe me,' he answered. 'It is a business like another, one gets accustomed to it.'

Petrograd. Towards evening it can be very beautiful. The canals have a character all their own, and though you may be reminded of Venice or of Amsterdam, it is only to mark the difference. The colours are pale and soft. They have the quality of a pastel, but there is a tenderness in them that painting can seldom reach; you find the dreamy blues, the dying rose, of a sketch by Quentin de Latour, greens and yellows like those in the heart of a rose.

They give the same emotion as that which the sensitive soul obtains from the melancholy gaiety of the French music of the eighteenth century. It is a quiet scene, simple and naïve, and it makes a pleasantly incongruous setting for those Russians of unbridled imaginations and wild passions.

My first teacher of Russian was a little man from Odessa covered with hair. He was almost a dwarf. I was then living at Capri and he used to come to my villa among the olive trees in the afternoon and give me a lesson every day. He was not a good teacher; he was shy and abstracted. He was dressed in rusty black and wore a large hat of fantastic shape. He sweated freely. One day he did not come, nor the next day, nor the day after; and on the fourth I set out in search of him. Knowing that he was very poor I had been rash enough to pay for his lessons in advance. I found my way to a narrow white alley in the town and was directed to a room at the top of the house. It was a tiny garret under the roof, baking hot, with nothing in it but a truckle bed, a chair and a table. I found my Russian sitting on the chair, stark naked, very drunk, with a huge flagon of wine on the table in front of him. When I went in he said to me: 'I have written a poem.' And without further ado, unconscious of his hairy nudity, with dramatic gestures he recited it. It was very long and I didn't understand a word.

Every nation forms for itself a type to which it accords its admiration, and though individuals are rarely found who correspond with it a consideration of it may be instructive and amusing. This type changes with the circumstances of the time. It is an ideal to which writers of fiction seek to give body and substance. The characteristics which they ascribe to this figment of their fancy are those which the nation at a given moment vaguely aspires to, and presently simple men, fascinated by these creatures of fiction, take them as their model and actually transform themselves, so that you may recognize in real life a type which you have seen described in novels. It is a curious thing that writers can create characters which men afterwards make their own. It is said that Balzac's people were truer to the generation after his own than to the generation he described, and no one can have wandered about the earth without encountering persons who had modelled themselves on the characters of Rudyard Kipling. It may be remarked that they show a deplorable taste. The type which seems most to captivate the fancy of the English to-day is that of the strong silent man. It is difficult to know when first he forced his way into English fiction; it may be that Jane Eyre's Rochester is the first example of him; he has since then been a constant favourite with women writers. He appeals to them, and to women generally, for a double reason; they feel in him the power to protect them for which they yearn, and his strength, submissive to their influence, flatters their innate desire for domination. Since he is more common in fiction and on the stage than in life and it is difficult to describe a man without making him express himself at length, silence, though part of his definition, is not the characteristic which is most noticeable; in fact he tends to be verbose. But in principle he is taciturn; a man of few words and of a smaller vocabulary; he is very practical, as is shown by the fact that he uses a great many technical terms when speaking to people who cannot be expected to understand them; he is embarrassed in general company and his manners leave much to be desired; but, strangely enough, though awkward in his dealings with his fellow countrymen, he has a singular gift with natives. At a loss in a drawing-room, he is a match for the subtle Oriental. He uses him kindly but firmly, as a good father does his children; he is upright, just and truthful. He is not much of a reader, but such literature as he studies is sound, the Bible, Shakespeare, Marcus Aurelius and the Waverley novels. He is not a conversationalist, but when he speaks it is to go straight to the point; his intelligence is good, but a little narrow. He knows that two and two make four, and it has never occurred to him that in some inexplicable way sometimes they make five. He has no patience with art and his philosophical attitude is naïve. He has never had any doubts about the 'things that matter', and indeed part of his strength lies in his never seeing that any question has more sides than one. His character is more excellent than his intellect. He has all the manly virtues and to these he adds a feminine tenderness. But it must not be supposed that he has no faults; it has been suggested that his manners are not always good, and sometimes he is even bearish; how great is the triumph then when he is softened by the grey-eyed English girl who wins his faithful heart! His temper, although under excellent control, is often shocking, and his arteries stand out on his hollow temples while he masters it. His morals vary. Sometimes he is very pure, but sometimes, contrariwise, he has been at one period of his life sadly dissolute. He is stern, perhaps ruthless when occasion demands, but he has a heart of gold. His appearance fits his character. He is tall and dark, very strong, muscular, lithe and slender. He has hawklike eyes, his curly hair is grizzled, especially on the temples, his chin is square, but his mouth is sensitive. He is a master of men. Such is the strong silent man who bears the white man's burden, the founder of our country's greatness, the Empire-builder, the support and mainstay of our power. He toils ceaselessly in remote and inaccessible places of the world; he guards the Marches of the Empire: you will find him at the Gates of India, in the lonely wastes of the Great Dominion, and in the tropical forests of Darkest Africa. No one can contemplate him without a thrill of pride. He is everywhere that is a long way off. It is that indeed which makes him endurable.

Fiction has never enriched the world with a more delightful character than Alyosha Karamazov, and just as he made people happy when they met him he cannot fail to make his readers happy too. He affects one like a June morning in England when the air is sweet with flowers and the birds sing and the salt breeze from the English seas is fresh on the uplands. You feel that it is good to be alive. And you feel it is good to be alive when you are in Alyosha's pleasant company. He has the rarest quality in the world, and the most beautiful, goodness, a native, simple goodness which makes all the gifts of the intellect a little trivial. For Alyosha is not very clever, he is ineffectual in action, and sometimes you must be impatient with him when the rough-and-tumble of the world demands a more decided attitude; he is not a man of action; indeed he is hardly a man at all, he has almost the inhumanity of the divine. His virtues are passive rather than active, he is meek and patient and long-suffering; he never judges others, he does not perhaps understand them, but he has infinite love for them. And that, I suppose, is the passion which fills his soul, a selfless, eager love, a love which makes that of sex horrible, which makes even the love of a mother for her child of the earth. Dostoievsky, a cruel man, for once was kind, and he made Alyosha as beautiful in body as he was in soul. He is merry like the angels who have never known the pains of earth. Sunshine walks with him. His sweet smile is worth the wit of others. He has a wonderful gift to soothe the troubled heart. His presence to those in pain is like the cool soft hand of someone you love when your brow is hot with fever.

The Democratic Convention began to sit to-day at the Alexandrevsky Theatre. It was representative of the working classes and it might be presumed that these delegates from all parts of Russia fairly well typified the classes they were sent by. Scanning their faces, it struck me that on the whole it was a peasant type of countenance; of course there were a great many Jews, with alert, wary eyes, and I suppose that among the vast number (there were nearly two thousand persons in the theatre) there were many rogues; but on the whole I had the impression not of degenerate, but rather of backward, loutish people: they had ignorant faces, and a vacuous look, the narrowness, the obstinacy, the uncouthness of peasants; and notwithstanding the collars and jackets of some, the uniforms of others, I felt they were very near to the slow-moving tillers of the soil. They listened to the speeches with apathy. The speeches were very long. The meeting, timed to begin at four, began in point of fact at five and continued till nearly midnight. Only five speeches were made in all those hours and each speech was of about the same length. The orators spoke with great fluency, but with a monotonous fervour; they were tremendously in earnest and they did not attempt to lighten their speeches with story or with jest; they did not even give the mind the relief of a plain fact, but confined themselves to generalization and exhortation; every speech was in effect a peroration.

There was once a professor of law who said to his students: 'When you're fighting a case, if you have the facts on your side hammer them into the jury, and if you have the law on your side hammer it into the judge.' 'But if you have neither the facts nor the law?' asked one of his listeners. 'Then hammer hell into the table.' answered the professor. These orators were hammering hell into the table all the time. But they were not impressive. You might see just such men addressing the meeting of the Radical candidate for a constituency in the South of London. Chernov, who is spoken of as as the evil genius of the revolution, a man who is feared on all sides and is supposed to have enormous influence, was a man without force or personality; rather short, with thick, coarse features and a shock of grey hair. He had the look of a socialist orator in any part of the world, and he spoke at inordinate length, with wearisome emphasis. Tsesetelli, the Minister of Foreign Affairs, spoke clearly and to the point, but in an undistinguished manner; it was the very ordinary speech of a very ordinary man. It is amazing that such mediocre persons should be in control of this vast empire, and I asked myself what it was in them that had raised them from the anonymous crowd whom they seemed to excel neither in character, force nor intelligence.

The only real enthusiasm aroused in the meeting was by Kerensky. I was curious to see the man who in so short a time has achieved a position of such fame and power; and here again I was puzzled, for strength is the one thing he obviously has not. I could not understand how his enemies could see in him Napoleonic designs. There is more of Saint-Just in him than of Bonaparte. He was seated in the middle of the imperial box when the chairman called upon him to speak, and he walked along the central aisle of the theatre to the stage. He was dressed in khaki and accompanied by two A.D.C.s. He was somewhat stouter than I had expected, clean-shaven, his hair cut *en brosse*; but what struck me most was his colour. One often reads of people being green in the face with fright and I had always thought it an invention of novelists. But that is exactly what he was. He walked quickly, and having reached the stage walked round the table at which the Council sat and shook hands with each of the delegates in turn. He gave a quick, spasmodic shake, and his face remained set in an anxious immobility. He had a strangely hunted look. He was obviously very nervous. It was a hazardous moment for him, because accusations had been freely made against him of complicity in the adventure of General Kornilov, and the Bolsheviks who had called the meeting together were hostile; it was notorious that this gathering might decide his fate, and if the extremists found themselves in a majority it was supposed that they would call upon him to resign in their favour. It was not known what he intended to do then; but the general impression was that he would refuse, remove his government to G.H.Q. and, leaving Petrograd to the Bolsheviks, rule the country with the help of the army. He began his speech by asking for what amounted to a vote of confidence. He spoke for an hour, fluently, without notes, amid constant interruptions. He was extremely emotional. There was a passage over the orchestra which led on to the stage, and down this he walked every now and then till he stood practically among the audience as though he sought to appeal to each man personally. His appeal was to the heart and not to the mind. The applause grew more frequent and the interruptions were more impatiently resented. The people seemed to feel that here was a sincere and upright man, and if he made mistakes they were honest. His voice was not attractive and he spoke at one pitch, without modulation; there was no light and shade in his oratory, and, I should have said, nothing to inspire. His only power seemed to be his seriousness and his disinterestedness. He finished, shook hands quickly with the delegates round the table and returned to his box amid thunderous cheers. He said a few more words from his box in answer to the applause and soon left the theatre. He had won the day.

The ballet. I saw in the fugitive beauty of a dancer's gesture a symbol of life. It was achieved at the cost of unending effort, but, with all the forces of gravity against it, a fleeting poise in mid-air, a lovely attitude worthy to be made immortal in a bas-relief, it was lost as soon as it was gained and there remained no more than the memory of an exquisite emotion. So life, lived variously and largely, becomes a work of art only when brought to its beautiful conclusion and is reduced to nothingness in the moment when it arrives at perfection.

Savinkov was sitting in a tavern drinking a cup of tea when a peasant came up to him and said: 'Where shall I find God?' He was more than a little drunk. Savinkov looked at him with a grave face, but with smiling eyes. 'In your heart, my brother,' he answered. The peasant said nothing for a time as the answer sank into his fuddled brain. 'Then what shall I do with my life?' he said. Savinkov replied with another question. 'How old are you?' The peasant seemed doubtful and he shrugged his heavy shoulders. 'Forty,' he said, a little uncertainly. 'That is a safe age to trust to one's instincts,' said Savinkov. 'You are strong and healthy. Do the work you know how to do; and for the rest trust to your inclinations. I know nothing else.' The peasant stood solidly on his two feet, with soft, kind eyes fixed on Savinkov; he rubbed his beard; then he made a low bow and went slowly away.

Savinkov. He appears to be a man of between forty and fifty, of medium height, slender, with a somewhat bald head; his features are ordinary, and his eyes are small and hard and set rather closely together. One can imagine that at times they would be very cruel. He was neatly dressed; he wore a stand-up collar, a quiet tie with a pin in it, a frock-coat and patent-leather boots. He had the prosperous look of a lawyer. There was nothing violent in his appearance. He gave me the impression of a cultivated man, somewhat commonplace, but not without a certain distinction. He was quiet, reserved and modest. It was not till he began to talk that I saw anything remarkable in him. He spoke in Russian and in excellent French, idiomatic and correct except for an occasional error in gender; he spoke slowly as though he were thinking out what he said, but it was clear that he possessed an admirable power of finding the exact words to express his ideas. His voice was soft and pleasant, his enunciation extremely clear. I had never heard such a captivating talker. He was grave when the subject needed gravity, humorous when there was occasion for it; there was such a reasonableness in what he said that it was impossible not to be affected; he was exquisitely persuasive; but the deliberation of his speech, the impressive restraint of his manner, suggested a determined will which made his ruthlessness comprehensible. I had come across no one who filled me with so great a sense of confidence.

He told me one or two curious anecdotes.

After the battle of July eighteenth when the Russian troops were shamefully defeated, Kerensky, who with him had watched their flight, asked him to come for a drive with him in his car. Savinkov, who was then Minister of War, thinking he wished to confer with him about means to repair the disaster, got into the car and they started. But Kerensky said nothing. He sat as one cowed and despairing. He opened his mouth only to make a hackneyed quotation from a second-rate poet; Savinkov could hardly believe his ears. What on earth was the connection between this sentimental line and the tragedy of their country? He concluded: 'It was characteristic of this man without education that he should comfort himself with such a bad poet.' An incident somewhat similar took place at the fall of Tarnopol; Savinkov, seeing the Russian troops flee precipitately, hurried to Kornilov to tell him what was happening. Kornilov betrayed not the smallest emotion; his answer came directly, without hesitation: 'Shoot them.' The way in which Savinkov told the story showed that here he recognized with rejoicing a man of spirit equal to his own.

Another anecdote. He was returning from the front with Kerensky, and at the station, on their arrival at Petrograd, a telegram was handed to the Premier. He glanced at it and passed it to Savinkov with the words: 'Will you see about this?' It was the request of a woman for mercy on behalf of her son, a soldier condemned to be shot for desertion. Now the matter was no business of Savinkov's, who had had nothing to do with the sentence and who had not the prerogative of mercy; Kerensky gave him the telegram in order to rid himself of a responsibility he dreaded. Savinkov finished: 'And the curious thing is that Kerensky never referred to the matter again; he never ventured to ask me what I had done.'

171

He described Kerensky as a man of words, not of acts, a vain man who would not suffer disagreement and so surrounded himself with sycophants, a man of morbid verbosity, who would make speeches *en tête à tête* with his ministers, who would make speeches to his aide-de-camp driving in a motor with him, a man of small education and of limited imagination, a man tired out and neurotic. 'If he had had imagination,' he said, 'he would surely not have installed himself with his womenkind in the Winter Palace.'

Kerensky. He looked very unhealthy. Everyone knew he was a sick man; and he spoke of himself, not without a suspicion of bravado, as a dying one. He had a rather large face; it was of a strange yellow colour and when he was nervous it went livid; the features were not bad, the eyes large and vivacious, but the general impression was of a plain man. He wore an odd dress, khaki, but it was not quite a military uniform, nor was it the dress of a civilian; it was nondescript and dingy. He came into the room followed by his A.D.C., with a quick step, and gave me a firm, hasty, mechanical handshake. He seemed fearfully on edge. Sitting down and talking incessantly, he took hold of a cigarette-box and played with it restlessly, locking and unlocking it, opening and shutting it, turning it round and round. His speech was rapid and emphatic; and his nervousness made me nervous too. He seemed to have no humour, but a lively and rather boyish sense of fun. It appeared that one of his A.D.C.s was a flirtatious youth and women were in the habit of ringing him up on the telephone which stood on Kerensky's desk. It was Kerensky's amusement to answer the telephone in place of the A.D.C. and, pretending it was the young officer speaking, to flirt violently with the unknown person at the other end. Tea was served and he was offered brandy, but as he was about to take it the A.D.C. expostulated, since alcohol was bad for him, and it was amusing to hear him, like a spoilt child, try to wheedle the young man into allowing him to drink just one glass. He was very merry and laughed a good deal. I could not make out what were the characteristics which had raised him in so short a while to so extraordinary a position. His conversation did not suggest a man of wide culture, hardly even a man of general education. His personality had no magnetism. He gave me no feeling of intellectual or of physical vigour. But it was impossible to believe that he owed his ascent merely to chance and held his position only because there was no one with whom to replace him. As the conversation proceeded – he talked on as though he were too tired to stop – something pathetic seemed to arise; I felt sorry for him and I got the idea that his power consisted perhaps in exciting a protective emotion; there was something appealing in him so that you felt inclined to help him; he had the quality which Charles Frohman had to an extraordinary degree, the quality of exciting in others the desire to do things for him. I saw nothing of the outrageous vanity which so many had told me of; on the contrary I found him simple and unaffected. It was impossible not to believe in his honesty; I felt that here was a man who was sincerely trying to do his best, and who was filled with a very pure enthusiasm to serve not so much his country as his fellow countrymen. His emotionalism was a strength in Russia, where the facile expression of feeling has an overwhelming effect, but it was rather disconcerting to English modesty. I could have wished his voice did not tremble quite so easily. It was a little embarrassing to hear such noble sentiments expressed with so much candour. But this is one of the differences between English and Russian which will always keep the two countries strange to one another. The final impression I had was of a man exhausted. He seemed broken by the burden of power. It was easy to understand that he could not bring himself to act. He was more afraid of doing the wrong thing than anxious to do the right one, and so he did nothing until he was forced into action by others. And then his great care was to avoid the responsibility which might be ascribed to him.

Gauguin. A fruit piece in the Gallery at Christiania. These are fruits, mangoes, bananas, persimmons, in which the colour is so strange that words can hardly tell what a troubling emotion they give; there are sombre greens, opaque like a delicately-carved bowl in Chinese jade and yet with a quivering lustre that suggests the palpitation of mysterious life; there are purples horrible like raw and putrid meat and yet with a glowing sensual passion that reminds one of the Roman Empire of Heliogabalus; there are reds, shrill like the berries of a holly – one thinks of Christmas in England and the snow and the good cheer and the pleasures of children – and yet by some magic softened till they are like the tender colours of a dove's breast; there are deep yellows that die with an unnatural passion into a green as fragrant as the spring and as pure as the sparkling water of a mountain brook. Who can tell what tortured fancy made these fruits? They seem to belong to some Polynesian garden of the Hesperides. There is something alien in them as though they grew in a stage of the earth's dark history when things were not irrevocably fixed to their forms. They are extravagantly luxurious. They are heavy with tropical odours. They seem to possess a sombre passion of their own. It is enchanted fruit to taste which might open the gateway to God knows what secrets of the soul and to enchanted palaces of the imagination. They are heavy with unknown dangers, and to taste them might turn a man to beast or god.

1919

They told him someone had said of him: 'He's smart, he doesn't give much away.' He beamed; he took it as a compliment.

She plunged into a sea of platitudes, and with the powerful breast stroke of a channel swimmer made her confident way towards the white cliffs of the obvious.

A married couple. She adored him with a selfish, passionate devotion, and their life was a struggle on his part to secure his soul and on hers to get possession of it. Then it was discovered that he had T.B. They both knew that this was her triumph, for thenceforward he would never escape her. He killed himself.

Jamie and his wife. Two stodgy people who do nothing but read novels. They live a perfectly monotonous life, but in the spirit, a life of romance. All their experiences are fiction. They had a baby and the baby died. Jamie hoped that his wife wouldn't have another. It disturbed the tenor of their lives. After the funeral they both settled down with a sigh of relief to the new novels that had just come from the library.

Arnold. For thirty years he had cultivated a pose till at last it became second nature to him. Then he was bored to death by it, but when he came to look into his heart for his real self he couldn't find it. Nothing was left but the pose. He went to France hoping to get killed, but he came back at the end of the war safe and sound, and there stretched before him then an illimitable emptiness.

Chicago. The hogs are driven into pens and they come squealing as though they knew what was before them; they are attached by a hind leg and swung from a moving bar which takes them to where a man in blue overalls splashed with blood stands with a long knife. He is a pleasant-faced young man. He turns the hog towards him and stabs it in the jugular vein; there is a gush of blood and the hog passes on. Another takes its place. Hog follows hog with a mechanical regularity which reminds you of the moving steps of an escalator. I was struck by the calm indifference with which the pleasant-faced young man killed them. It was like a grim caricature of the Dance of Death. They come, struggling and screaming, the poet, the statesman, the merchant prince; and no matter what ideals, what passions or high endeavours have been theirs, they are hurried on by a remorseless fate and none escapes.

The activity is intense as the hog is passed by a machine from one man to another; one scrapes off such hair as is left after the hog has gone through one machine, another cuts out the bowels, a third slices off the hams. There was not a moment's pause, and I wondered what would happen if a man fell out and missed his appointed task. There was one old man, grey-bearded, who lifted a huge chopper and mechanically cut off the hams. The movement of the chopper, so deliberate and regular, yet so unceasing, was strangely mysterious. They told me he had been doing that very same thing for thirty years.

Wabash Avenue. Many-storeyed buildings white. red and black, but dingy, with their fire-escapes like strange parasites on monstrous mushroom growths. Long lines of motors along the kerbs. The dull roar of trains on the elevated, the hurried, agitated string of street cars as they thunder along crowded with people, the sharp screech of motor horns and the shrill, peremptory whistle of the cop directing the traffic. No one loiters. Everyone hurries. Street-cleaners in their white uniforms, artisans in dingy overalls, brown or blue. The mixture of races, Slavs, Teutons, Irish with their broad smiles and red faces, Middle-Westerners, dour, long-faced, strangely ill at ease, as though they were intruders.

H.B. went down to stay in the country. His next-door neighbour was a very quiet prim little old lady; becoming acquainted with her, he gradually connected her with the heroine of a celebrated murder which had excited the world fifty years before. She had been tried and found not guilty, but the evidence was so damning that notwithstanding the verdict the general opinion was that she had in point of fact committed the crime. She discovered that he had found out her identity, taxed him with it and presently said to him: 'I suppose you want to know whether I did it or not. I did, and what's more, if it were all to happen again I'd do it again."

An Italian, driven by hunger, came to New York and in due course got work on the streets. He was passionately attached to the wife he had left in Italy. Rumour reached him that his nephew was sleeping with her. He was seized with rage. He hadn't the money to return to Italy, but wrote to his nephew to come to New York, where he could earn good wages. The nephew came, and on the night of his arrival the husband killed him. He was arrested. The wife was brought over for the trial and in order to save him confessed what wasn't true, that the nephew had been her lover. The man was sentenced to a term of imprisonment and after no very long while paroled. His wife was waiting for him. He knew that she hadn't been unfaithful to him, but her confession was as great a burden on his honour as if she had been. It rankled. It shamed him. He made her violent scenes, and at last, hopeless, because there was nothing else to do, because she loved him, she told him to kill her. He drove his knife into her heart. Honour was satisfied.

When I have travelled through America I have often asked myself what sort of men those were whom I saw in the parlour-cars of trains or in the lounge of an hotel, in rocking-chairs, a spittoon by their side, looking out of a large plate-glass window at the street. I have wondered what their lives were, what they thought of and how they looked upon existence. In their ill-fitting, ready-made clothes, gaudy shirts and showy ties, rather too stout, clean-shaven, but wanting a shave, with a soft hat on the back of their heads, chewing a cigar, they were as strange to me as the Chinese and more impenetrable. Often I have tried to speak with them, but I have found no common language in which I could converse with them. They have filled me with timidity. Now that I have read *Main Street* I feel that I am no longer quite unfamiliar with them. I can give them names. I know how they behave when they are at home and what they talk about. I have enriched my knowledge of human nature. But the author of *Main Street* has done something more than depict with accuracy the inhabitants of a small town in the Middle-West, and I cannot make up my mind whether he has done it knowingly or by accident. He has described a very curious circumstance, the beginnings in America of the social distinctions which in Europe make up so important a part of life. And it is interesting to see this arise when in Europe the war is thought to have abolished so many distinctions of class. The story of *Main Street* is very simple; it is the description of the marriage of a lady with a man who is not a gentleman. He is an excellent fellow, but she suffers much because his ways are vulgar and the people among whom she has to live are common. In England a woman in such a case would have been at once conscious of the social difference and would have hesitated to marry. Her friends would have said to her: 'My dear, of course he's a dear good chap, but he's not a gentleman and you can't possibly be happy with him.' And much else of the story hangs on the various levels of village society; the tradesman looks down on the farmer and the farmer on the hired man. There could not be more class-consciousness in an English village; but in an English village each man knows his station and accepts it without rancour. It looks as though every civilization as it grows complicated and stable gave rise to a minute difference of classes, and to acknowledge them frankly conduced to ease of mind. In the community described in *Main Street* every man allows with his lips that every other is as good as he, but in his heart he does not think it for a moment. The banker does not ask the dentist to his house and the dentist will not hobnob with the tailor's assistant. The lip-service which is given to equality occasions a sort of outward familiarity, but this only makes those below more conscious of the lack of inward familiarity; and so nowhere is class-hatred likely to give rise in the long run to more bitter enmity.

1921

Haddon Chambers. I was told this morning that Haddon Chambers was dead, and I said: 'Poor chap, I'm sorry'; but it occurred to me immediately that I spoke according to a foolish convention. Haddon Chambers had made a successful job of life according to his own lights. He had enjoyed himself. His day was over and unless his jaunty spirit had found new resources of philosophy he had nothing much to look forward to that was attractive to a man of his temper. He died in a happy moment. If he is remembered at all it will be, not for his plays, but for his phrase: 'the long arm of coincidence'. That may well last as long as the language. He was a little man, shrivelled in his dapper clothes, who reminded you somehow of a dead leaf; and like a dead leaf he used to blow into the places he was used to frequent, tarry, without giving you the impression that he was settled even for a moment, and then with a singular aimlessness blow out again. He seemed to have no material attachments. He came and went without intention as though he were the sport of a perfectly indifferent chance. At the first glance he looked a youngish man, but presently you saw that in reality he was old, old; his eyes in repose were weary and he gave them brightness only by an-effort of will; his face had an unnatural smoothness as though it were massaged and nourished with cold creams; he looked like someone who had been long buried and then dug up again. It made you think that he was much older than he really was. He never told his age. He clung to youth with a seriousness which he showed in no other of the affairs of life. He had the reputation of a Don Juan, and this he valued much more than any that his plays had brought him. One of his affairs at least had been notorious, and he rejoiced to the last in the fame of it. He liked to pretend that he was engaged in constant intrigues, and with innuendoes, hints, broken phrases, raisings of the eyebrow, winks, shrugs of the shoulder and waves of the hand would give you to understand that he was still pursuing his amorous career. But when he went out from his club, very spruce in clothes a little too young for him, ostensibly to a rendezvous, you had an inkling that it was in truth to dine by himself in the back room of some restaurant in Soho where no one he knew would be likely to see him. Since he wrote plays I suppose he must be counted as a man of letters, but surely there can have been seldom a man of letters who cared less for literature. I do not know whether he ever read: certainly he never spoke of books. The only art in which he seemed at all interested was music. He attached no great importance to his plays; but it exasperated him to have his best play, *The Tyranny of Tears*, ascribed to Oscar Wilde. For my part I cannot imagine how such a notion could ever have been as widely spread as it certainly was. No one could have had it who had any feeling for dialogue or any discrimination in humour. Oscar Wilde's dialogue was succinct and pointed, his humour well bred and urbane: the dialogue

in *The Tyranny of Tears* is loose, pertinent rather than sparkling, and it has no epigrammatic quality; the humour smacks
of the bar parlour rather than of the drawing-room. Its wit is
due to its aptness rather than to any verbal ingenuity. It had
the very stamp and idiosyncrasy of Haddon Chambers. He
was a sociable creature, and when I seek for a characteristic
impression with which to leave him I see him lounging at a
bar, a dapper little man, chatting good-humouredly with a casual
acquaintance of women, horses and Covent Garden opera, but
with an air as though he were looking for someone who might
at any moment come in at the door.

1922

Things were easier for the old novelists who saw people all of a
piece. Speaking generally, their heroes were good through and
through, their villains wholly bad. But take X for instance. She
is not only a liar, she is a mythomaniac who will invent maliciou
stories that have no foundation in fact and will tell them so
convincingly, with such circumstantial detail, that you are almost
persuaded she believes them herself. She is grasping and will
hesitate at no dishonesty to get what she wants. She is a snob and
will impudently force her acquaintance on persons who she
knows wish to avoid it. She is a climber, but with the paltriness
of her mind is satisfied with the second rate; the secretaries of
great men are her prey, not the great men themselves. She is
vindictive, jealous and envious. She is a quarrelsome bully. She
is vain, vulgar and ostentatious. There is real badness in her.

She is clever. She has charm. She has exquisite taste. She
is generous and will spend her own money, to the last penny,
as freely as she will spend other people's. She is hospitable and
takes pleasure in the pleasure she gives her guests. Her emotion
is easily aroused by a tale of love and she will go out of her way
to relieve the distress of persons who mean nothing to her. In
·sickness she will show herself an admirable and devoted nurse.

She is a gay and pleasant talker. Her greatest gift is her capacity for sympathy. She will listen to your troubles with genuine commiseration and with unfeigned kindliness will do everything she can to relieve them or to help you to bear them. She will interest herself in all that concerns you, rejoice with you in your success and take part in the mortifications of your failure. There is real goodness in her.

She is hateful and lovable, covetous and open-handed, cruel and kind, malicious and generous of spirit, egotistic and unselfish. How on earth is a novelist so to combine these incompatible traits as to make the plausible harmony that renders a character credible?

In this connection it is instructive to consider Balzac's *Le Cousin Pons*. Pons is a glutton. To satisfy his ignoble craving he thrusts his company at dinner-time on people who plainly resent it, and rather than go without good food and good wine will submit to the coldness, the acidulous greeting of his unwilling hosts and the sneers of their servants. He wilts when he has to eat at home and at his own expense. The vice is disgusting and the character can only excite aversion. But Balzac demands your sympathy for him and he gets it with ingenuity. In the first place he makes the people he sponges on vile and vulgar; then he dwells on his hero's faultless taste, for he is a collector, and on his love of beauty. He will deny himself not only luxuries, but necessities in order to buy a picture, a piece of furniture or of porcelain. Balzac again and again insists on his goodness, his kindness, his simplicity, his capacity for friendship, till little by little you forget his shameful greed and the abject sycophancy with which he tries to repay the good dinners he gets only to feel deep sympathy for him and to view with horror his victims, who after all had a lot to put up with but to whom Balzac has not allowed a single redeeming trait.

I've known Mrs A. for years. She's American and married to a diplomat who had been *en poste* in Petersburg before the war. I met her in Paris the other day. She told me she'd just had an odd experience. It had upset her. She had run across a Russian friend whom she had known rich before the revolution and whose parties she had frequently been to. She was shocked to see her poorly dressed and down at heel. She gave her ten thousand francs to buy herself new clothes which might help her to get a position as a *vendeuse* or something like that. A week later Mrs A. met her again, but in the same old frock, the same old hat and the same old shoes. She asked her why she hadn't bought herself a new outfit. The Russian rather shame-facedly told her that every one of her friends was poor and shabby, and she couldn't bear the idea of being the only one among them who was well dressed, so she had invited them all to a grand dinner at the Tour d'Argent and after that they'd gone to *boîte* after *boîte* till every penny was spent. They got home at eight in the morning, broke, tired, but happy. When Mrs A. went back to the Ritz and told her husband, he was cross with her for wasting the money. 'You can't do a thing for people like that,' he said. 'They're hopeless.' 'Of course he was right,' she said when she told me the story, 'and I was mad too, but you know, somehow or other, I can't help having a sort of sneaking admiration for her.' My friend looked at me ruefully. 'I feel it shows a spirit that I haven't got and never can have,' she sighed.

Charlie Chaplin. He is of an agreeable exterior. He has a neat figure, admirably proportioned; his hands and feet are well shaped and small. His features are good, the nose rather large, the mouth expressive and the eyes fine. His dark hair, touched with white, is waving and abundant. His movements are singularly graceful. He is shy. His speech has in it still a hint of the Cockney of his early youth. His spirits are ebullient. In a company in which he feels himself at ease he will play the fool with a delightful abandon. His invention is fertile, his vivacity unfailing, and he has a pleasant gift of mimicry: without knowing a word of French or Spanish he will imitate persons speaking in one or the other of those languages with a humorous accuracy which is wildly diverting. He will extemporize dialogues between a couple of women in the Lambeth slums which are at once grotesque and moving. Like all humour they depend on a close observation, and their realism, with all its implications, is tragic; for they suggest too near an acquaintance with poverty and squalor. Then he will imitate the various performers in a music hall of twenty years ago or the amateurs at a cabman's benefit in a public house on the Walworth Road. But this is mere enumeration: it omits the unbelievable charm that graces all his actions. Charlie Chaplin will keep you laughing for hours on end without effort; he has a genius for the comic. His fun is simple and sweet and spontaneous. And yet all the time you have a feeling that at the back of it all is a profound melancholy. He is a creature of moods and it does not require his facetious assertion: 'Gee, I had such a fit of the blues last night I didn't hardly know what to do with myself' to warn you that his humour is lined with sadness. He does not give you the impression of a happy man. I have a notion that he suffers from a nostalgia of the slums. The celebrity he enjoys, his wealth, imprison him in a way of life in which he finds only constraint. I think he looks back to the freedom of his struggling youth, with its poverty and bitter privation, with a longing which knows it can never be satisfied. To him the streets of southern London are the scene of frolic, gaiety and extravagant adventure. They have to him a reality which the well-kept avenues, bordered with trim houses, in which live the rich, can never possess. I can imagine him going into his own house and wondering what on earth he is doing in this strange man's dwelling. I suspect the only home he can ever look upon as such is a second-floor back in the Kennington Road. One night I walked with him in Los Angeles and presently our steps took us into the poorest quarter of the city. There were sordid tenement houses and the shabby, gaudy shops in which are sold the various goods that the poor buy from day to day. His face lit up and a buoyant tone came into his voice as he exclaimed: 'Say, this is the real life, isn't it? All the rest is just sham.'

Sarawak. On the horizon was a row of little white clouds, the only clouds in the sky, and they had a curious gaiety. They looked like a row of ballet girls dressed in white, waiting at the back of the stage, alert and merry, for the curtain to go up.

The sky was grey, and against the greyness hung black, fantastic clouds, and the high sun, breaking through the greyness, touched their summits with silver.

Sunset. Suddenly the rain stopped and the heavy clouds that straggled about the mountain seemed to set upon the sun with the fury of Titans fighting the divine Apollo, and the sun, vanquished but magnificent in its fall, transfigured the black clouds with glory. And they seemed to pause for a moment, as though aghast at the spendour with which the death throes of the god had covered them; and then on a sudden it was night.

The river is broad, yellow and turbid. At the back of the sandy shore grow the casuarinas, and when the breeze stirs their lace-like foliage they make a sound as of people talking. The natives call them talking trees and say that if you stand under them at midnight you will hear voices of unknown people telling you the secrets of the earth.

A green hill. The jungle reached to its crest, an intoxication of verdure, and the luxuriousness was such that it left you breathless and embarrassed. It was a symphony of green, as though a composer working in colour instead of with sound had sought to express something extraordinarily subtle in a barbaric medium. The greens ranged from the pallor of the aquamarine to the profundity of jade. There was an emerald that blared like a trumpet and a pale sage that trembled like a flute.

The yellow river under the breathless sun of midday had the white pallor of death. A native was paddling upstream in a frail dug-out so small that it hardly showed above the surface of the water. On the banks of the river, here and there, were Malay houses on their piles.

Towards evening a flight of egrets flew down the river, flying low, and scattered. They were like a ripple of white notes, sweet and pure and springlike, which an unseen hand drew forth, like a divine arpeggio, from an unseen harp.

S. A boy of eighteen who has just come out. A rather good-looking youth, with blue eyes and curly chestnut hair that grows thickly on his neck. He is trying to grow a moustache. He has a charming smile with him. He is ingenuous and *naïf*. He has the enthusiasm of youth and the mannerisms of a cavalry officer.

The mangrove swamp. Along the coast and at the mouth of the river grow mangroves and nipah. The nipah is a long-leafed dwarf palm, like those palms which in old pictures you see carried on Palm Sunday. They grow at the water's edge, reclaiming the soil, and when they have made fresh, fruitful earth they die down and the jungle takes their place. They are the pioneers preparing the country for the traders and the motley crowd of humanity that come after them.

The Sarawak River. The mouth is very broad. On each side are mangrove and nipah washed by the water and behind the dense green of the jungle, and in the distance, darkly silhouetted against the blue sky, the rugged outline of a mountain. You have no sense of gloom, or of being shut in, but of space and freedom. The green glitters in the sunshine and the sky is blithe and cheerful. You seem to enter upon a friendly, fertile land.

A blue sky, not pale with the languor of great heat, nor violent like the skies of Italy, but as though Prussian blue were mixed with milk; and like little sailing boats on the sea white clouds, shining in the sun, pass leisurely.

A room. The walls were of unstained wood and on them hung photogravures of Academy pictures, Dyak shields, parangs and huge straw hats with a symmetrical decoration in gay colours. Long cane chairs. Pieces of Brunei brass ware. Orchids in a vase. The table was covered with a dingy Dyak cloth. On a rough wooden shelf were cheap editions of novels and old travel books in battered leather. In one corner a shelf crowded with bottles. Rattan matting on the floor.

The room opened on to a veranda. It was only a few feet from the river, and from the bazaar on the opposite bank you heard the beating of a gong for some Chinese festivity.

The chik-chak. It is a small brown lizard which gives the sound from which it gains its name. You can hardly believe that so loud a noise can come from so small a throat. You hear it at night, a curiously human sound that breaks upon the silence suddenly, and there is something derisive about it. You might think it was chuckling with amusement at the white men who come and go and leave all things as they were.

In the early morning the colours are brilliant, yet tender, and then as the day wears on they grow tired and pale. They are then only the various tones of the heat. It is like a Chinese melody, in the minor key, which exacerbates the nerves by its monotony. The ear awaits a resolution which never comes.

The prisoners are engaged in public works, and you see them, under the guardianship of a Sikh, on the roads, taking their work not too hardly, and those in chains, because they have previously escaped, are to all appearances not much inconvenienced by them.

The jungle. There is no sign of a pathway and the ground is thickly strewn with decaying leaves. The trees grow dense, trees with enormous leaves and trees with the feathery foliage of the acacia, coconut trees and the areca palm with its long, straight white stem, bamboos and wild sago like huge bunches of ostrich feathers. Here and there, white and naked, is the skeleton of a dead tree; and its whiteness against all the green is startling. Here and there, rival kings of the forest, tall trees, with profuse and heavy foliage, soar above the common level of the jungle.

Then there are the parasites, great tufts of green leaf growing in the fork of a tree, flowering creepers that cover a tree like a bridal veil; sometimes they wind a sheath of splendour round the tall trunks and throw long arms of flowers from branch to branch.

In the early day all this green is blithe and exhilarating. There is nothing sombre or oppressive in it, but in the passionate wildness of all that growth a strange excitement. It has the daring abandon of the maenad rioting along in the train of the god.

Going up the river. High overhead fly a pair of doves and a kingfisher darts rapidly across the water, a flash of colour, a living jewel, brilliant like a Chinese porcelain. Two monkeys sit side by side on a branch with their tails hanging down; another monkey leaps from branch to branch. There is the ceaseless sound of the cicadas, and the sound has a sort of fury. It is as continual and monotonous as the rushing of a brook over a rocky bed. Then suddenly it is silenced by the loud singing of a bird whose notes are those of an English blackbird.

At night the frogs croak, croak, croak, such a racket; and now and then some singing bird of the night breaks in upon it with a few short notes. The fireflies give the shrubs the look of a Christmas tree all lit up with tiny candles. They sparkle softly; the radiance of a soul at peace.

The river narrows and it is like a leafy reach of the Thames.

The fever bird. It has three notes, and it just misses the fourth which would make the chord, and the ear waits for it maddeningly.

The Bore. We saw it coming from a good way off, two or three large waves following one another, and it didn't look very alarming. It came nearer, very quickly, with a roar like the roar of a stormy sea, and I saw that the waves were much larger than I had thought. I didn't like the look of them, and I tightened my belt so that my trousers shouldn't slip down if I had to swim for it. Then in a moment the Bore was upon us. It was a great mass of water, eight, ten, twelve feet high, and it was quite plain at once that no boat could weather it. The first wave dashed over us, drenching us all and half filling the boat with water, and then immediately another wave struck us. The boatmen began to shout. They were prisoners from the up-country jail and they wore their prison clothes. They lost control of the boat; the force of the water turned it round so that we were broadside on as we were carried on the crest of the Bore. Another wave dashed over us and we began to sink. Gerald, R. and I scrambled from beneath the awning under which we had been lying, and suddenly the boat gave way under us and we found ourselves in the water. It was surging and storming round us. My first impulse was to swim for the shore, but R. shouted to Gerald and me to cling to the boat. For two or three minutes we did this. I expected that the waves would pass as the Bore swept up the river and that in a few minutes at the outside we should find ourselves once more in calm water. I forgot that we were being carried along with the Bore. The waves kept dashing over us. We were hanging on to the gunwale and the base of the frame work which supported the rattan mats of the awning. Then a bigger wave caught the boat, and it turned over, falling upon us, so that we lost our hold. There was nothing then but a slippery bottom to put our hands to, and as the keel came within reach we made a desperate grab at it. The boat continued to turn, like a wheel, and then we caught hold of the gunwale with a greater sense of security, only to feel the boat turn again, forcing us under water, and the whole business repeated itself.

This went on for I don't know how long. I thought it was because we were all clinging to the side of the boat, and I tried to get some of the crew to go round to the other side; I thought that if half of us remained on one side while half went over to the other, we could keep the boat bottom down and so easily hang on; but I could make no one understand. The waves swept over us, and each time the gunwale slipped out of my hand I was pushed under, only to come up again as the keel gave me something to cling to.

Presently I began to get terribly out of breath, and I felt my strength going. I knew I couldn't hold out much longer. I thought the best thing was to make a dash for the bank, but Gerald begged me to try to hold on. The bank now didn't look more than forty or fifty yards away. We were still being carried along among the seething, pounding waves. The boat went round and round and we all scrambled round it like squirrels in a cage. I swallowed a good deal of water. I felt I was very nearly done. Gerald stayed near me and two or three times gave me a hand. He couldn't do much, for as the side of the boat fell over us we were equally helpless. Then, I don't know why, for three or four minutes the boat held keel downwards, and we were able to hold on and rest. I thought the danger was past. It was a precious thing to be able to get one's breath. But on a sudden the boat rolled right round again, and the same thing repeated itself. The few moments' respite had helped me, and I was able to struggle a little longer. Then again I became terribly out of breath and I felt as weak as a rat. My strength was gone, and I didn't know if I had enough now to try to swim for the shore. Gerald by this time was nearly as exhausted as I was. I told him my only chance was to try to get ashore. I suppose we were in deeper water then, for it seemed that the waves were not so turbulent. On the other side of Gerald were two of the crew, and somehow they understood that we were down and out. They made signs to us that now we could risk making for the bank. I was dreadfully tired. They caught hold of a thin mattress as it floated past us, it was one of those that we had been lying on, and they made it into a roll, which they used as a life-belt. It didn't look as though it would be much use, but I took hold of it with one hand, and with the other struck out for the shore. The two men came with Gerald and me. One of them swam by my side. I don't quite know how we reached it. Suddenly Gerald cried out that he could touch the bottom. I put down my legs, but could feel nothing. I swam a few more strokes, and then, trying again, my feet sank into thick mud. I was thankful to feel its beastly softness. I floundered on, and there was the bank, black mud into which we sank up to the knees.

We scrambled up with the help of roots of dead trees that stuck out of the mud, and when we came to the top found a little flat of tall rank grass. We sank down and for a while lay there stretched out and exhausted. We were so tired that we couldn't move. We were covered with black mud from head to foot. After a time we stripped off our things and I made myself a loin cloth out of my dripping shirt. Then Gerald had a heart attack. I thought he was going to die. I could do nothing but let him lie still and tell him it would pass over. I don't know how long we lay there, the better part of an hour, I should think, and I don't know how long we were in the water. At last R. came along in a canoe and fetched us off.

When we got to the Dyak long-house on the other side where we were to spend the night, although we were caked with mud from top to toe, and were in the habit of having a swim three or four times a day, we couldn't bring ourselves to go into the river, but washed ourselves perfunctorily in a pail. None of us said anything, but we certainly all felt that we didn't want to have anything more to do with the river that night.

Looking back, I was surprised to notice that not at any moment had I been at all frightened. I suppose the struggle was so severe that there was no time for any emotion, and even when I felt my strength going and thought that in a moment or two I should have to give up, I am not conscious that I had any feeling of fear or even distress at the thought of death by drowning. I was so tired that it seemed to me rather in the nature of a relief. Later in the evening when I was sitting in a dry sarong in the Dyak house and from it saw the yellow moon lying on her back it gave me a keen, almost a sensual pleasure. I couldn't help thinking that I might at that moment have been a corpse floating along with the tide up the river. And next morning when we started off again to go down stream I found an added pleasure in the cheerful sky and the sunshine and the greenness of the trees. The air was singularly good to breathe.

The Dyak House. It was very long, built on piles, with a thatched roof. Access was obtained by climbing up the trunk of a tree which had been rudely notched into steps. There was a veranda outside, the floor of which was made of bamboos attached with rattan; and within a long common-room with a platform and the rooms in each one of which lived a family. At the sides of the common-room stood the large jars which are the Dyaks' wealth. When we came in, clean mats were unrolled and laid down for us to sit on. Chickens flew about. A monkey was attached to one of the posts. Dogs wandered around. Beds were made up for us on the platform. Through the night cocks crowed and with the dawn they made an infernal racket. Then the noise of the household began again. The men set out for their work in the rice-fields. The women went down to the river to get water. The sun had scarcely risen and the long-house was already as busy as a hive.

The Dyaks are rather small, but very trimly built, with brown skins, large shining eyes flat in the skull like the eyes of Coptic mosaics, and flat noses. They had ready, sweet smiles and engaging manners. The women are very small, shy, with something hieratic in their immobile faces, pretty, with dainty little figures when they are young. But they age quickly, their hair goes grey, and the skin hangs loosely on their bones, all wrinkled and shrivelled; and their dried breasts are pendulous. There was an old, old woman, quite blind, who sat in a corner like an idol, upright on her haunches, taking no notice of anyone. The busy life passed her by and she remained absorbed in memories of the past. The preparation of the rice is left to the women. There is an absolute division of labour, and it would never occur to a man to do anything that immemorial custom has established as woman's work. The women wear nothing but cloth reaching from the waist to the knee. Round their arms is curled silver wire and many have silver wire curled round their waists. It looks like a huge watch spring. They carry their children on their backs, making a seat for them from a shawl tied round their necks. The men wear silver bracelets, ear-rings and rings, and in full dress they are handsome and jaunty. Many of them have long hair hanging down their backs; and the slightly feminine appearance it gives them is strange and ambiguous. For all their ready smiles and pleasant manners you feel in them a latent savagery which is a little startling.

Under the long-house pigs rustled around devouring garbage, and chickens and ducks kept up a constant clatter. From the house to the river a pathway was made of roughly-hewn planks so that you should not have to walk in the mud of the track, but when the tide is low you have to climb up slippery banks of mud, dark and slimy, into which you sink knee-deep.

When I got back to Kuching I wrote to the Resident with whom we had been staying and asked him if he could see his way to commuting the sentences of the two prisoners who had saved my life. He wrote back and told me that he had set one of them free, but was afraid he could not do anything for the other, since on his way back to Simiangang he had stopped off at his own village and killed his mother-in-law.

An eastern river. On either bank the jungle spread densely, and under the full moon it was blacker than the night, silent with a silence in which was something omnious. You shuddered as you thought of the dark, violent things which its thick foliage shrouded. It seemed to wait expectantly. But in the clear sky the moon proceeded leisurely: it was like the squire's lady, portly in her Sunday best, sailing up the aisle of the village church. Then in the east, beneath a ragged fringe of cloud, a faint redness appeared. On the placid river a sampan glided silently, and against the water you saw the dim figure of the standing fisherman. On the bank a solitary light gleamed friendly amid the jungle wildness, and you guessed that a grass hut stood there clinging to the water's edge and pressed upon fiercely by the lush extravagance of palm and strange-named tree and creeping plant. Now the redness in the East lurid. The ragged clouds were torn and tortured: the sun was rising unpeacefully as though he strove desperately with unknown, dark and merciless powers. And when you looked up the river it was day; but when you looked back, the moon shone tranquilly and the night lingered serene.

L. He is a little over forty, of about the middle height, thin, very dark, slightly bald, with black hair and large eyes *à fleur de tête*. He has not the look of an Englishman, but rather of a Leventine. He speaks, without modulation, on one note. He has lived so long on outstations that he is shy and silent in company. He has a native wife whom he does not care for and four half-caste children whom he is educating in Singapore to be clerks in Government offices in Sarawak. He never wants to go to England, where he feels himself a stranger. He speaks Dyak and Malay like a native; he was born in the country and knows the native mind better than he knows the English. He got engaged to a girl on one of his leaves in England, but the thought of his native family harassed him so that he broke off the engagement. He would much sooner be on an outstation than in Kuching. He seldom smiles. He is a morbid, melancholy man, very conscientious, and always afraid of doing wrong. When he talks, without humour, he is verbose and dull. Life is a blind alley.

The bazaar at Kuching. The bazaar consists of narrow streets with arcades like those of Bologna and each house is a shop in which you see the thronging Chinese pursuing the busy life of the Chinese town, working, eating, talking. On the banks of the river are the native huts, and here, living their immemorial lives, are the Malays. As you wander in the crowd, as you linger watching, you get a curious, thrilling sense of urgent life. You divine a happy, normal activity. Birth and death, love and hunger; these are the affairs of man. And through that press of people passes the white man who rules them. He is never part of the life about him. So long as the Chinese keep the peace and pay their taxes he does not interfere with them. He is a pale stranger who moves through all this reality like a being from another planet. He is no more than a policeman. He is the eternal exile. He has no interest in the place. He is only waiting for his pension, and he knows that when he gets it he will be unfit to live anywhere but here. In the club they often discuss where they shall live when they retire. They are bored with themselves, bored with one another. They look forward to their freedom from bondage and yet the future fills them with dismay.

A planter. He was at Cambridge and after taking his degree decided to be a planter. He has been out ten years. He is a bachelor. He was ruined by the slump. He made two thousand dollars in the boom and put it into rubber, but now most of the estates in which he invested his money have gone back to jungle. He is a little man with irregular features, soft dark eyes and a soft voice, very shy, with a gift of mimicry and a love of music. He can play after a fashion all kinds of instruments. He collects Malay silver. There is something pathetic about him. He lives alone in a very untidy bungalow. On the walls are innumerable pictures of women in all states of undress. On the rough shelves are modern novels.

Mrs T. A blonde. Owing to the heat her hair is straight, but it is rather pretty hair, very fair, flaxen; and she has blue eyes, a little pale and already inclined to be tired although she cannot be more than six and twenty. Full-face she is almost pretty in her colourless fashion, but she has a very weak, small, insignificant chin, and in profile there is something sheeplike about her. Her skin has been clear and fresh, but now like one of the tropical days it is faded. She wears cotton and muslin frocks, blue or pink, open at the neck, with short sleeves. Her usual ornament is a string of white coral beads. On her head a Philippine straw hat.

Mrs N. Fair, fat and forty. She is a large, dark woman, with bright eyes and a bold, friendly manner. She gives you the impression that she might have been a chorus girl; as a matter of fact she comes from a family that has been busied with the East for a hundred years. She is stout, growing stouter all the time, to her dismay, but she cannot resist food, and she devours cream and potatoes and bread with gusto.

Singapore: Opium Dream. I saw a road lined on each side with tall poplars, the sort of road that you see often in France, and it stretched in front of me, white and straight, immensely far; I saw farther than I had ever thought it possible to see, and still the white road continued with green poplars on either side. And then I seemed to go along it, rapidly, and the poplars fled past me more quickly, infinitely more quickly than the telegraph poles fly past when you are in an express train; and still they went and still they were ahead of me, the long rows of poplars. Then, on a sudden, there were no more poplars, but shady trees with large leaves, chestnuts and planes; and they were spaced out, and I went at no breakneck speed, but leisurely, and presently I came upon an open space and then, as I looked down, far below me, was the grey calm sea. Here and there a fishing-boat was sailing into harbour. Yonder, on the other side of the bay, stood a trim and tidy granite house with a flagstaff in the garden. It must have been the coast-guard's.

He had been Resident in one of the Federated Malay States for twenty years. He lived in almost regal state. He was very odd and fierce. He was autocratic, violent and brutal. He had a Malay wife and by her and other women a great number of children. At last he retired and married a woman in Cheltenham where he had settled down, and his only desire thenceforward was hers, to get into the best society.

The D.s asked me to dinner to meet some friends of theirs, husband and wife, who were spending a few days in Singapore. The man was Resident somewhere in British North Borneo. Mrs D. told me that he had been a fearful drunkard and took a bottle of whisky to bed with him every night which he finished before morning. He became so tiresome that the Governor sent him home on leave and told him that if he didn't sober up by the time he came back he would have to dismiss him. The man was a bachelor, and the Governor advised him to find a nice girl in England and marry her, and she would keep him straight. At the end of his leave he came back married and a reformed character. He never touched a drop of alcohol.

They came to dinner. He was a big, fat man, with a very naked face, rather bald, prosy and pompous; she was smallish, dark, neither young nor pretty, but alert and evidently competent. She was very lady-like. She was the sort of woman whom you meet by the dozen at Tunbridge Wells, Cheltenham or Bath – born spinsters who seem never to have been young and who will never, you think, grow old. They have been married five years and seem very happy. I suppose she had married him just to be married.

I never saw them again and they never knew what they had let themselves in for when they came to dinner that night. They suggested to me a story which I called 'Before the Party'.

Java. At the station there was a group of dejected people, three men and two women, handcuffed and guarded by Javanese soldiers. The prisoners were native Christians. Eight of them had gone to a village to convert the inhabitants to Christianity. They expounded their doctrines of peace and good will to all men, and the headman sought to argue with them. The argument grew hot, and presently the chief evangelist struck the headman. A fight started. The women joined in and the headman was killed. This turned into a general scrummage as the result of which seven persons of the village were killed and three evangelists.

Thursday Island. The Browns, man and wife, run the hotel. She is a little stoutish woman in open-work blouses, with marcelled dark hair. She is fond of a joke. She has keen, rather cunning eyes and a nose which is suspiciously red. She may once have been pretty. Like her husband she is full of wild-cat schemes for making a fortune. He is a man of the middle size, about forty, with thin long hair that waves about over his head. He has a curious looseness of limb and of gesture so that he seems to be on springs. He has followed many professions. He began as a barber, then was a professional runner, he has been a bookmaker and a trainer, a miner, a tobacconist and a barber again. He is very frank about his running experiences, in which he made a lot of money. It seems to be a somewhat crooked sport and he tells stories of running under a false name, of not winning when the bookmakers made it worth his while and so forth. He conducts the hotel very negligently and is only interested in a mining property on an adjacent island where he expects to find gold. He never drinks. He has a daughter by a former marriage called Queenie who waits at table. She feels herself superior to such work and takes the orders as if they were veiled insults. But when one of the guests chaffs her she hits him over the head with her menu and says: 'Get along with you.' The housemaid is a dried-up maiden of thirty with a sallow face and sharp features. She goes about with her fringe in curl papers. She has been a barmaid and looks upon it as beneath her dignity to do the housework. She is very fond of gossiping about the various people on the island.

C. He owns a twenty-ton ketch and a couple of cutters which he used for pearling till, owing to the slump, the industry grew unprofitable. He is a man of six feet high, strongly built, stout, with a round face and honest blue eyes. His manner is slightly shy, but he is good-natured and considerate. His hair is closely cropped except for a little curly lovelock on his forehead. He is between thirty-five and forty. When he is sailing his ketch he wears very old and ragged ducks and a singlet, but when he goes ashore he puts on yellow boots, a pair of grey trousers, and a white coat, a stengah shifter, which he leaves unbuttoned, a starched

collar no matter how hot the weather is, and a black knitted tie
which he arranges to look as though it went round his neck by a
neat contrivance which he fastens on to his collar stud. As he
walks along with a slight roll you would tell him anywhere for
the master of a small vessel.

The *Dinton*. A ketch fifty-five feet long. The crew consisted of C.
and four Torres Straits islanders, black, with crisp curly hair and
fine figures. They are dressed in patched, dirty trousers, singlets
and battered felt hats. Tom Obi is grey and solid; the others are
young; Henry is a blood, rather handsome, dashing and boastful.
Utan, with nothing on but a lava-lava, does the cooking on a fire
of sticks in the hold, and here are the crew's bunks. The cabin is
aft, and through it runs the main mast; it is so low that you can't
stand upright in it; and the ceiling is blackened by the smoky
hanging lamp. There is room for two men to sleep lengthwise
and one across the hatch. Two dinghies are wedged between the
bulwarks and the hold.

We were to start at nine in the morning, but C. was late and
when he came discovered that a spare jib had been left behind,
so two of the crew were sent to his house to fetch it. We cast off
and slipped away with the tide. There was a stiff breeze, but the
sun was shining and the sky was blue. It was exhilarating to
speed along under the mainsail and the jib. We expected to get to
Mobiag that evening. It was a distance of forty-five miles. We
ran down between Thursday Island and Prince of Wales Island,
and we had lunch, which we ate on the deck house, cold beef,
pickles, boiled potatoes, and a sponge cake. We drank tea. When
we got out of shelter of the land we found the monsoon blowing
hard, and there was a heavy sea. C. had the foresail set and the
water cask lashed down. Now and then we were caught in a
squall and when a sea struck us a shower of spray swept along the
deck. The waves, crested with white, looked very big, and in that
little boat one was very near the water. We were passing small
islands all the time, and as we passed each one I wondered if I
could swim to it if we capsized. After some hours we reached the
island of Badu, and C. said he would anchor there and go to

Mobiag next day. When we rounded the island we were protected from the wind and it was more comfortable. There was an anchorage, and we found ten or a dozen pearlers which had been driven in by the bad weather. They were Japanese, but one who was an Australian, with a black crew, and when we anchored we sent a dinghy off to fetch him. We gave him a cup of tea and asked him to come back to dine and play bridge with us. We went ashore and bathed. Our dinner consisted of a king-fish we had caught on the way, cold meat and apple pie. We drank tea, and whisky and soda out of tin panikins; and after we had done played bridge on the deck house by the bright light of a hurricane lamp. T. (the Australian) told us that the weather was terribly bad farther north and said that he had nearly been capsized. He was purposing to wait till the storm moderated; anyhow the water was too dirty for pearling. He was of about my height, and though quite young, looked dried-up. He was thin, fair, with a weather-beaten wrinkled face, false teeth and blue eyes. He wore a pair of dark pants and a singlet. At about nine we were all sleepy and he left us. The night was clear and bright, the moon nearly full, and in that sheltered spot there was no wind. We rigged up a sail to make a shelter and put our mattresses on the deck and lay down.

Next morning we set sail early to take advantage of the out-flowing tide, but we hadn't gone far before we struck a sand-bank. The tide was going out, and we stuck there till it turned and floated us off. We sailed between islands and soon found ourselves in the open sea. Mobiag, an uneven, hazy mass, stood away in the distance. The wind was stronger even than the day before and the sea ran high. We sailed through islands, in muddy water, and there were reefs all about. One of the men stood on the jib-boom and kept a look-out. Each time a sea dashed over us we ducked to avoid the spray. Presently there was a dull scraping sound and we knew we had struck a reef. We bumped over and were again in deep water. The look-out man with a gesture of one arm or the other guided C. at the helm. He was very anxious. We struck another reef and again bumped off. Then we sailed out to avoid them.

Mobiag is surrounded by a double reef, and we were aiming for the end of one to bear up between the two and so get round the island to where there was an anchorage. We got to the end of the outer reef and sailed across till we were within a few yards of the inner one, veered about – the ketch turned almost in her own length – and tacked back to the outer reef. It was blowing hard and we had all our sails set. There was a quivering and rattling of the sails as we put about. This we did five or six times, gradually getting to the end of the island. The jib sail was torn to tatters and flapped with loud smackings against the mast. We were soaked to the skin. At last we made for a channel between Mobiag and a small island where our anchorage was. The tide was coming in against the wind, and this made the sea very heavy. I was frightened. The ketch rolled like the devil and righted herself each time with a jerk. I watched a heavy wave ride towards us, break, flooding the deck, and I expected the next wave to break over us before the ketch had time to recover, but with an almost human agility she avoided it and rode triumphant on. Then the outer island gave us protection and we sailed bravely to the anchorage.

We got into a dinghy and went ashore. There, in a hollow, among coconut palms, at the edge of the beach of a little cove, C. had a cottage. The skeleton of a cat lay at the door. After our wetting it was good to get into dry clothes and have a cup of tea. We wandered about the island. The huts of the islanders nestled prettily among the coconuts. That night the wind blew wildly, whistling through the coconuts, and it made such a racket that I couldn't sleep. Next day the crew spent the morning loading great stones from the beach into the dinghy to add to the ballast. In the afternoon they went up to the village and didn't return till night. Tom Obi came to the cottage and said the weather was very bad, so C. decided to wait another day. The coconuts were writhing in the wind, and looking out to sea we saw a squall dark in the distance rushing on to break into thin rain on the island. The clouds were scudding across the sky. We played cards. The villagers notwithstanding the heavy sea went out in cutters and in the evening came back with four sea-cows. Everyone on the island assembled to watch the batch being cut up, and when this was done went off with great lumps of red meat. It tastes like beef-steak not so tender as it should be.

The schoolmaster. He is a man between fifty and sixty, tall and spare, with a much-wrinkled face; his grey hair grows thickly on his head, and he has a grey moustache and a week's growth of grey beard on his chin. His teeth are badly broken and discoloured. He talks indistinctly, partly owing to his lack of teeth and partly owing to the heavy moustache, so that it is an effort to listen to him. He is dressed in a khaki stengah shifter, a pair of ragged pepper-and-salt trousers, old tennis shoes and a shapeless felt hat. He is very dingy and dirty. He has lived on Mobiag for fifteen years in a shabby bungalow on the water-front among the coconut trees. It is of planks covered with a roof of corrugated iron. The cane chairs are rickety. On the walls are a number of photographs and coloured advertisements. On a little shelf are his books, cheap editions of popular novels and magazines. His wife has native blood in her. She is a dark women, wizened, with grey curly hair and a stoop. She wears a torn white skirt and a not very clean white blouse. When I went into their house a dozen native girls of just under fifteen, buxom and nimble, were seated on the floor taking a sewing lesson.

The missionary. He is a very thin man with a shock of grey hair and blue eyes. He generally wears grey trousers and a singlet, but when he wants to dress up puts on a clerical collar with a black frontpiece over his singlet, and a white coat. In his library are cheap novels and theological works. He has a ketch in which he travels from island to island, for his parish consists of eight islands. He is at home very little. His wife has short wavy hair, and if she did not wear spectacles and were nicely dressed she would be a pretty woman. She is a very bad cook and keeps her house in a slovenly way. She is shy with strangers.

In front of the veranda were casuarina trees, and through them you saw the sea and the island beyond. Long after the sun set there was a blood-red glow over the sea and the casuarina trees were silhouetted against it. They were lace-like and graceful and unreal. The picture reminded you of a Japanese print. At last the fitful breeze swayed them a little more and there sprang into sight, only to disappear again, a white star.

The casuarina trees were like a veil of phantasy that pleasant thoughts obtrude between you and the sight before your eyes.

Next morning we started for Deliverance. C. wanted to put in there to deliver stores. The wind was lighter than the day before. The superficial clouds still sped swiftly across the sky against, as it were, a background of dark heavy clouds that seemed hardly to move. The sun shone brightly. I sat on deck in a shirt and a pair of ducks, with my feet bare, and read. At one time we had the wind dead fair and C. set the mainsail and the foresail butterfly-wise. Deliverance is a low-lying island, and at first one saw only a dimness on the horizon, then the tops of trees. We had to sail round in order to find shelter to anchor. There is no opening in the reef and we were obliged to anchor outside a mile or more from the island. The sea was choppy and it took over an hour to row ashore. We had to bail out all the time with an empty fruit tin.

Back on board we had a shark-line out with a piece of dugong as bait, and suddenly there was a great commotion in the water. We drew the line in. There was a struggle and a flurry. We saw a shark. C. fetched his revolver and we drew the shark to the surface and near the side. C. fired and there was a stain of blood in the water. The struggle went on and C. put six shots into it. Then a rope was passed round it, over the head and below the dorsal fin, with a noose, and this was attached to the pulleys. We hoisted it over the side and it fell heavily on the deck. It was not quite dead and lashed spasmodically with its tail. Utan took a tomahawk and gave it whacking blows on the skull, then a long knife and slit open its belly. In the stomach were the bones of a turtle. We cut out the huge liver. Then we cut off a piece of the shark, baited the hook and flung the line overboard. In a few minutes another shark was hooked. Soon we had three huge sharks from fourteen to eighteen feet long. The decks were horribly greasy and bloody. Early next morning we cast them overboard and set sail for Merauke. C. wanted to make oil from their livers for the masts and spars, and all day two of the crew were cooking chunks of liver in a kerosene tin over a fire of sticks. The stench was awful.

There were shoals between Deliverance and Merauke, so that we couldn't make a bee-line, but had to go due west for fifty miles. The wind was abeam and the ketch rolled horribly, dipping down to the gunwale and righting herself with a jerk. This went on for hours. Then the turbid water showed that we had reached the shoals. We took soundings every quarter of an hour and watched for broken water. The swell was not so heavy and we rolled less. We were far out of sight of land and we passed no other craft. We seemed very small in that desert of waters. The afternoon wore on and the soundings showed that we had eight fathoms; we had passed the shoals and we turned north. The wind was fair and the sea calmer; it was lovely then to sail on an even keel. Twice we saw turtles basking on the surface. The breeze grew lighter and lighter. There were heavy white clouds on the horizon but they were motionless; they might have been clouds in a picture. The sun set, and the light gradually faded from the sky. Night fell and the stars came out one by one. After supper we sat about the deck smoking. The air was balmy. The moon rose slowly, forcing her way through the clouds. It was enchanting to sail so through the night. I slept in snatches and each time I woke it was with a sense of delight. About two in the morning C. had the mainsail taken down and we sailed with only the foresail.

I awoke again at dawn. It was cool but not cold on deck. There was no sign of land. The sun was pleasant as it came up and warmed one. It was delicious to smoke cigarettes in that limpid morning. An hour or two later we saw land. It was flat and low. We sailed on until the outline of the coast was clear, a wooded country, and through the glass we descried little fishing-villages. We ran along looking for the Merauke river. We didn't know where it was, and it made one feel like one of the old explorers; we took soundings, and tried to judge by the shape of the coast-line where we were. We knew there was a light at the entrance to the river and we kept a look-out for it. We sailed for hours, feeling our way along, and at last we saw weed floating on the water, muddier now, and C. said that must mean we were near the river. We sailed on and then made out an opening in the coast line, very vaguely, and after a bit a thin white streak like a flagstaff which was the light. We saw a buoy in the distance and steered for it. The tide was flowing in, and though the breeze was light we began to move quickly. There was the mouth of the river before us and we sailed up, the tide carrying us, in fine style.

We saw the red roofs of the town, ketches at anchor, and a jetty. We lowered the sails and anchored. We had arrived.

Merauke has a neat Dutch look. It has not the sordid aspect of a similar town in a British colony. The Government offices, frame-built, with roofs of corrugated iron, one or two large sheds for merchandise, and the Controleur's house are on the front. At right angles to this is the one street of the town and there the Chinese traders live. During our stay we had our meals in the store of one of them. It was a treat to eat curry after living for a week on dugong, corned beef, coarse fish and canned fruit.

In the muddy dry creeks there are hundreds of mudfish, from little things a couple of inches long to fat brutes of eight or ten. They sit looking at you with large round malevolent eyes and then make a dash and bury themselves in their holes. It is extraordinary to see them scudding over the surface of the mud on their flappers. The mud is alive with them. They give you an impression in miniature of what the earth must have been in long-past ages when such creatures, gigantic in size, were its inhabitants. There is something uncanny and horrible about them. They give you a loathsome feeling that the mud itself has mysteriously come alive.

Dobo (Aroe Islands). This is a rather sordid little town of two streets with Chinese and Japanese stores. The native Malay village is built on piles at the water's edge. In the harbour are the pearling cutters. The men of the Celebes Trading Company have a large untidy frame house, but they spend most of their time on the Company's schooner, coming in to Dobo only when the steamer brings mail.

Cardan. The son of an English remittance man and a Polynesian woman. An enormous fellow, tall and fat, with flashing eyes and very white teeth, rather bald, but with curling hair round his ears and at the back of his neck. He talks eagerly with a kind of spluttering explosiveness. He is very hearty, laughs uproariously, and his conversation is made up of Australian oaths, scatological and obscene.

Tanal. A little town at the water's edge of houses on piles crowded with Chinese, Arabs and Malays. From the veranda of the resthouse you see the water through the tall casuarina trees, the island opposite, and one or two houses. Flowering shrubs bloom with a wanton profusion. Enormous butterflies, gaily painted, flit from shrub to shrub. Green parrots, with red or yellow heads, ripple, a flash of brilliant colour, across the blue sky. Towards evening the birds burst into loud song. Their notes are wild and strange. In the distance you hear the beating of drums and perhaps the playing of a wooden pipe. At sunset there is a red glow over the island that faces you.

The Kai Islands. You approach through a defile of low-lying, small wooded islands. It is as though you were going through a labyrinth. The sun rises and the sea is calm and blue. It is so lovely, so peaceful, so solitary that it fills you with awe. You have the feeling that you are the first ever to have burst into that silent sea and you hold your breath in anticipation of you know not what.

Banda. It is approached by a narrow inlet between two high islands thickly wooded. Opposite the town is the volcano overgrown with rough shrubbery. In the harbour the water is deep and clear, and at the water's edge are warehouses and thatched houses on piles.

The streets of Banda are lined with bungalows, but the place is dead, and they are empty and silent. People walk about, the few you see, quietly, as though they were afraid to awaken the echo. No voice is raised. The children play without noise. Now and again you catch a sweet whiff of nutmeg. In the shops, all selling the same things, canned goods, sarongs, cottons, there is no movement; in some of them there is no attendant, as though no purchaser could possibly be expected. You see no one buy or sell.

There are few Chinese, for they don't settle where no trade is, but many Arabs, some in smart Cairo fezzes and neat duck suits, others in white caps and sarongs. They are dark-skinned, with a Semitic look, and they have large shining eyes. There are a great many half-castes, Malay and Papuan, and of course numbers of Malays. Now and then you see a Dutchman, deeply bronzed, or a stout Dutch woman in loose pale draperies.

The old Dutch bungalows are thatched, with very high, pointed roofs, and the roof juts out, supported by Doric or Corinthian pillars of brick covered with plaster, to make a broad veranda. In the verandas are round tables with stiff Dutch chairs and hanging lamps. The floor is tiled or of white marble. Inside the house the rooms are dark, stiffly furnished in a Dutch way, with bad paintings on the walls. The parlour runs right through the house and on each side of it are bed-rooms. Behind is a walled garden. The whitewash of the wall is peeling, and from damp in places green. The garden is wild and overgrown with weeds. There is a confusion of roses and fruit trees, creepers, flowering shrubs, bananas, with a palm or two, a nutmeg and a breadfruit tree. At the back are servants' quarters.

As you walk about you come now and again upon a long white wall crumbling away and within it are ruined buildings. This has been a Portuguese convent. Along the shore, beyond the Portuguese fort, are the trim new houses of Dutch officials.

There are two Portuguese forts. One is a little away from the sea, surrounded by a moat in which grows a tangle of trees and shrubs; but only these massive walls of great grey stones remain, and the quadrangle is a jungle of tropical vegetation. Opposite the fort is a large open space reaching down to the sea where huge trees grow, casuarinas, kanary trees and wild figs. They were planted by the Portuguese, and here I suppose they took their ease in the cool of the evening.

Higher up on a hill, in a commanding position, is another fort, grey and bare, surrounded by a deep moat. It is in a fair state of preservation. The only door is about twelve feet from the ground, and is reached by a ladder. Inside the square walls is another fort with a well in the centre. It has large chambers with late Renaissance doors and windows, well proportioned but scantily ornamented, where presumably the officers of the garrison lived.

The forest. Enormously tall kanary trees give shade to the nutmegs. Underfoot there is no tangle of the bush, but only decaying leaves. You hear the boom of great pigeons as large as chickens, and the screech of parrots. Occasionally you come across miserable huts in which live ragged Malays. It is humid and sultry.

They say that in the old days the merchants were very rich and vied with one another in extravagance. They had carriages so that they might slowly drive in the evening along the sea front and round the square. There were so many vessels that sometimes the harbour was full, and the newcomers had to wait outside till the departure of a fleet gave them a chance to enter. They used to bring marble from Holland as ballast and huge blocks of ice, for they came without a cargo to fetch the precious spices from the island.

Afternoon in the tropics. You have tried to sleep, but you give it up as hopeless and come out, heavy and drowsy, on to your veranda. It is hot, airless, stifling. Your mind is restless, but to no purpose. The hours are leadenfooted. The day before you is unending. You try to cool yourself by taking a bath; it serves but little. It is too hot to sit on the veranda and you throw yourself once more on your bed. The air under the mosquito curtain seems to stand still; you cannot read, you cannot think, you cannot repose.

The cool of the evening. The air is soft and limpid. You have an extreme sense of well-being. Your imagination is pleasantly but not exhaustingly occupied with image after image. You have the sense of freedom of a disembodied spirit.

Macassar Harbour. The sun sets magnificently, yellow, then red and purple; and in the distance a little island grown over with coconut trees floats in radiance. The sea in its vast expanse shines like burnished copper. You try to think how to describe the dazzling spectacle. Its splendour a little unnerves you and you feel a bit wobbly about the knees, but at the same time it fills your heart with its own glory and if you could sing you would burst into song. The Quintet in the *Meistersinger*? No, a Gregorian chant. It is a death in which there is no sorrow but only fulfilment.

That is what these Eastern cities can best offer you, their harbours with shipping, tramps, passenger-boats, schooners with an exotic air (something in them still of the galleons which first entered those distant waters) and fishing-smacks; that, the sunrise and the sunset.

1923

T. He is a dug-out who after the war came out to Ceylon to be the secretary of a club on the strength of having run a regimental mess. He is a short stumpy man with legs very much too short for a long body. He looks absurd in very wide trousers and a long loose homespun coat, both much the worse for wear. He gives you the impression that he was a cavalryman, but in point of fact he was in the K.O.Y.L.I. His hair is dark and thin and plastered down on his skull, but he has an enormous flowing and luxuriant moustache. He prides himself on playing bridge very well, and criticizes everyone with whom he plays. He is fond of talking of the titled persons he has known and of the generals and field-marshals with whom he was hail-fellow-well-met.

The Snatcher. He is a man of little more than fifty, but he looks very old and frail. He is bald and his hair and moustache are white. He has a very red thick nose. When he is seated you have the impression of a little hunched-up man, and when he stands up you are surprised to see that he is more than commonly tall. He is a great fisherman and talks incessantly of his pursuit. He generally has flies in his pockets. He is much interested in butter-flies and is bringing out a book on the butterflies of Ceylon. He drinks a great deal and talks willingly of the drinking-bouts in which he has taken part. I don't know why he is called the Snatcher.

The Jungle. There is a moment just before sundown when the trees in the jungle seem to detach themselves from the great mass of forest and become individuals; then you cannot see the wood for the trees. In the magic of the hour they appear to gain life of a new kind so that you can almost imagine that they enclose spirits and with the sunset will be capable of changing their places. You feel that at some uncertain moment a strange thing will happen to them and they will be fantastically trans-formed. Then the night comes, the moment has passed, and once more the jungle takes them back; the trees again become part of the wood and they are still and silent.

A planter's house. The two-storey bungalow is placed on the crest of a little hill and it is surrounded by a garden in which are lawns of some sort of coarse herbage, bright yellow cannas, hibiscus and flowering shrubs. Behind the bungalow is a huge tree with red flowers. From the veranda there is a long narrow view of hill planted with rubber. There is a small formal drawing-room at the back, but the living-room is a large open veranda, furnished with estate furniture, large chairs, with extensions for the legs, cane chairs, a table or two, and some shelves in which are cheap and ragged editions of vapid novels. The bedrooms are upstairs; they are very poorly furnished with iron beds, painted deal chests-of-drawers and a washstand with broken crockery which does not match. At meals the glass is coarse, the plate is shabby, and the crockery is of the cheapest kind. The dinner is elaborate, with soup, fish, roast and sweet, but everything is badly cooked and served in a slovenly and unappetizing fashion.

Rangoon. They were father and son, both skippers of tramps belonging to a Chinese firm. The father idolized his trim, smart, handsome boy and was horrified when he fell in love with a Burmese girl, but not just in love, head over ears in love. He was infatuated. He went native, began to smoke opium and eventually lost his job. The older man got the idea that the girl had cast a spell over the boy and determined to save him. One day she was found drowned. No one knew how she had come by her death, but everyone believed that the father was responsible. The boy was broken-hearted. He went all to pieces, and the passionate affection that he had had for his father turned to a deadly hatred.

Mandalay by moonlight. The white gateways are flooded with silver and the erections above them are shot with silhouetted glimpses of the sky. The effect is ravishing. The moat in Mandalay is one of the minor beauties of the world. It has not the sublimity of Kilauea nor the spectacular picturesque of the Lake of Como, it has not the swooning loveliness of the coastline of a South Pacific island, nor the austere grandeur of parts of the Peloponnesus, but it has a beauty which you can take hold of and enjoy and make your own. It is a beauty which does not carry you off your feet, but which can give you constant delight. Those other beauties need the frame of mind to be enjoyed and appreciated, but this is a beauty suited to all seasons and all moods. It is like Herrick's poems, which you can take up with pleasure when you are out of humour for the *Inferno* or *Paradise Lost*.

F. He is a big fat man, with scanty grey hair, but his red face is unlined and round, so that he looks sometimes almost boyish.

He has a small grey toothbrush moustache. His teeth are very bad, and the only one you see, a long yellow one in the middle of his mouth, hangs loosely and looks as if it would come out with a sharp pull. His face is shiny with sweat. In mufti he wears a khaki suit, a tennis shirt with a loose open collar and no tie. He has a game leg caused by a bad wound during the war and walks with a pronounced limp. His only interest in life is horses. He speaks of them as skins and talks of nothing else all day long. He races a great deal, keeping his own ponies, and is a byword, for he never wins a race. He is jovial and hearty, but gives you the impression that he is up to all the tricks of the race-track and would hesitate at little to bring off a coup.

E. He describes himself as country-born, and because he has probably been exposed to a good deal of mortification on that account insists that he is proud of it. His father was first mate on a tea clipper running to China, who eventually settled in Moulmein and married a Burmese. E. came to Mandalay as interpreter in 1885 and has remained there ever since, first in the Government service and then in a business of his own, selling jade, amber and silk. When I went to see him I was taken into a room which served both as a parlour and as a shop. It was crowded with cheap European furniture, upholstered chairs and sofas, occasional tables and what-nots, and here and there were cabinets in which was displayed a certain amount of second-rate jade and amber. There was no fan, and the place was hot and stuffy and mosquito-ridden. He kept me waiting a long time, while he was dressing himself up. Then he came in, a tall thin man with white hair, a sallow dark skin and a flat nose. He talked a great deal in a loud rasping voice; he seemed to like the sound of it. He spoke in a formal elaborate way, using in conversation words which we are accustomed to see only in print. He always chose the long word rather than the short one. He had a passion for the hackneyed phrase. Whenever he referred to anybody and however often, it was always by his full title. Thus he spoke of General Sir George White, the Hero of Ladysmith, and of General Sir Harry Prendergast, V.C.

G. He is a tall man of over six feet, slender, not exactly handsome, but of prepossessing appearance. He has a thin sunburnt face with sunken cheeks; his eyes are blue and smiling. He is clean-shaven, but for a small toothbrush moustache. His hair, cut short, is hardly grey. He is loose-jointed and his gestures are easy and graceful. He is dressed without affectation, but well; his clothes hang on him loosely, but are well cut. He is a cavalryman and you can imagine that in uniform he must be a striking figure. He speaks with a singular drawl, in a rather humorous fashion. He is dryly ironic. He is an amateur of horseflesh, a great sportsman, and talks easily of all the unusual games that he has played.

T. He is a tall thin man with a sallow, clean-shaven face and spectacles. This gives him an odd air of a student, and you would think that he was a literary journalist rather than a jungle-wallah. He has a shy and apologetic manner. He has lived so much alone that he speaks very little. He is dressed in khaki shorts, stockings, and a khaki shirt. He is by profession a miner and has discovered a jade mine in the north of Burma, where he expects to make his fortune. He comes down to Mandalay for the wet season, but the rest of the year he spends up at his mine with no other white man within seven miles of him.

1929

Borneo. H. is dressed in a khaki shirt and khaki shorts. He wears brown shoes and stockings that come to just below the knee. He is a man of about the middle size, fat, with a red face shining with sweat and a hooked red nose. He has blue eyes and fairish hair receding on the forehead. He talks almost entirely in catchwords, especially when he is with people who are drinking. It is his way of showing that he is a good fellow. But when he is alone with you he speaks more naturally, and like a gentleman. He keeps a couple of cats and a dog. He comes from a family of clergymen.

A. He is a Welshman with quite a marked Welsh accent, a thin, slovenly, clean-shaven man, with outsticking ears and irregular features. He is neither good-looking nor healthy of appearance. He has a sardonic humour and a way of insincerely flattering people, and it gives him a certain amusement when he sees that they are taken in by his soft sawder. He is badly and untidily dressed. He plays the piano well and is fond of classical music. Whenever he is out of temper he soothes himself by playing. He gives you the impression of being a country boy of rather humble origin who by his cleverness at school and in examinations entered the Civil Service. He has in his room a lot of school prizes bound in the usual way. He is fond of reading French and has a small collection of modern French novels, but speaks it badly.

The Sultan. It was arranged that we should be received by the Sultan in his audience chamber at ten, and as we walked along we saw him and his suite coming out of the place where he lives, which is above and at the side of the audience chamber, and we waited for a moment to allow him to enter. He was accompanied by two middle-aged men and a suite, all higgledy-piggledy, with a man holding an umbrella over his head. The audience chamber was a long low room with a gaudily-painted throne at one end. In front of this was a table with half a dozen dining-room chairs round it, and from this, on each side of the table, two rows of chairs ran down the hall. We were introduced to the Sultan and then to the two regents. The Sultan is a little boy of thirteen with a long face like a horse, a pale ivory skin, a large mouth which shows his long teeth and gums when he smiles, and very quick beady eyes. He was dressed in yellow silk, a coat, trousers and sarong, and on his head he wore a black fez decorated with an appliqué pattern of gold cloth enriched with imitation diamonds. Round his neck were a number of gold strings and chains and a large gold medal. The regents, who are his close relations, wore blueish-grey patterned silk handkerchiefs made into a kind of turban on their heads, and dark trousers, bajus and sarongs. One of them had a very pronounced squint and wore spectacles of blue grass. The younger brother of the Sultan, a little pale-faced boy of eight, was carried in by an attendant on whose lap he sat throughout the audience. The Sultan looked every now and then at the cross-eyed regent to see what he was to do, but seemed to have self-assurance and to be not at all shy. He sat in an arm-chair at the head of the table, with the regents on one side of him and the British Resident and ourselves on the other. Behind him stood a group of officials in very shabby clothes. One of them bore a state sword of execution and there was another who bore a spear, a third with a cushion and a fourth with the apparatus for chewing betelnut. Large native cigarettes were handed round, about the size of an ordinary candle, coarse Borneo tobacco wrapped in nipah palm leaves; but they smoked easily and coolly. The rest of the councillors sat on chairs on each side of the hall and appeared to be listening intently to the conversation that went on at the round table. At the side of the throne behind the Sultan stood two enormous burning candles in large brass candlesticks, and these were supposed to indicate the purity of the Sultan's sentiments towards us. The little boy, the Sultan's brother, stared with all his eyes. The regent on behalf of the Sultan paid us elaborate compliments, and then the Resident on my behalf made a long speech telling them all about me and who I was. After this there was a little desultory conversation, each side trying to think of something to say. Then after a final compliment from the regent and a graceful return from the Resident we took our leave.

The hill behind the Residency is covered with all manner of trees, but the haphazard arrangement, due to the chance of nature, has the effect of an artful devising. It looks like a jungle-covered hill in an old Chinese picture.

We went over the cutch factory. It is built by the side of the river at the bottom of a hill. A variety of sheds, on piles, of roughly-hewn logs covered with a corrugated iron roof. Behind it grow bananas, papayas and various trees. It has a rough and ready air and gives you the impression of having been erected higgledy-piggledy as occasion arose. It is sloppy and untidy and has none of the trimness of a factory in England or America. Cutch is a material used for tanning made from the bark of the mangrove tree, and as you walk about the factory there is a slight odour of tan. There are huge vats in which the bark, which has been previously broken to pieces by a complicated machine, is washed in water and boiled till the tannin has been extracted, and when the cutch is finally ready it comes out in a thick; reddish brown viscid liquid which looks like molasses. This then dries out and is made into large, very hard cakes. The manager and his two assistants live each in his own bungalow on a hill and they have a little club which they all go to as evening draws in. The club consists of one long room in part of which is a billiard-table and in the rest a small bar, a bridge-table, and a table on which are piled-up papers like the *Daily Graphic* and the *Mirror*, and magazines like the *Royal* and the *Strand*. The club is looked after by one boy who serves out drinks and in the interval acts as billiard-marker. It is very grubby. The manager is a fattish man with horn-rimmed spectacles and false teeth, clean-shaven, with a bronzed, squarish face. He has been here for five and twenty years and is said to have great influence on the natives. He has a way of interspersing his conversation with fragments of bad French. He is said to be kindly and reliable. The three men who compose the staff get on very badly together. They have fearful quarrels. The engineer is a man getting on for thirty, who speaks with a broad Scotch accent so that it is not easy for the Englishman to understand what he says. He is of about middle height, dressed in shabby grey drill and a ragged tennis shirt. He has a good-looking attractive face with blunt, but not unpleasant, features, and blue eyes which you may think are just bleary with drink, but if you look at them with imagination have an enigmatic and tragic look. They give you the impression of being oddly puzzled as though they had seen things out in the East which the man could not understand, and you might think to yourself that this raw, simple, uneducated Scot had become aware of something strange which had knocked him off his balance and left him adrift on the sea of life. He is said to be a very heavy drinker and when drunk is objectionable and violent. The third man is small but big-boned, sandy-haired, with a large nose, and extremely taciturn.

Labuan. You land at a little pier and come upon the main street, which runs along in front of the sea. It consists of Chinese and Jewish shops which have this peculiarity: often two or three trades are conducted in one shop, and you will see on one side of the door in the open window a dentist's chair or a hairdresser's establishment and in another a watchmaker working at his bench, while in the rest of the shop they sell canned goods. There are three or four shops of Jewish traders from Baghdad. In one, a regular jack-of-all trades of a shop, with everything that you might find in a pedlar's pack for sale, there was reclining on a bench at the back a Jewess of amazing, of almost unbelievable beauty. Half lying, half sitting, in an attitude of lazy abandonment, she had nothing on but a faded pink dressing-gown. Her white feet were naked. She had a lovely oval face, ivory in colour, a mass of very black hair and magnificent, ox-like eyes. She might have stepped right out of one of the Arabian Nights. There was about her a sensual languor and a voluptuousness which took your breath away. Her husband was a tall, emaciated, bearded Jew in spectacles, such as you might easily see in the East End of London; sharp, cunning and obsequious.

F.M.S. Dawn at sea. I happened to awake as day was breaking and went on deck. The hills of Perak were grey and above them were grey clouds, and as the sun rose for a moment it coloured the clouds pink and gold so that they looked like the sarongs of Trengganu.

Ricebirds. The ricebirds fluttered disorderly, a white flock, like haphazard thoughts that pass through the mind without reason or sequence.

The Resident Councillor. He is a little man, between fifty and fifty-two, with grey hair and bushy grey eyebrows. He has a good profile and you can imagine that in youth he was good-looking. His blue eyes are tired now and his mouth with its thin lips is peevish. He speaks as though he had no teeth in his mouth and it is difficult to understand his mumbling. He is said to be very shy, but gives you the impression of being merely ignorant of social usages. It embarrasses him to introduce one person to another. He cannot summon up enough courage to leave a party until someone else has made a move. He is conscientious and hard-working, but stupid. He is the kind of official who is always afraid of doing the wrong thing, and bound up in silly prejudice and red tape. Though he has been here for thirty years, he speaks little Malay and takes no interest in the country or in anything else but doing his work so that his superiors may have no cause for complaint against him, and getting away as soon as he is entitled to a pension. His mind is so occupied with trifles that he cannot give any attention to general topics. His concerns are purely local and are confined to the club and the comings and goings of the people in his district.

Planters. For the most part they seem to belong to two classes. The greater number of them are rough and common men of something below the middle class, and they speak English with a vile accent, or broad Scotch. They have vulgar minds, occupied only with rubber and its price and the sports of their club. Their wives are either very genteel and anxious to be ladies, or else blatant, noisy and hail-fellow-well-met. There is another class of planter who has been to a public school and perhaps a university. He has become a planter because he had no means of earning a living in England, and rubber planting is apparently the only occupation at which a man can earn a salary without training or experience. He is often a little anxious to impress on you the fact that he is a gentleman born, but except that he leads a slightly different life when he goes to England on leave, his conversation and his interests are exactly the same as those of the others. Among all planters there seems to be the same feeling towards the Government officials, and this is a combination of awe, envy, contempt and petulance. They sneer at them behind their backs, but look upon a garden party or a dinner at the Resident's house as an event in their lives. You would have to go far to find among the planters a man of culture, reading or distinction.

F.M.S. Mac was staying at the rest-house and was over from Dutch Borneo where he lives, in the hope of selling to the Dunlop Company rubber lands belonging to some Dutch Malays. But he was prepared to sell anything that anyone would buy, and he spent much of his time trying to get a young Eurasian to purchase a motor-car and seeking to interest some Jews in Singapore in black diamonds, of which he claimed to be able to get mining rights in Borneo. He has been in various parts of Malaya for the last thirty-five years and has followed a great number of occupations. He came out first as a missionary and then became a Government official, doing surveying work for Perak; after that he was a planter and then a miner, and he has been agent for a number of European firms. He seems to have succeeded in nothing and now is a man of hard on sixty. He is tall and heavily-built and walks in a clodhopperish sort of fashion as though his boots were heavy with clay. He has a dark red face and blue eyes, red at the rims. He gives you an impression of low cunning. His stories of the F.M.S. are mostly about the people who in one way and another have done him down, and he gives you the impression that he is the only honest man in a world of rogues. The one story he told me which was of any value was of a woman who married a man and, finding out that three or four half-caste children in the village were his, arranged with the headman to have them drowned in the river. There was probably not a word of truth in it, but he told it with a sardonic humour which made it effective.

O. He is the secretary of the club, a little hunch-backed man of about fifty who was a planter for many years. He has much more knowledge of the world and of literature than most of them, and speaks with a lively scorn of the complaints which the planters' wives make of the pains of exile. He says that of course all planters belong to the lower middle classes, and most of their wives, instead of having a house with plenty of servants and a motor-car, would at home be serving behind a counter.

G. R. He is the Government engineer. He is a very small, dapper fellow with clean-cut features and grey hair. He is precise in his manner. He is very much the soldier and the gentleman, and has a house in the Isle of Wight to which he proposes to retire next year. He wants to find some occupation and suggests chicken-farming, which he hopes will take up his time and bring him ten per cent on his outlay. He is the typical dug-out with a great respect for all the prejudices of the military caste. You can imagine how well he will fit in with the retired soldiers when he finally settles down at Ventnor.

P. He is a great big burly fat Irishman with a double chin. He has the red face, curly hair and blue eyes of his nationality, and speaks with a brogue. He has been thirty-five years in the state, having come out first as an ordinary policeman. He is now head of the police. He has recently married again, a handsome Belfast girl of the barmaid type, younger than his own daughter. He rolls about in a jolly good-humoured way. He took us over the gaol. Here we saw the prisoners, the long-sentence men with irons on their legs, engaged on various tasks. Some were preparing rice for the cooking, and others were carpentering. In two little cells we saw a couple of men who were condemned to death, and they sat cross-legged on their beds clothed in nothing but a prison sarong, which is a strip of dingy white cotton, made by the prisoners, with a prison mark on it. They were doing nothing. They stared into vacancy. We were told that during the last three days before their execution they are given five dollars a day which they can spend on any food, drink or smoke they choose. On the morning of the execution they are taken across the courtyard where they have a bath, then are put in a room where they have breakfast, and are then taken up a small flight of narrow stairs to the execution chamber. A white cap is put over their heads. They are turned with their faces to the wall. The rope attached to an iron ring in the ceiling is placed round their necks and the bolt of the trap on which they are standing is drawn. We were shown this by a little vulgar Cockney, with broken and discoloured teeth, who is married to a Japanese wife. I asked him if he did not find an execution very horrible, but he laughed and said it didn't interfere with his night's sleep. He told me that one man who was to be hanged next day, when he was asked if there was anything he wanted, said 'Yes, I want a woman.' The head of the police chuckled. 'Damned sporting of him,' he said. 'Of course I wouldn't have minded, but it wouldn't have done, you know. I'd have had the whole community down on me like a ton o' bricks.'

It was curious to see the prisoners having their bath, which they have twice a day. They come in batches to a large tank, each provided with his pail, and at the word of command sluice themselves four times, rub themselves down, and then again at the word of command sluice themselves four times more. Then they hurriedly put on dry sarongs and make way for the next batch.

The areca trees outlined against the night were slim and elegant. They had the gaunt beauty of a syllogism.

L. K. He is known as Powder-puff Percy. He has been at Balliol, and is much better educated and more widely read than the planters and the Government officials with whom he must spend his life. He started as a cadet and has now become a schoolmaster. He is a very good bridge-player and an excellent dancer. They complain of him that he is conceited, and he has aroused a furious antagonism in the community. He wears his clothes with a certain dash and he is a good and amusing talker in the Oxford manner. He is slangy in a smart way and at the same time cultured. He has a vocabulary of his own. He is good-looking with something of an intellectual face, and he might be a young don or a professional dancer at a night club.

C. was a donnish, studious man, precise, respectable and dull. His wife was frivolous and flirtatious. He was able, and occupied a prominent position in Singapore. Near them lived a woman with her beefy, hearty husband. She was prudish, and as respectable and dull as C. They were both middle-aged. One day to the amazement of everyone in the colony they eloped. The abandoned partners instituted divorce proceedings and eventually married again. C. was deprived of his job and lives in England, in penury, with the woman he ran away with. The only flaw in the satisfaction of Singapore is that the pair are reported to be immensely happy.

As I walked along I thought of a broad road which I see sometimes in a dream, a road winding over the hills just as this one did that I was on; it leads to a city which, I know not why, I am eager to reach. Men and women are hurrying along the road, and often I have awakened to find myself up and half across my room in my desire to be of their number. The city is plain to see, standing on the top of a hill, surrounded by battlemented walls, and the road, broad and white, can be seen winding up to its great gates. The air is fresh and sweet and the sky is blue. They press on, men, women and children, not talking with each other, for they are intent on their purpose, and their faces shine with expectancy. They look neither to the right nor to the left. They hurry and their eyes are eager and bright. I do not know what they await. I only know that they are impelled by some urgent hope. The city reminds one a little of those cities of El Greco which stand on the brow of a rocky hill, cities of the soul, seen tremulously in a flash of lightning that tears across the darkness of the night. But those are cities of narrow, tortuous streets, and the dark clouds encompass them round about. In the city which I see in my sleep the sun shines and the streets are broad and straight. I know vaguely what the men are in those cities of mystics, the manner of them and the peace they offer to the tortured heart; but what kind of men they are in this city of mine and why it is that all those others on the road so passionately seek it, I do not know. I only know that it imports me urgently to go there, and that when at last I slip through its gates, happiness awaits me.

Lines.

I could not bear the thought that I should ever lose you
Or that our lives might ever be disjoined,
But yet I know that in your wanton heart

There was for me nor love nor tenderness.
To many another I saw you give unwanted kisses,
But when I sought to break the chain that bound me
You twined your slim soft arms about my neck
And would not let me go.
Humbly I thanked you when you feigned to love me.
I bought your grudging lips for gold.
And now the love I thought would last till death is dead.
Ah, where is that high power that you had
To make the heavens golden with a smile
Or with a careless word to cloud the summer day?
In weariness, and not in death or parting, is
The bitterness of love. Spent is my passion
Like a river dried up by the sun's fierce rays.
I look into my empty heart and shrink dismayed:
My soul is like a desert, and the wild wind blows
In its silent, barren spaces.
The night-birds build their nest amid the tombs
Of kings. My eyes rest on you sadly. I regret
My pain, my rapture, my anguish and my bliss.

1930

The Boarding House at Nicosia. The food is the typical English
food that you would get in a private hotel in Bayswater. Soup,
fish, roast and a sweet, which is either a trifle or a cabinet
pudding; and on Sundays a savoury of stuffed eggs. There are
two bathrooms fitted with a geyser, which heats the water with
wood. The rooms are furnished with little iron beds and cheap
furniture painted white. There are on the floor strips of rug
that look like horse-blanket. The drawing-room has large
chintz-covered chairs and tables covered with Maltese drawn-
work. The light is bright and inconveniently placed for reading.
Here in the evening the guests collect and play hearts for infinitesimal sums. There is a lot of noise and chaff. The proprietor is a

small fat Greek, who speaks not very good English, and he is assisted in the dining-room by a scrubby Greek boy with fine eyes and a gold tooth.

The guests. A military man, an ex-Dragoon, very gentlemanly and good form. He is tuberculous and spends his time in *pensions* on the Riviera or wandering about the Near East. He is tall and thin with sharp features and thinnish hair plastered down on his head. An elderly, fat lady with white hair, extremely gay and flirtatious. She is what is called a man's woman, and exchanges chaff across the dining-room with the other guests. She laughs a great deal and is very skittish. A business man from Egypt with his stout wife. He has a red face and greyish hair done like a private soldier's; he might have started in the ranks. An elderly man with gold-rimmed spectacles who is slowly going round Europe studying social welfare. He writes articles for minor papers and is getting material for a book on the social conditions of the working classes. He talks of nothing else. He has a large fund of old stories which he is constantly trying to tell, and which the other people are always preventing him from telling. There are two slim ladies in delicate health who live much in their bedrooms. The other women think it odd that they should have cocktails brought them before each meal. A small stout old man with a pointed white beard and spectacles, who has spent forty-two years in Japan. His business was shaken by the earthquake and ceased to pay, so it was dissolved. He came back to England to settle with his daughter and bought a house in Harrow, proposing to live with her and her husband for the rest of his life. He had seen practically nothing of her since she was six months old when she was sent back to Europe, and when he came to settle down with her he found that they were complete strangers. Friction arose, and so, leaving her the house, he came out to the Near East. He regrets Japan and would like to go back, but feels he cannot afford any longer to live there as he had been used to. He goes to the club here, reads the papers and plays billiards. In the evening at the hotel he plays patience or listens to the conversation. He very seldom joins in, apparently feeling a little out of it, but he chuckles at the chaff that passes to and fro. He is just waiting for death. With all of them chaff is the staple conversation. The price of the *pension* is ten shillings a day.

New York. She was the secretary of a wealthy woman, and she lived in a small hotel in which lived also the father of an English poet. She had a passionate admiration for the poet, and for his sake befriended his father, who was poor, alcoholic and really rather disreputable. He loved his son and was proud of him. Then the poet came to New York to stay with her employer. She felt sure that he could not know in what poverty his father lived, and as soon as he found out would do something to relieve his distress. But the days passed and he made no sign of wishing to see his father, and at last, one day when she was answering letters for him, she told him that she knew his father, that they lived in fact in the same hotel, and that his father wanted terribly to see him. 'Oh?' he said and went on with his dictation. She was horrified. She felt obliged to tell the old man. He chuckled. 'He's ashamed of me,' he said. 'He's a lousy poet,' she said indignantly. 'No,' he answered, 'he's a lousy man; he remains a great poet.'

It is essential for a writer unceasingly to study men, and it is a fault in me that I find it often a very tedious business. It requires a great deal of patience. There are of course men of marked idiosyncrasy who offer themselves to your observation with all the precision of a finished picture, they are 'characters', striking and picturesque figures; and they often take pleasure in displaying their peculiarity, as though they amused themselves and wanted you to share their amusement. But they are few. They stand out from the common run and have at once the advantage and the disadvantage of the exceptional. What they have in vividness they are apt to lack in verisimilitude. To study the average man is an affair of quite another sort. He is strangely amorphous. There is someone there, with a character of his own, standing on his own feet, with a hundred peculiarities; but the picture is hazy and confused. Since he does not know himself, how can he tell you anything about himself? However talkative, he is

223

inarticulate. Whatever treasures he has to offer you he conceals with all the more effectiveness that he does not know they are treasures. If you want to make a man out of these crowded shadows, as a sculptor makes a statue from a block of stone, you want time, patience, a Chinese ingenuity and a dozen qualities besides. You must be ready to listen for hours to the retailing of second-hand information in order at last to catch the hint or the casual remark that betrays. Really to know men you must be interested in them for their own sake rather than for yours, so that you care for what they say just because they say it.

The Outward Man. One of the difficulties that confronts the novelist is how to describe the appearance of his characters. The most natural way is of course the formal catalogue, the height, the complexion, the shape of the face, the size of the nose and the colour of the eyes. This may be given all at once or mentioned as occasion arises, and a salient trait by repetition at apposite moments may be impressed upon the reader's attention. It may be given when the character is introduced or when interest has already been excited in him. In any case I do not believe that the reader gets any clear impression. The older novelists were very precise in their enumeration of their characters' physical parts, and yet if any reader could see in the flesh the person whom the author has thus elaborately described I do not believe he would recognize him. I think we seldom form any exact image in our minds as a result of all these words. We have a clear and precise picture of what the great characters of fiction looked like only when an illustrator like Phiz with Mr Pickwick or Tenniel with Alice has forced his own visualization upon us. The cataloguing of characteristics is certainly dull, and a good many writers have tried to give liveliness to their description by an impressionistic method. They ignore the facts altogether. They scintillate more or less brightly on the subject of their characters' appearance and expect you from a few epigrammatic phrases, from the way he strikes a vivacious onlooker, for instance, to construct in your mind a human being. Such descriptions may often be read with a pleasure which you cannot get from a sober enumeration of traits, but I doubt whether they take you much further. I have a notion that their vivacity often conceals the fact that the author has no very clear picture in his mind of the character he is inventing. They shirk the difficulty. Some writers seem unconscious of the importance of physical characteristics. It appears never to have struck them how great is their influence on character. The world is an entirely different place to the man of five foot seven from what it is to the man of six foot two.

1933

Monserrat. Like a poem, harsh and difficult, of a poet forcing his verse to strange harmonies and wrestling with his medium in the effort to make it carry a significant beauty and a power of thought that words are incapable of expressing.

Zaragoza. The chapel was dimly lit with candles on the altar, and at the altar steps two or three women and a man were kneeling. Above the altar was a Christ on the Cross in polychrome and almost life-size. With his low brow, thick black hair and short, straggling black beard he had the look of a peasant of the Asturias. In a dark corner of the chapel, away from the others, a woman knelt, with her hands not joined in the common way of prayer, but with the palms open towards the altar, the arms a little away from her body, as though on an invisible platter she were bearing the offering of an anguished heart. She had a long face, smooth and unlined, and her great eyes were fixed upon the image over the altar. There was an infinite pathos in her posture, that of a suppliant, helpless and defenceless, who sought aid in her confused distress. You would have said that she could not understand why this pain had been given her to bear. I did not believe that it was for herself she prayed, but for another that she interceded. A child in danger of death, a husband, a lover in prison or exile? She remained strangely still, and her eyes, unblinking, were set fast on the face of the dying Christ. But it was not to the living presence of which the image was no more than a crude symbol, it was literally to the grim, realistic figure, the work of human hands, that she made her passionate plea. There was in her eyes utter submission, resignation to the will of God, and yet a complete and intense confidence that from that wooden statue relief and succour might come if she could but move the heart within the wooden body. Her face shone with the radiance of her faith.

There is nothing to say of Murillo (except that he is not so bad as Valdes Leal) but that his pictures are very good furniture for sacred buildings. From any other standpoint they are profoundly insignificant. He has a pleasing talent for composition, his colour is soft and pretty; he is loose, sentimental, graceful and superficial. And yet when you see these paintings in the places for which they were painted, dimly lit and magnificently framed, in a chapel of which the rich tones complete their colour, you cannot deny that they have something. They appeal to an over-wrought, sickly devotion, the other side of the Spanish violence, crudity and brutishness. They appeal to the faculty of shedding abundant tears, the love of children, the casual admiration of a pretty girl and the half superstitious charitableness, which are to be found in the average Spaniard.

La Celestina. It can be read with interest, but it can hardly to-day excite. Its importance is historical. It was, it appears, the forerunner both of the picaresque novel and of the Spanish drama. Certain of its characters have been repeated and emphasized by a number of succeeding authors. But the terms in which historians of literature speak of it are exaggerated, and to describe it as a great masterpiece is absurd. The intrigue is inane. The dialogue is praised for its naturalness and doubtless it is written in an easy and idiomatic language; but every one of the persons expresses himself in the same fashion, with a constant use of the wise saws which is the curse of Spanish literature and which even Cervantes overdid. The humour is all of a pattern and consists in the rank absurdity of putting moral apophthegms in the mouth of the old procuress who is the chief character, and the most living, of the tragi-comedy. But it is seldom that this provokes even a smile. One would have to be very easily moved to mirth to laugh. Some of the scenes are gay and lifelike. You can approve them, but you are never carried away by them. Though the story concerns the love of a young cavalier and a high-born damsel and there is much to-do about the extremity of their emotion, there is never a thrill of passion from the first page to the last. It is a love story from which love is absent. Of course it is a mischance that Calisto should be a fool and Melibea a half-wit; a half-wit, however, with the culture of a blue-stocking, for when she is about to throw herself from the top of a tower in desperation at her lover's death, she pauses to deliver, after Plutarch, a series of reflections on the mutability of human things, with examples drawn from classical story.

It is a book that owes its celebrity rather to the accident of time than to intrinsic excellence.

Seville. When you are in the country towards evening the light has just that warm golden glow with which Murillo surrounds his saints, and the little white clouds on the horizon are like the cherubs that surround the Virgin in glory.

The crowd in the bull-ring. A thousand paper fans of all colours fluttered in the heat; it looked as though a swarm of butterflies had suddenly started into life.

Valdes Leal. It is all fluid. The design has a vague sweep of no significance. It give you the impression of a badly blurred photograph. These people have no bones in their bodies. Valdes Leal had no power of composition and his pictures have no architecture; the vast canvases seem to be filled at haphazard. The colour is dull and conventional. It must be admitted that he had a certain imagination, but it was the inept, exaggerated imagination of the counter-reformation.

Andalusia. The moon leaned low against the sky like a white-faced clown lolling against a circus wall.

The harvest moon flitted in and out of the trees as the car sped by, like a fat gay woman playing hide and seek with a grotesque but rather appealing archness.

The hoots of the motor-horns and the roar of the exhausts pierced the night like the jagged peaks of the mountains in Japan against the unclouded sky.

M. P. He threw his bread on the waters in the confident hope that it would be returned four-fold, but in case providence were inattentive, took care to attach a string to it, so that if need be he could pull it back.

In the development of every art there is an interval between the charm of naïveté and the elegance of sophistication, and it is then that perfection is produced. But in this interval is also produced dullness. For then artists are in complete command of their medium, and their personality must be out of the ordinary if they are to avoid the tediousness of realism.

Compare the springlike delightfulness of Raphael's early works and the sumptuous power of the *stanze* of the Vatican with the emptiness of the pictures when he painted like Giulio Romano.

In perfection there is always the malaise of the degeneration which will succeed it.

The artist has by his nature the detachment and freedom which the mystic seeks in the repression of desire.

The artist, like the mystic who seeks to attain God, is detached in spirit from the world.

Intense activity blunts the doer to the sense of sin; it is only when his activity is thwarted that his conscience has opportunity to gnaw.

The art of the Renaissance gives you all it has to give at once. It has peace, healthiness and serenity. It more nearly reached perfection than any other style. It is stimulating, but not to the imagination, rather to the general sense of well-being. It gives you the feeling of physical contentment that a sunny morning does in spring.

Cordova. Plaza del Potro. It is a long, narrow place, with small white houses on each side of it, and at the end the river. Towards the upper end is a fountain with a prancing horse on a pedestal. Hither come the neighbours with earthenware jars to fetch water. They take it from jets through a hollow bamboo. Donkeys and horses are watered from the basin. On the left as you look up from the river is the Posada. From the front it looks a modest house; it has two storeys, it is whitewashed and has a large door which is closed at night. But inside is a great courtyard, very roughly paved and uneven. There are stables, each just large enough for a single horse, beside which the groom or boy could sleep. There are no more than two or three horses now. One of the stalls is occupied by an itinerant flower-seller who comes in chanting his *pregon*. In the broad archway that leads from the street to the courtyard girls are ironing linen. There are two small kitchens for common use. The upper storey is reached by rough stone stairs. There is a wooden balcony all around, jutting out, with a rickety balustrade, and this balcony gives access to the rooms. Here Cervantes lived.

La Mancha. The oak trees. They stretch for miles along the gently undulating country. They are not very high and magnificence is not theirs, but they look immensely sturdy, and their trunks are gnarled and twisted, so that they give you an impression of violent effort. They have battled with rugged energy against the assaults of time and wind and rain.

Then for miles as far as the eye can reach you have the monotonous lines of the furrows.

Sometimes you pass a peasant ploughing his field with a wooden plough, like the ploughs they used in Roman times, drawn by two mules. Sometimes you pass a peasant on a donkey, or another, with his son riding pillion, on a horse. The wind blows cold and they are huddled in their brown blankets. Sometimes you pass a shepherd, wrapped up, guarding a flock of sheep that nibble the scanty grass, or, more scattered and active, a herd of goats. They are spare old men, the shepherds clean-shaven, with small, sharp, pale eyes, and their earthy faces are thin and lined and astute; and the bitter cold of winter, the heat of summer, seems to have dried them up. Their movements are slow and you guess that they are sparse of words.

In the villages the houses, built of stones and clay, have the colour of the barren soil, and they look like temporary shelters that soon will crumble away again into the ground on which they have been built.

Alcalá de Henares. It has a large plaza with arcades, and a street with arcades and two-storey houses of modest appearance. It is an empty, dead little town. Down the street wander few people, a cart with a great hood drawn by a mule, a huckster on horseback with his two big baskets on either side. The university, with its handsome patio, has a plateresque façade of no great importance. The other streets are narrow and grey and silent.

Las Meniñas. The first thing that strikes you is its gaiety, and then you realize that this comes from the warm light of common day that miraculously envelops the figures. Velasquez painted no picture in which his cheerful, equable nature is more evident. It has the *alegria* which is the Andalusian's most cherished and characteristic grace.

Velasquez's dwarfs and fools are painted in the Shakespearian spirit, with frank amusement, gaily and without the slightest feeling for the horror of their deformity or the misery of their lot. His sunny temper made him look upon these loathsome, aborted creatures with the good humour of one who knows that the Almighty had created them to be the playthings of princes.

Velasquez suggests in none of his portraits a criticism of his sitters. He takes them at their face value. His charm seems joined to a sort of gay heartlessness. I suppose no one can deny his wonderful skill; the dresses of some of these infantas are amazing, but while one admires one has a slight sense of uneasiness and asks oneself whether this marvellous skill is worth very much. It reminds one of a writer who says things with exquisite sobriety, but says nothing of any great consequence. There is no reason to depreciate breadth in favour of depth, but it is hard to resist the impulse to do so. Velasquez may be superficial, but he is superficial on the grand scale. How beautifully he places his figures on the canvas so that they make a pattern charming to the eye! He was the greatest court painter that ever lived.

London. The barber. He got his job when he was sixteen. He was then a well-grown boy big enough to pass for the eighteen which he said he was, with a mop of curly fair hair the luxuriance of which had encouraged him to enter his trade. He was fond of reading poetry and on Sundays – in those days a barber worked six days a week – he made pilgrimages to the various places which were connected with the poets he was at the time interested in. He visited Chalfont St Giles while he was reading *Paradise Lost*; he had seen the birthplace of Keats and the house in which Coleridge had lived; he went to Stoke Poges and wandered in the churchyard which had suggested Grey's *Elegy*. He had a delightful and naïve enthusiasm. All his spare money he spent on books. He had his midday meal at an A.B.C. and while he ate his scone and butter and drank a glass of milk thumbed a precious volume. It was at an A.B.C. that he first saw the young lady who afterwards became his wife. She worked in a dress-maker's shop in Dover Street. Then he had a son. While he was courting her his wife had admired him because he was so well-read, but when they were married it made her impatient to see him constantly poring over a book. When he got back from his work and they had eaten their supper she wanted him to take her out for a walk or go to the pictures. They had been married for seven or eight years when the war broke out. He enlisted, and by the influence of one of the men whom he had shaved habitually was sent out to Russia with armoured cars. He was away for the duration of the war. The end of it found him in Rumania. At last he came back and returned to his job. He was a young man still. He was thirty-three. The prospect of cutting hair and shaving chins for the rest of his life dismayed him, but he did not know what else to do. That was all he knew, how to shave chins and cut hair. His wife thought he ought to be thankful to have a good job to come back to. He did not get on so well with her as he had done before he went away. She thought him crotchety and fanciful. He was impatient because she was so well satisfied with the life she led. He saw that he would never escape from the necessity of earning a decent living so that he could support her and the boy. The boy was ten now. He began to loathe his customers. I asked him if he still read. He shook his head. 'What's the good?' he said. 'It'll never get me anywhere.' 'It'll take you out of yourself,' I replied. 'Perhaps it will. But I've always got to come back.' He had only one thing left, the determination to give his son the freedom that was denied to himself. He was beaten, he had no longer any hope; but savagely, vindictively, he looked forward to his son revenging him vicariously for the loss of his own illusions. When the son grew up he went into the hairdressing business, but for ladies, because it pays better.

The Recipe. The young are earnest. He was a young man with a pugnacious but rather attractive face and a shock of thick brown hair, brushed straight back from his forehead, to which he sought by the lavish application of oil to give the fashionable sleekness. His inclinations were vaguely literary and he asked me how to make an epigram. Since he was in the flying corps it seemed natural enough to answer: 'You merely loop the loop on a commonplace and come down between the lines.' His brow puckered as he turned my reply over in his mind. He was paying me the compliment of giving it his serious attention: I only wanted the tribute of a smile.

Once a lady who had a son of a literary bent asked me what training I should advise if he was to become a writer; and I, judging by the inquirer that she would pay little attention to my answer, replied: 'Give him a hundred and fifty a year for five years and tell him to go to the devil.' I have thought of it since and it seems to me it was better advice than I imagined.

On such an income a young man will not starve, but it is small
enough for him to enjoy little comfort; and comfort is the writer's
bitterest foe. On such an income he can travel all over the world
under conditions which will enable him to see life in aspects more
varied and multicoloured than a man in more affluent circumstances is ever likely to happen upon. On such an income he
will be often penniless and so constrained to many pleasant
shifts to earn his board and lodging. He will have to try his hand
at a variety of callings. Though very good writers have led
narrow lives they have written well in spite of their circumstances
rather than on account of them; many old maids who spent
much of the year at Bath have written novels, but there is only
one Jane Austen. A writer does well to place himself in such
conditions that he may experience as many as possible of the
vicissitudes which occur to men. He need do nothing very
much, but he should do everything a little. I would have him
be in turns tinker, tailor, soldier, sailor; I would have him love
and lose, go hungry and get drunk, play poker with roughnecks
in San Francisco, bet with racing touts at Newmarket, philander
with duchesses in Paris and argue with philosophers in Bonn,
ride with bull-fighters in Seville and swim with kanakas in the
South Seas. No man is not worth the writer's knowing; every
occurrence is grist to his mill. Oh, to have the gift, to be twenty-
three, to have five years before one, and a hundred and fifty a
year.

They're both dead now. They were brothers. One was a painter
and the other a doctor. The painter was convinced that he had
genius. He was arrogant, irascible and vain, and he despised
his brother as a philistine and a sentimentalist. But he earned
practically nothing and would have starved except for the money
his brother gave him. The strange thing was that though bearish
and uncouth in manner and appearance he painted pretty-pretty
pictures. Now and then he managed to have an exhibition and
always sold a couple of canvases. Never more. At last the doctor
grew conscious of the fact that his brother wasn't a genius after
all, but only a second-rate painter. It was hard for him after all

the sacrifices he'd made. He kept his discovery to himself. Then he died, leaving all he had to his brother. The painter found in the doctor's house all the pictures he had sold to unknown buyers for twenty-five years. At first he couldn't understand. After thinking it over he hit upon the explanation: the cunning fellow had wished to make a good investment.

For an English audience the extremity of love is always somewhat ridiculous. To love more than moderately is to find oneself in a farcical situation.

Middle Age. I think I have been more than most men conscious of my age. My youth slipped past me unnoticed and I was always burdened with the sense that I was growing old. Because for my years I had seen much of the world and travelled a good deal, because I was somewhat widely read and my mind was occupied with matters beyond my years, I seemed always older than my contemporaries. But it was not till the outbreak of the war in 1914 that I had an inkling that I was no longer a young man. I found then to my consternation that a man of forty was old. I consoled myself by reflecting that this was only for military purposes, but not so very long afterwards I had an experience which put the matter beyond doubt. I had been lunching with a woman whom I had known a long time and her niece, a girl of seventeen. After luncheon we took a taxi to go somewhere or other. The woman got in and then her niece. But the niece sat down on the strapontin leaving the empty seat at the back beside her aunt for me to sit on. It was the civility of youth (as opposed to the rights of sex) to a gentleman no longer young. I realised that she looked upon me with the respect due to age.

It is not a very pleasant thing to recognize that for the young you are no longer an equal. You belong to a different generation. For them your race is run. They can look up to you: they can admire you; but you are apart from them, and in the long run they will always find the companionship of persons of their own age more grateful than yours.

But middle age has its compensations. Youth is bound hand

and foot with the shackles of public opinion. Middle age enjoys freedom. I remember that when I left school I said to myself: 'Henceforward I can get up when I like and go to bed when I like.' That of course was an exaggeration, and I soon found that the trammelled life of the civilized man only permits of a modified independence. Whenever you have an aim you must sacrifice something of freedom to achieve it. But by the time you have reached middle age you have discovered how much freedom it is worth while to sacrifice in order to achieve any aim that you have in view. When I was a boy I was tortured by shyness, and middle age has to a great extent brought me a relief from this. I was never of great physical strength and long walks used to tire me, but I went through them because I was ashamed to confess my weakness. I have now no such feeling and I save myself much discomfort. I always hated cold water, but for many years I took cold baths and bathed in cold seas because I wanted to be like everybody else. I used to dive from heights that made me nervous. I was mortified because I played games worse than other people. When I did not know a thing I was ashamed to confess my ignorance. It was not till quite late in life that I discovered how easy it is to say: 'I don't know.' I find with middle age that no one expects me to walk five and twenty miles, or to play a scratch game of golf, or to dive from a height of thirty feet. This is all to the good and makes life pleasant: but I should no longer care if they did. That is what makes youth unhappy, the vehement anxiety to be like other people, and that is what makes middle age tolerable, the reconciliation with oneself.

By imagination man compensates himself for his failure to get a complete satisfaction from life. Eternal necessity forces him to renounce the gratification of many of his most radical instincts, but renunciation comes hardly to man; and balked of his desire for honour, power, love, he cheats himself by the exercise of fantasy. He turns away from reality to an artificial paradise in which he can satisfy his desires without let or hindrance. Then in his vanity he acribes to this mental process a singular value. The exercise of the imagination seems to him the sublimest activity of man. And yet to imagine is to fail; for it is the acknowledgement of defeat in the encounter with reality.

The Novelist's Material. The danger always lies in wait for the novelist that with increasing knowledge of the world which offers him his subject matter, with a more comprehensive grasp of the ideas which enable him to give it coherence, and with a more exact command of the technique of his art, he may outgrow his interest in the varieties of experience which on the whole make up his material. When advancing years, wisdom or satiety prevent him from giving an excessive consideration to affairs which concern the generality of men, he is lost. A novelist must preserve a child-like belief in the importance of things which common-sense considers of no great consequence. He must never entirely grow up. He must interest himself to the end in matters which are no longer of his age. It needs a peculiar turn of mind in a man of fifty to treat with great seriousness the passion of Edwin for Angelina. The novelist is dead in the man who has become aware of the triviality of human affairs. You can often discern in writers the dismay with which they have recognized this situation in themselves, and you can see how they have dealt with it: sometimes by looking for significance in different subject matter, sometimes by deserting life for fantasy, and sometimes, when they have been too deeply engaged with their past to disentangle themselves from the snares of reality, by turning upon their old material with a savage irony. So George Eliot and H. G. Wells deserted the seduced maiden and the amorous clerk for sociology; so Thomas Hardy turned from *Jude the Obscure* to *The Dynasts*; and Flaubert from the love affairs of a provincial sentimentalist to the cruelties of *Bouvard et Pécuchet*.

The Work of Art. When I watch the audience at a concert or the crowd in a picture gallery I ask myself sometimes what exactly is their reaction towards the work of art. It is plain that often they feel deeply, but I do not see that their feeling has any effect, and if it has no effect its value is slender. Art to them is only a recreation or a refuge. It rests them from the work which they consider the justification of their existence or consoles them in their disappointment with reality. It is the glass of beer which the labourer drinks when he pauses in his toil or the peg of gin which the harlot takes to snatch a moment's oblivion from the pain of life. Art for art's sake means no more than gin for gin's sake. The dilettante who cherishes the sterile emotions which he receives from the contemplation of works of art has little reason to rate himself higher than the toper. His is the attitude of the pessimist. Life is a struggle or a weariness and in art he seeks repose or forgetfulness. The pessimist refuses reality, but the artist accepts it. The emotion caused by a work of art has value only if it has an effect on character and so results in action. Whoever is so affected is himself an artist. The artist's response to the work of art is direct and reasonable, for in him the emotion is translated into ideas which are pertinent to his own purposes, and to him ideas are but another form of action. But I do not mean that it is only painters, poets and musicians who can respond profitably to the work of art; the value of art would be much diminished; among artists I include the practitioners of the most subtle, the most neglected and the most significant of all the arts, the art of life.

My first book, published in 1897, was something of a success, Edmund Gosse admired it and praised it. After that I published other books and became a popular dramatist. I wrote *Of Human Bondage* and *The Moon and Sixpence*. I used to meet Gosse once or twice a year and continued to do so for twenty years, but I never met him without his saying to me in his unctuous way: 'Oh, my dear Maugham, I liked your *Liza of Lambeth* so much. How wise you are never to have written anything else.

The Dying Poet. He was so ill that the friend who was taking care of him felt he should telegraph for his wife. She was a painter of sorts and had gone to London for a one-man show she was giving in a minor gallery. When he told the sick man that he had sent for her, he was angry. 'Why couldn't you let me die in peace?' he cried. Someone had sent him a basket of peaches.

'The first thing she'll do on getting here is to take the best peach in the basket and while she eats it she'll talk of herself and the success she's had in London.'

The friend went to fetch her at the station and brought her to the apartment.

'O, Francesco, Francesco,' she cried, as she swept into the room. His name was Francis, but she always called him Francesco. 'How terrible! Oh, what beautiful peaches. Who sent you them?' She chose one and dug her teeth into the juicy flesh. 'The private view. Everyone was there that one's ever heard of. An enormous success. Everyone admired the pictures. I was surrounded with people. They all said I had real talent.'

She went on and on. At last the friend told her that it was late and she must let her husband go to sleep.

'I'm absolutely exhausted,' she cried. 'Such a journey. I had to sit up all night. It was horrible.'

She went to the bedside to kiss the sick man. He turned his face away.

He was a shipping clerk. He went to work at fourteen and for twenty-two years worked in the same firm. At the age of twenty-eight he married a wife who after a year or two had an illness which left her a permanent invalid. He was a devoted husband. He began to steal the insurance stamps, not so much because he wanted the money, though it enabled him to get little delicacies for his wife, but because it amused him to think that he was not the respectable, reliable clerk his employers thought him. Then his thefts were discovered, and knowing that he would be discharged and perhaps sent to prison and there would be no one to look after his wife, he killed her. When she was dead he put a pillow under her head and an eiderdown over her body. Then he took her pet dog to a vet's to have it painlessly destroyed, for he couldn't bear to kill it himself. He went to a police station and gave himself up.

T. He was a tall man, thin without being cadaverous, and he walked with a slight stoop. I suppose he was between forty-five and fifty, for his curling hair, though abundant, was very grey,

and his clean-shaven, neat face was much lined. It had little
colour. He wore gold-rimmed spectacles. He was unobtrusive.
He spoke in a low voice, seldom unless he was spoken to, and
though he never said an intelligent thing he never said a foolish
one. He was a trusted man in one of the most important corpora-
tions in America, and it was his trustworthiness that chiefly
attracted your attention. It was plain that he was not a very clever
fellow, but certainly he was a very honest one. He was sober in
his habits. He had a wife whom he was attached to and two
children of whom he was agreeably proud. You could have
safely wagered that he had never in his life done anything which
he had reason to regret. He was satisfied with the firm he worked
for, satisfied with his position in it, which was honourable without being conspicuous, satisfied with the house he lived in, the
city he worked in and the train service that took him daily to his
occupation. He was an extremely capable employee. He was a
rivet in a huge machine and was content to be a rivet. The great
levers, the vast revolving wheels, the gigantic cylinders never
suggested to him that it was possible to be anything but a rivet.
He was a man extraordinary only in that he was ordinary to
such a supreme degree.

It was a house-party. The post had just come in. Her hostess
gave her a letter and she recognized her lover's writing. She
opened it and began to read it. Suddenly she was aware that her
husband was standing behind her and reading the letter over her
shoulder. She read to the end and then handed it to her hostess.
   'He seems very much in love,' she said, 'but if I were you I
wouldn't let him write to you in that way.'

If you have a little more money than other people you must
expect them to exploit you and sponge upon you; but it is
exasperating that they should take you for such a fool that you
don't know what they're about, and if they get away with it, it's
only because you let them.

Ernest P. He was a young Frenchman, of good family, very
brilliant and expected by his family to have a distinguished

career. He was to go into the diplomatic service. At twenty he fell madly in love with a girl eight years older than himself; but she married a more suitable person. It broke him up. To the consternation of his family he threw up the studies which would enable him to pass the necessary examinations and took to social service in the slums of Paris. He became deeply religious (his family were free-thinkers) and immersed himself in the literature of mysticism. There were troubles in Morocco at the time, and he joined a dangerous expedition and was killed. All this had a shattering effect on the woman he loved, on his mother and his friends. They were deeply disturbed. They felt that here among them had lived one in whom there was something of a saint. His sweetness, his goodness, his piety, his nobility of soul made them ashamed – and afraid.

I thought there was a moving story to be written on these bare facts, and I was interested in the influence the life and death of this poor boy had on those who had been in contact with him; but it was too difficult for me to cope with and I never wrote it.

People will sometimes forgive you the good you have done them, but seldom the harm they have done you.

The writer must be playful and serious at the same time.

In the foam at the wake of the ship the phosphorescence, little gleams of light, was like the sardonic winking of the eyes of the dead that lie at the bottom of the sea.

Sunset. The sun was setting strangely behind an archway of heavy clouds, and below the arch the sky, pale green and gold, shone like the entrance way into magic, mystic realms. It reminded you of Watteau's *Embarquement pour Cythère*. It offered the imagination hope and unknown joy. Then the sun sank below the horizon and the arch crumbled away; and now the clouds, dark against the lurid afterglow, were like the ruins of a great city, ruins of palaces and temples and vast buildings. The hope and confidence of a few minutes were shattered like the pillars of Gaza and despair settled on the heart.

The Shilling Shocker. Their authors have little honour among men and yet they are benefactors of their kind. They are conscious of the small esteem in which the world holds them and they refer to their works deprecatingly, with a shrug and a smile. They hasten to disarm your scorn by assuring you that they are not dupes. They are timid of praise. They are afraid to believe that you are serious. And yet they are deserving of praise. There are times when your mind is not attuned to good literature; there are times when your brain is weary, but restless; times when the classics bore you, when you are harassed or unhappy; there are railway journeys; there is sickness: then what can be more comfortable than a good shocker? You plunge into murders, robbery, treacheries and blackmail, imprisonments and hairbreadth escapes, opium dens, thieves' kitchens, artists' studios, sumptuous hotels; you foregather with forgers, crooks, gunmen, detectives, adventuresses, stool pigeons, convicts, persecuted heroines and falsely accused heroes. Standards of excellence are not the same here as in other forms of art. Improbability is no bar to your enjoyment, economy of invention is a defect, graces of style are out of place, humour is damning. It is fatal if a smile should ever force its way to your unwilling lips: you must read with a high, with an intense and with a pitiless seriousness. You turn the pages with a nervous hand. The hours race by. You have defeated time. And then you have the ingratitude to throw aside the book with a sneer and look down upon its author. It is graceless.

Since he was a philosopher by profession I asked him to explain something that I had never been able to understand. I asked him whether the statement that two and two make four means anything. I couldn't see that four was anything but a convenient synonym for two and two. If you look out *violent* in Roget you will see that there are something like fifty synonyms for it; they have different associations and some by the number of their syllables, the collocation of their letters or the difference of their sound may be more suitable for use in a particular sentence than others, but they all *mean* the same thing. Roughly, of course, for no synonym is quite precise; and four may be a synonym not only for two and two, but for three and one and for one and one and one and one. My philosopher said he thought the statement that two and two make four had a definite meaning, but he didn't seem able to tell me exactly what it was; and when I asked him whether mathematics was ultimately anything more than an immensely elaborate Roget's *Thesaurus* he changed the conversation.

1936

St Laurent de Maroni. The director is a short stout man with large shining eyes, in a clean white uniform, with the cross of the Legion of Honour on his tunic. He has exuberant gestures and speaks with a strong accent of the Midi. He is a jolly, vulgar, ignorant man; but kindly and tolerant. He got his job by political influence. His salary is sixty thousand francs a year, but there are probably large perks. He likes the job because he can live cheaply and save money. He looks forward to retiring in ten years and building himself a house on the Riviera.

His wife is plump and rather pretty, but run to seed; her mother has a *bureau de tabac* at Cette; she and her husband were *amis d'enfance*. She wears almost always the same dress of blue foulard with white spots. It brings out the colour of her blue eyes. She is ingenuous, inclined to be flirtatious, but proud of, and in love with, her fat husband.

The commandant of the camp is a tall man, a Parisian, fair rather than dark, earnest, shy and very well-mannered. He is deeply interested in penology and reads a great deal. He has the notion that much can be done by appealing to the better nature of the convicts. He looks for amendment in them.

An old *surveillant* at St Jean. Short thick white hair and a heavy white moustache. A lined sun-burned face. He is against capital punishment, for he thinks no one has the right to take another's life. He tells a story of how a doctor had arranged with a man who was to be guillotined to blink three times if he could after his head was cut off, and says that he saw him blink twice.

When a man is sentenced to death the sentence has to be confirmed by the minister in Paris. No execution takes place on Sunday. If two or more are to be guillotined at the same time the least guilty is executed first so that he should not suffer the added horror of seeing his mates die. The convict does not know that he will be executed till the warder comes in with the words: Have courage, etc. When there are executions the other convicts are depressed and nervous, and they go about their work sullen and silent.

When the head has fallen the executioner takes it up by the ears and shows it to the bystanders, saying: *Au nom du peuple français justice est faite*. At the side of the guillotine is a large wicker basket covered with some black material and into this the body is put. The knife falls with lightning speed and the blood spurts over the executioner. He is given a set of new clothes after each execution.

The director's house. A large white frame house, with official furniture, a chandelier in the middle of each room, and stiff, uncomfortable chairs in the drawing-room. It faces the sea and has a large veranda which is used as a parlour. The garden, with its bougainvillaea, crotons, cassias, papaias and flame of the forest, has the bedraggled look of a garden in the banlieue belonging to a retired tradesman.

The punishment cells. They are long and narrow and they contain a wooden pallet for a bed, a stool and a small table fixed to the wall. They are hot, and lit only by an opening over the heavy door. The convicts sentenced to solitary confinement are locked in and let out for an hour morning and evening. The cells at the end of the corridor are pitch black, for the light only comes in by the door at the entrance to the passage.

Most of the convicts live in dormitories of fifty or sixty beds, but there are a certain number of cells either above the dormitories on the first floor or in a separate courtyard, and these are given to well-behaved prisoners who ask for them. Sometimes, however, they dislike being alone and ask to be put back into the dormitories. In each of these cells there is a hammock and a small table on which the convict keeps his bits and pieces, a shaving-mop, a razor, a hair brush and a photograph or two. On the walls they tack illustrations from the picture papers.

The convicts. They are dressed in striped pink and white py-jamas and wear a round straw hat and shoes with wooden soles and leather-tops, but no socks. Their hair is cut short and cut very badly. Their food consists of grey bread, two good-sized loaves a day, soup made of bones and meat, potatoes and cabbage-tops, beef a ration of cheese if they are well-behaved, and a ration of wine. They make their cigarettes out of little blue packets of coarse tobacco. They sit about on the verandas or steps of the house, chatting and smoking, or wander, some alone, some in charge of a warder, and work desultorily. They are emaciated notwithstanding their abundant food, they suffer from fever and hook-worm, and they have staring eyes. They don't look quite sane. Rum is the great luxury and they all have knives.

No warder dares go into a dormitory at night, after lock-up, or he wouldn't come out alive.

The gateway of the prison is open all day long and they saunter in and out at liberty.

The *porte-clefs*, under-warders, almost officials, are well-behaved convicts; and they live in separate quarters and wear felt hats instead of straw. They are not liked by the others, and not seldom get themselves killed.

The executioner, a convict, has two mongrel dogs trained to guard him, and they prowl about the compound at night. He has his own little house near the director's. The other convicts don't speak to him and his food is fetched from the prison kitchen by his assistant. He spends his leisure strolling in the public garden and fishing, and he sells his fish to the director's wife.

The guillotine is in a small room within the prison, but it is reached by a separate door from the outside. To make sure that it will work well a banana stem is used for practice because it is of the same thickness as a man's neck. From the time a man is strapped up to the time his head is off, it takes only thirty seconds. The executioner gets a hundred francs for each execution.

The previous executioner disappeared and they thought he had run away. He was found three weeks later hanging to a tree with knife thrusts in his body, and he was only found because a flock of vultures, *urubus* they are called, were seen clustering round a tree. He had known the convicts were out to kill him and had asked to be sent to Cayenne or back to France. They had caught him and after stabbing him to death had carried him into the jungle.

The *relégués*, habitual criminals, are sent to St Jean not exactly under sentence, but to be kept there for the protection of society. They catch butterflies and beetles which they mount in boxes and sell, or make ornaments out of buffalo horn. In one part of the camp there is a newspaper kiosk, just like a kiosk in a small French station, with books for hire and papers a month old neatly set out. Over it is written *Le crédit est mort*. In another part is a small theatre with a stage and rough scenery painted by the *relégués*.

The sea is shark-infested, and they say with a laugh that the sharks are the best jailers.

I spent today inquiring into the motives of the murders which had caused the convicts to be sentenced to what is virtually life-long imprisonment, and I was surprised to discover that though on the surface it looked as though they had killed from love, jealousy, hatred, in revenge for some wrong or merely in a fit of passion, when I asked a little further it was borne in upon me that not far below the surface the motive was pecuniary. In one way or another money was at the bottom of every murder I inquired into but one. The exception was a young lad, a shepherd, who had raped a little girl and when she cried out, afraid people would hear, he had strangled her. He is only eighteen now.

Martinique. In 1902 Mt Pelée erupted and overwhelmed the town of St Pierre. Forty thousand people lost their lives. There had been some volcanic activity shortly before and an eruption north of St Pierre in which a number of people were killed. Then a few days later without warning a mass of fire, like a flaming whirlpool, swept over St Pierre and destroyed the ships in the harbour. A fall of molten lava and ashes followed the flames, accompanied by dense gases which asphyxiated those who had so far escaped. All who could fled from the town, whole families together, and strangely enough the gases swept over them irregularly so that a group in front escaped and a group behind, whereas a group between them was overcome and perished.

I asked my friends what effect the catastrophe had on those who were saved. I wanted to know whether the fearful danger and the miraculous escape had had a spiritual or a moral effect on them, whether it changed their lives afterwards, whether their faith was strengthened or weakened, whether they became better men or worse. Everyone gave me the same answer. It had no effect on them at all. Most of them were ruined, but after they had recovered from the shock they took up their lives as best they could and as though nothing had happened. They were neither more nor less devout, neither better nor worse. I suppose it is because there is a resilience in man, a power of forgetfulness, or perhaps merely an obtuseness, that he has been able to survive the countless horrors that have encompassed him since first he came into existence.

West Indies. A girl came out as governess to the children of some English people settled on the island, and after a while she was asked in marriage by a planter. On the face of it, it was a good match for her; he was well-off, a very good fellow and well-liked. He was slightly coloured, and on this account was not a member of the club; but in his outlook, his habits, his manner, he was as white as any white man. The girl was as much in love with him as he was with her, but her employers urged her not to be in a hurry and persuaded her to go home to England for six months so that she might make certain of her own mind. She came back at the end of this period and the pair were married, but on the understanding that they should have no children. The planter was a good husband, a passionate lover and a pleasant companion, and she was completely happy. Then he contracted typhoid. He was very ill, and the girl nursed him with the help of his old black nannie. She had a queer feeling that something was happening to him that she couldn't account for; he seemed to collapse morally rather than physically. He seemed to be infected with the superstitions which she knew prevailed among the coloured people. One day he refused to see the English doctor. 'The only one who can cure me is old nannie,' he said irritably. When she expostulated he told her roughly to shut up. 'You don't know what you're talking about.' That night they turned her out of the room and the nurse went in with three old men, all black, and one of them carried a white cock under his arm. She stood outside the door and heard strange incantations, and then a sort of flutter, it might have been of wings, and she realised that they were killing the white cock. When the coloured people came out of the room and she could go in again she saw that the sick man's forehead and cheeks and chin, his breast, hands and feet had been smeared with blood. She knew then that for all his clear honey-coloured skin, his wavy red hair, at heart her husband was a Negro. Two or three days later she discovered she was pregnant.

1937

Sincerity in literary judgements is terribly hard to achieve. It is almost impossible to form one's own opinion of a work without being to some small extent at least influenced by critical or common opinion. What adds to the difficulty is that with regard to works of acknowledged greatness common opinion has given them some part of their greatness. To try to read a poem with the eyes of the first reader who read it is like trying to see a landscape without the atmosphere that clothes it.

Much of Henry James is what the French, whom he so extravagantly admired, dismiss with a shrug of the shoulders as *littérature*. He did not live, he observed life from a window, and too often was inclined to content himself with no more than what his friends told him they saw when *they* looked out of a window. But what can you know of life unless you have lived it? Something escapes you unless you have been an actor in the tragi-comedy. In the end the point of Henry James is neither his artistry nor his seriousness, but his personality, and this was curious and charming and a trifle absurd.

Would anyone think he could get a useful knowledge of motorcars by reading a novel of which the scene was a motor works and the characters car-manufacturers; and do you think the soul of man is less complicated than the engine of a car?

Poe supposed he could obtain novelty and originality by taking thought. He was wrong. The only way to be new is constantly to change yourself, and the only way to be original is to increase, enlarge, deepen your own personality.

Give us this day our daily bread, the devout pray. One would have thought it was an insult to a benign and omnipotent being to beg him for the bare necessities of life. When we treat our neighbour with common civility it is no favour we grant him; it is his right.

Truth is not only stranger than fiction, it is more telling. To know that a thing actually happened gives it a poignancy, touches a chord, which a piece of acknowledged fiction misses. It is to touch this chord that some authors have done everything they could to give you the impression that they are telling the plain truth.

There are books that are at once excellent and boring. Those that at once leap to the mind are Thoreau's *Walden*, Emerson's *Essays*, George Eliot's *Adam Bede* and Landor's *Dialogues*. Is it a chance that they belong very much to the same period?

The writer should have a distinguished and varied culture, but he probably errs when he puts its elements into his work. It is a sign of naïveté to put into a novel your views on evolution, the sonatas of Beethoven, or Karl Marx's *Das Kapital*.

Shyness: a mixture of diffidence and conceit.

He had had so little love when he was small that later it embarrassed him to be loved. It made him feel shy and awkward when someone told him that his nose was good and his eyes mysterious. He did not know what to say when someone paid him a compliment, and a manifestation of affection made him feel a fool.

Thirty years after. A lined, haggard, sallow face. A boring chatter-box. Stupid gush about her children and her house. Trivial, trivial. Every now and again an arch look that seemed to tell him that she remembered how mad he had been about her. He was ashamed to think that for that fool he had walked up and down the street in which she lived on the chance of meeting her, and had waited in an agony of suspense for the postman's knock that might bring him a letter from her, and that to sit beside her he had sat through dreary musical comedies and had acted amusement and delight so that she should be pleased with him. For her he had pretended to take interest in actors and actresses, in gossip of the most inane sort; and the worst of it was that he had not only pretended, he really had been interested because she was. However stupidly she talked he was charmed to listen to her. For her he had abased himself to ask for favours that he would have been ashamed to ask for himself.

Remorse. He was desperately in love with a woman and jealous of another man who was in love with her too. He was an honest and upright man and he prided himself on his integrity. But in his jealousy he played a despicably mean trick on his rival and so disposed of him. He married the woman. But little by little he became obsessed with the beastly, dishonourable thing he had done. It tortured him. He came to hate the woman for whose sake he had done it.

Two men were sitting in the lounge of a hotel at Worthing and they were discussing a murder that the papers were full of. A man, sitting near them, listened to their conversation, and asked if he might join them. He sat down and ordered drinks. He told them what he thought of the murder they had been talking about. 'It's the motive you've got to go for,' he said. 'When once you've found the motive it's only a question of time before you find the murderer.' Then without warning, as though he were saying something quite ordinary, he said : 'I don't mind telling you that I committed a murder once.' He told them that he had done it just for fun and he described the thrill. Since there was no motive for it he knew he could never be discovered. 'Someone I'd never seen in my life,' he said. He finished his drink, got up, nodded to them and went out through the swing doors. He left them flabbergasted.

1938

India. Major C. He was a tall, broad-built man, with close-cropped brown hair. It was hard to guess his age. He might not have been more than thirty-five and he might have been fifty. He had a clean-shaven face, rather large, but with small features and a short blunt nose. He had an expression of peaceful happiness. He spoke slowly, but fluently, in rather a loud voice. He smiled a great deal and laughed frequently. His manner was cheerful. He was very polite and anxious to do what he could to be pleasant. It was hard to tell if he was intelligent or a little stupid. He was certainly not widely read. There was something of the boy scout about him which was disconcerting; he was childishly pleased when the Yogi came into his room and sat on his chair, and he told me several times that he enjoyed privileges that no other inmate of the Ashrama was accorded. His attitude was a little like that of the schoolboy inclined to boast because he is in the headmaster's favour.

He has been living at the Ashrama for two years and by special favour has been allowed to build his own little shack with a kitchen behind it. He has his own cook. He does not eat meat or fish or eggs, but has a store of tinned goods from Madras to help out with the curry and curds that his cook prepares for him. He drinks nothing but tea.

In this one room is a pallet bed, a table, an arm-chair and another chair, a small bookcase in which are perhaps fifty books. They are translations of works on the Vedanta, the Upanishads and so forth, books by the Yogi and books about him. On the walls are a few small pictures, one of Leonardo's Christ, a few, hideous, of Vishnu, cheap coloured prints and a photograph of the Yogi. The walls are painted green. On the floor a rattan mat.

He wears a sort of Chinese coat and Chinese trousers of white cotton and goes barefoot.

He has an intense adoration for the Yogi and says that he looks upon him as the greatest spiritual figure that the world has known since Christ.

He is somewhat reticent about his past. He said he had no one close to him in England and had travelled a great deal in years gone by, but now, having arrived there, he had reached his goal and would travel no more. He said that he had found peace and (over and over again) that the presence and the sight of the Yogi gave him a spiritual serenity which was beyond all price. I asked him how he spent his day. In reading, he said, taking his exercise (he has a push-bike and cycles regularly eight miles a day), and in meditation. He spent many hours a day sitting in the hall with the Yogi, though often he did not speak more than a few words to him in a week. But he was a strong man in the prime of life, and I asked him whether his natural energy had sufficient outlet.

He said that he was fortunate in that he was one of the few persons who had a real desire and liking for meditation; and that he had always practised it. He added that meditation was a strenuous exercise and after spending some hours in it one was physically exhausted and had to lie down and rest. But I could not get from him exactly what he meant by meditation. I could not understand if he was actively thinking of a certain subject. When I put before him the Jesuit contemplation of a particular theme, such as the Passion, he said it was not that at all. He said his effort was to realize the self in him in communion with the universal self, to separate the I that thinks from the self, for that, he said, is the infinite. When he had done that, and really seen, or felt, that the divine in himself was part of the infinite divine he would have reached enlightenment. He was of a mind to stay there till this happened or till the Yogi died.

It was hard to make up one's mind what sort of a man he was. He was certainly very happy. I had thought to discover something of the truth about him from what he looked like and from what he said, but I came away completely puzzled.

Hyderabad. Passing along the road by car to Hyderabad from Bida I saw a large crowd, the usual Indian crowd, women in bright saris, men in dhoties, ox wagons, cows – I thought it was a small market, but my bearer told me it was the place where a healer lived and all these people were gathered from the surrounding villages to have their ills cured and women, if they were sterile, to be made fertile. I asked if I could go and see him. The driver told me he was a well-to-do contractor in Hyderabad who had felt the call to live the life of a Sadhu and had given over his fortune to his family and settled in that spot. He lived under a peepul tree and tended a small wayside shrine to Siva. We made our way through the crowd. There must have been three or four hundred people. Sick men were lying on the ground. There were women with sick children in their arms. When we got near the shrine the healer came forward and greeted us by humbly doing obeisance to us. He was dressed in a grubby white turban, a shirt without a collar, the ends hanging over his grubby dhoty. He had silver ear-rings in his ears. He was clean-shaven, but for a short stubble of grey moustache. Small, perky, quick in his movements, gay, bustling and cheerful. He looked not at all like a saint but like any wide-awake, active shopkeeper in the bazaar. You would have thought him an obvious fake, but for the fact that he had given up his house and belongings and accepted nothing for his ministrations. He lives on the rice and fruit that people bring him and gives away everything he does not need. He insisted on giving us some coconuts. He heals by saying a prayer to the god in his shrine and by the laying on of hands. I was much embarrassed when as I was leaving he asked me to give him a blessing. I told him I was not the proper person to do that, but he was insistent, and so, feeling hypocritical and very foolish, with all those people looking on, I did what he wanted.

The Sufi. He lived in a little house in a poor quarter of Hyderabad. It was almost a slum. There was a veranda, and we waited there to find out from our guide if the holy man would see us. Taking off our shoes before we entered, we were ushered into a smallish room, divided into two, as far as I could see, by mosquito-netting, and I surmised that the part we could not see was his sleeping apartment. The greater part of the space in which we sat was taken up by a sort of dais or platform, about eighteen inches from the ground, covered with cheap rugs, and on these was a rattan mat on which the saint sat. He was very old, very thin, with a ragged white beard; he wore a fez, a white cotton coat and white trousers; and his feet were bare. His eyes looked very large in the extreme thinness of his face in which the cheek-bones stood out above the sunken cheeks. He had long beautiful hands, but fleshless, and his gestures were profuse, graceful and expressive. Though so old and so frail, he seemed full of energy and talked with animation. He was cheerful. The expression of his face was very sweet and kindly. I do not know that he said anything remarkable. I know nothing of Sufism and so perhaps was more surprised than I should have been to hear him speak of the self and the supreme self in the same strain as the Hindu teachers speak. The impression I carried away was of a very dear, tender, kindly, charitable and tolerant old man.

A Holy Man. Sir Akbar Hydari sent his car to fetch him and at the appointed hour he entered the room. He was richly dressed and wore a great scarlet cloak of fine material. He was a middle-aged man, tall, of a handsome presence, and his manner was courtly. He spoke no English and Sir Akbar acted as interpreter. He talked fluently and well and his voice was sonorous. He said the things I had heard from others twenty times before. That is the worst of the Indian thinkers, they say the same things in the same words, and though you feel that it should not make you restive, for if they possess the truth, as they are convinced they do, and if the truth is one and indivisible, it is natural enough that they should repeat it like parrots, there is no denying the fact that it is irksome to listen interminably to the same statements. You wish at least they could think of other metaphors, similes, illustrations than those of the Upanishads. Your heart sinks when you hear again the one about the snake and the rope. Custom has too much staled it.

I asked him how I could acquire the power of meditation. He told me to go into a darkened room, sit on the floor cross-legged and fix my eyes on the flame of a candle, emptying my mind of every thought so that it was a complete blank. He said that if I would do that for a quarter of an hour a day I should presently have some extraordinary experiences. 'Do it for nine months,' he said, 'then come back and I will give you another exercise.'

That evening I did as he had directed. I took the time before I began. I remained in that state for so long that I thought I must have by far exceeded the quarter of an hour he had prescribed. I looked at my watch. Three minutes had passed. It had seemed an eternity.

A week or two ago someone related an incident to me with the suggestion that I should write a story on it, and since then I have been thinking it over. I don't see what to do. The incident is as follows. Two young fellows were working on a tea plantation in the hills and the mail had to be fetched from a good way off so that they only got it at rather long intervals. One of the young fellows, let us call him A, used to get a lot of letters by every mail, ten or twelve and sometimes more, but the other, B, never got one. He used to watch A enviously as he took his bundle and started to read, he hankered to have a letter, just one letter, and one day, when they were expecting the mail, he said to A: 'Look here, you always have a packet of letters and I never get any. I'll give you five pounds if you'll let me have one of yours.' 'Right-ho,' said A and when the mail came in he handed B his letters and said to him: 'Take whichever you like.' B gave him a five-pound note, looked over the letters, chose one and returned the rest. In the evening, when they were having a whisky and soda after dinner, A asked casually: 'By the way, what was that letter about?' 'I'm not going to tell you,' said B. A, somewhat taken aback, said: 'Well, who was it from?' 'That's my business,' answered B. They had a bit of an argument, but B stood on his rights and refused to say anything about the letter that he had bought. A began to fret, and as the weeks went by he did all he could to persuade B to let him see the letter. B continued to refuse. At length A, anxious, worried, curious, felt he couldn't bear it any longer, so he went to B and said: 'Look here, here's your five pounds, let me have my letter back again.' 'Not on your life,' said B. 'I bought and paid for it, it's my letter and I'm not going to give it up.'

That's all. I suppose if I belonged to the modern school of story writers, I should write it just as it is and leave it. It goes against the grain with me. I want a story to have form, and I don't see how you can give it that unless you can bring it to a conclusion that leaves no legitimate room for questioning. But even if you could bring yourself to leave the reader up in the air you don't want to leave yourself up in the air with him.

I went to lunch with the heir apparent and his wife, the Prince and Princess of Berar. During luncheon the prince talked to me of my journey. 'I suppose you've been to Bombay?' he asked. 'Yes,' I answered, 'I landed there.' 'And were you put up for the

Yacht Club?' 'Yes,' I said. 'And are you going to Calcutta?'
'Yes.' 'I suppose you'll be put up at the Bengal Club?' 'I hope so,'
I replied. 'Do you know the difference between them?' the prince
asked. 'No,' said I innocently. 'In the Bengal Club at Calcutta
they don't allow dogs or Indians, but in the Yacht Club at Bombay they don't mind dogs; it's only Indians they don't allow.' I
couldn't for the life of me think of an answer to that then, and
I haven't thought of one since.

The Swami. He was dressed in the saffron robes of the monk, but
pinkish rather than yellow, with a turban of the same colour and
a cloak. It looked an unduly hot costume. He wore white socks
and very neat brown shoes, rather like dancing pumps. He was a
tallish man, inclined to corpulence, with a large fleshy face,
handsome shining eyes behind his gold-rimmed spectacles, and a
large sensual mouth. He spoke loudly in a resonant voice, which
when he lectured was apt to be a trifle rasping. He smiled a great
deal. His manner had an unctuous benevolence. He gave you
the impression of being more than commonly self-satisfied. He
was glad of adulation and fond of talking about himself. I asked
him on one occasion whether he didn't regret the pleasures that
men in the world enjoy. 'Why should I?' he answered. 'I had
them all in a previous life.'

The Fakirs. The ceremony took place in a Moslem cemetery
where one of the saints of the order had been buried some
centuries back. The head of the order was a full bodied man with
a hooked nose and a clever, commanding expression. He wore
an Arab cloak of fine brown stuff and on his head a neat white
turban. In front of where he sat was a small brazier containing
burning charcoal into which he constantly dropped incense,
and the various instruments the dervishes were to use in their
display.

They were seated in a row opposite him and about four or
five yards away. They were of all ages; one could not have been
more than fourteen, some were young men; the most important were, from the Indian standpoint, old, with great beards and
grey hair. They were a wild-looking lot with their long hair,

the coloured voluminous rags they wore, their ear-rings and chains.

The proceedings began with a long prayer which the head of the order chanted and in which at intervals the others joined with cries. Then one of them advanced and took a skewer, perhaps two feet long, passed it over the incense and had it touched by the head man, then he put it through his cheek and pushed it through till it came out for at least two inches on the other cheek. He walked round to show himself and then with precaution took it out. He lightly rubbed the places where the skewer had gone in and come out and not only was there no blood, but there was no wound. Another came forward, took another skewer, passed it through his neck, behind the windpipe, and withdrew it. Then one took a short blunt dagger and after certain extravagant gestures and shouting gouged his eye out. He walked around with the ball of the eye hanging down his cheek, a revolting spectacle, then replaced it, rubbed it a little and appeared none the worse. Another passed a skewer through the skin of his abdomen, and still another through his tongue. They seemed to suffer no pain. The performance went on for perhaps half an hour and ended with another long prayer. One or two bled a very little, a drop or two, but the bleeding quickly stopped.

The occultist. He was a little man with a round face and bespectacled round eyes, very fluent in conversation. He had been in the war and emerged with the rank of major. He had travelled a great deal. He was a Christian and a student of Paracelsus and of Eliphas Levi. He distinguished between white magic and black. He had a contempt for miracles, but claimed to be able to levitate. His contention was that any demonstration made merely to satisfy curiosity lessened the agent's powers. His were purely spiritual. He asserted that he could heal the sick, but said that his wife (who came to my house with him) had much greater powers than he. She was an Indian in a sari, not quite young, silent and watchful. When they left she told me that I would sometimes see her and that when she appeared to people it was always in a dark blue sari.

It may be that it is the I in us which is the cause of all our wickedness, but it is the cause too of our music, our painting, our poetry. And so what?

Ahmed Ali, Sir Akbar's secretary, told me the following story. He said that a woman who had been bitten by a scorpion was brought to him and he was told that if he wrote the number 16 on the ground and rubbed it with a shoe she would be healed. Not believing in it, he did so and nothing happened. She went away and then someone pointed out that he had written not 16, but 13. Since then he had written 16 and had cured several people.

A Yogi wanted to cross a river and had not the penny to pay the ferryman, so he walked across the river on his feet. Another Yogi hearing of this said the miracle was only worth the penny it would have cost to cross by ferry.

A Yogi wanted to go somewhere by train, but having no money, asked the station-master if he could go for nothing; the station-master refused, so the Yogi sat down on the platform. When it was time for the train to go it would not start. It was supposed that something was wrong with the engine, so mechanics were sent for and they did all they knew, but still the train could not go. At last the station-master told the officials of the Yogi. He was asked to get in the train and it immediately started.

The occultist and Ahmed Ali both agreed that there was a station-master on the line who could heal snake bites, and they said that if anyone was bitten he had the right to telegraph free of charge to the station-master, who telegraphed back and cured the patient.

I gave a small dinner party. Six people. They were philosophers, pundits and scholars. The conversation turning on the power a Yogi can obtain by discipline and mortification, they told me of one who had let himself be buried at the bottom of a dry well and had told people to open it in six months. If the top of the head was warm they would know he was alive and should revive him, if it was cold they would know he was dead and could burn him. They did this and found he was alive. He soon revived and is now living hale and hearty sixteen years later. They had all either seen him or known people who had. They accepted the incident as certain.

The peacock. We were driving through the jungle. It was not thick and presently we caught sight of a peacock among the trees with its beautiful tail outspread. It walked, a proud, magnificent object, treading the ground with a peculiar delicacy, with a sort of deliberation, and its walk was so elegant, so wonderfully graceful that it recalled to my memory Nijinsky stepping on to the stage at Covent Garden and walking with just such a delicacy, grace and elegance. I have seldom seen a sight more thrilling than that peacock threading its solitary way through the jungle. My companion told the driver to stop and seized his gun.

'I'm going to have a shot at it.'

My heart stopped still. He fired, and I hoped he'd miss, but he didn't. The driver jumped out of the car and brought back the dead bird which a moment before had been so exultantly alive. It was a cruel sight.

We ate the breast for dinner that night. The flesh was white, tender and succulent; it was a welcome change from the scraggy chickens which are brought to the table evening after evening in India.

Benares. Nothing can be more impressive than to saunter down the Ganges by boat in the evening just before the sun sets. It is thrilling to look at the city with the two minarets of the mosque standing up against the pale sky. A wonderful sense of peace descends upon you. There is a great silence.

Then in the morning before the sun rises you drive through the city, the shops still closed and men under rugs lying asleep on the pavement; a scattering of people are going down to the river, with brass bowls in their hands, for their prescribed bath in the sacred water. You get on to a houseboat, manned by three men, and slowly row down by the ghats. It is chilly in the early morning. The ghats are unevenly peopled. One, I don't know why, is crowded. It is an extraordinary spectacle, the throng on the steps and at the water's edge. The bathers take the ritual bath in different ways. For some of the boys it is a lark and they dive into the water, come out and dive in again. For some it is a ceremony that must be gone through as quickly as possible, and you see them make the motions of devotion mechanically and gabble through their prayers. Others take it solemnly. They bow to the rising sun and, their arms outstretched above their heads, utter their prayers with unction. Then, the bath over, some chat with their friends and you guess that the daily obligation offers an opportunity to exchange news and gossip. Others sit cross-legged in meditation. The stillness with which some of them sit is strangely impressive: it is as though in that throng they sat in a temple of solitude. I saw one old man whose face was decorated with great rings of white ash around his eyes, a broad oblong patch on his forehead and square patches on his cheeks, so that he looked as if he were wearing a mask. Many of the bathers, having taken their bath, carefully scrubbed and polished the brass bowl in which they were going to carry back to their houses the lustral water.

It is a moving, a wonderfully thrilling spectacle; the bustle, the noise, the coming and going give a sense of a seething vitality; and those still figures of the men in contemplation by contrast seem more silent, more still, more aloof from human intercourse.

The sun rises higher in the heaven and the grey light which had bathed the scene grows golden, and colour clothes it with a motley radiance.

He was a sturdy little man, who walked with a jaunty perkiness, with a round bald head, bright blue eyes, with a lot of wrinkles round them, and a cheerful expression. He was the Government engineer. He built roads, dams, bridges. His bungalow faced the river. The drawing-room was furnished with comfortable arm-chairs and a carved Indian table in the middle; on the walls were fussy carvings in wood of mythological scenes, heads of animals he had shot, and framed photographs. There was a little strip of garden between the veranda and the river, and one tree grew in it that struck me by its beauty. Its leaves were not dense, so that you saw the branches very plainly and they made an exquisite pattern against the sky. I remarked on its loveliness, but the engineer had evidently never noticed it; I think he thought it rather funny of me to speak about it.

We were talking of shooting and he mentioned that he had once killed a monkey. 'I'll never shoot another,' he said. 'I was making a road and all the coolies struck, there were six hundred of them; the foreman was ill and they were afraid he was going to die; they'd made up their minds to go away and leave the work. I did everything I could to get them to stay, and at last they said they would if I'd kill a monkey so that they could have the blood in its heart, because they could cure the foreman with it. Well, I couldn't have the work stopped, so I took my gun and walked along the road. There were generally a good many monkeys playing about, black-faced ones, and after a time I saw one. I aimed and fired, but I only wounded it. It ran up to me for protection, crying, crying just like a child.'

'Did the foreman recover?' I asked.

'Well, in point of fact he did. Anyhow I got the road finished.'

Van H. He is a man of about sixty, a big fellow with a big stomach, a large fleshy face and a large nose, a grey beard and grey hair. His eyes are blue. He speaks willingly, correctly, but with somewhat of an accent. His voice is loud and he has a jovial manner. He can never have been goodlooking as a young man and now, in his shabby, careless clothes, with all that fat, though a man of some presence from his size, he has no dignity, nor is he striking or impressive. He has been in the East for over thirty years. He went out first to Java. He is a considerable linguist, a Sanscrit scholar; he is widely read in the religions of the East and in the philosophy of Greece. Here, not unnaturally, he is chiefly interested in Heracleitus and on his shelves is all the extant literature concerned with him. The flat is filled with books. On the walls are Tibetan banners and here and there pieces of Tibetan brass. He lived for a longish time in Tibet. He is a man who likes his food and enjoys his glass of beer. Under the influence of Leadbitter he became a theosophist, went to India and was for some years librarian at Adyar, but then quarrelled with Mrs Besant. When I asked him what he thought of the notion of Mahatmas he said that he thought the evidence in proof of their existence and of their non-existence was about fifty per cent on one side and fifty per cent on the other. Though he has long since lost his belief in theosophy, he has still a great admiration for Leadbitter and believes that he had supernatural powers. I think he has now a real faith in Buddhism.

When in Java as a young man he engaged a servant. He travelled with him for nine months and then the boy told him his story. He was a descendant of one of the Javanese sultans, married, with a child; his wife and child died and, heartbroken, he retired into the jungle to lead the life of a Sadhu. He eventually joined a company of charcoal-burners and lived with them for several months. At last they said to him that this was no life for the descendant of a prince and persuaded him to go and see a strange man. This was a tea planter, a Javanese, of about forty, who was generally believed to be, not a reincarnation of a celebrated rebel who had vanished into obscurity on defeat (as Nana Sahib did), but the man himself, still alive after more than a hundred years. This man had told him to go to Batavia, where he would find a white man whom for the nine months he would be there he was to serve. He told him on what day he would arrive. The fact that all this turned out exactly as the tea planter had foretold interested van H. and he went to see him. He found an ordinary-looking man, who was greatly revered by the people, but who would say nothing about himself; he would neither confirm nor deny that he was the ancient hero he was thought to be. When van H. asked him what had made him say the exact things that had made the servant come to Batavia and take a place with him, the answer was: 'There is a knowledge that comes from the head and there is a knowledge that comes from the heart. I looked in my heart and told what I saw there.'

A young officer on a P. and O. on the way home was seen on deck busily reading books on the Taj Mahal. He was asked why and he answered: 'Well, I was stationed at Agra for four years and I never saw it, but I know that when I get home everyone'll ask me about it, so I thought I'd better mug it all up before I got there.'

Taj Mahal. Notwithstanding my expectations and all the pictures I had seen of it, when I got my first and proper view of it, the view from the terrace of the gateway, I was overcome by its beauty. I recognized that this was the authentic thrill of art and tried to examine it in myself while it was still vivid. I can understand that when people say something takes their breath away it is not an idle metaphor. I really did feel shortness of breath. I had a queer, delightful feeling in my heart, as though it were dilated. I felt surprise and joy and, I think, a sense of liberation; but I had just been reading the Samkhya philosophy in which art is regarded as a temporary liberation of the same sort as that absolute liberation in which all Indian religion ends, so it may be that this was no more than a reminiscence that I transferred to my actual feeling.

I cannot enjoy the same ecstasy over a beautiful thing twice over, and next day when I went to the Taj again, at the same hour, it was only with my mind that I enjoyed the same sight. On the other hand I got something else. As the sun was setting I wandered into the Mosque. I was quite alone. As I looked from one end along the chambers into which it is divided I had an eerie, mysterious sense of its emptiness and silence. I was a trifle scared. I can only put what I felt into words that make no sense: I seemed to hear the noiseless footfall of the infinite.

Sundaram. It is terribly difficult to describe an Indian. Perhaps because you know so little about his antecedents and environment, perhaps because you know so few Indians, relatively, so that you cannot compare your impressions of one with another; or perhaps it is because their personalities are fluid, as it were, without marked idiosyncrasies; or it may be, of course, that they only show you what they want to, or what they think will please and interest you. Sundaram was a Madrassi, a thick-set, plumpish man, of the middle height for a European, not very dark in colour; he was dressed in a dhoty, a white shirt and a Gandhi cap. He had a short, thick nose and a rather large mouth with fleshy lips. An engaging, ready smile. I had a notion that he was a little pleased to talk of all the very grand people he had known, but that seemed his only vanity. He was most kind. He was a puritan and he told me he had never been in a theatre or a cinema in his life. He had poetic sensibility; landscape and rivers, flowers, the sky by day and the sky by night were a delight to him. He had no logical sense and no interest in discussion. He had accepted his beliefs from the heritage of India and directly from his Guru and was glad to discourse about them at length, but was not concerned with their reasonableness. He did not mind if his ideas contradicted one another. He took his ground on feeling and intuition. In these he had implicit trust. He carried out rigorously all the precepts concerning food, bathing, meditation and so on of the orthodox Hindu. He nourished himself chiefly on milk, fruit and nuts. He told me that once when he was occupied on a serious piece of intellectual work he had lived on milk alone for six months and had kept silence. He talked of renunciation, of the Absolute and of the God that is in all of us – God is everything, we are all God – with intense sincerity. He had at his fingers' ends a number of convenient metaphors, the metaphors that have been current in India for centuries, and used them effectively; it was clear that to him they were an adequate means of reasoning. A beautiful image about the Ganges had for him all the force of a syllogism. He was evidently devoted to his wife and children and proud of them. The children were beautifully mannered. He gets up at five every morning and meditates. He considers this the most propitious hour. I saw him with some of the students of the university. He was extremely nice to them, but not with the slightly cloying affectionateness that you sometimes see in missionaries with their converts; he was natural and human.

The Empire Maker. He was a general, white-haired, with a white toothbrush moustache, tall, well covered but not fat, with a red face, blue eyes and an egg-shaped head. Every morning he went out at six for a ride, and he had a rowing-machine in his room so that he could take some exercise when he came in before he had his bath; as soon as the heat had a trifle diminished he was on the tennis court, and he played strenuously, a very good game (his boast was that he could hold his own against fellers half his age and he preferred singles because they gave you more exercise), till the darkness made it impossible to see the ball; then he went back to his room and rowed on his rowing-machine for a quarter of an hour before bathing. 'You have to keep fit in this country,' he constantly said and complained: 'I can't get enough exercise.' He had been in India for thirty years. 'The only thing that makes India possible is the shootin'. I've had a lot of Shikaris who were first-rate fellers, I mean you could trust them as much as if they were English, first-rate sportsmen, keen as mustard, I mean, except for their colour pukka white men. I'm not exaggeratin', you know. It's a fact.'

Ashwarth. He told me that when he was studying philosophy at college, he could not understand it when his teacher told him that everything was one. How could one say that one was that table and that table was oneself? It didn't seem to mean anything. And then one day he understood. He went to see the great falls that are in Mysore, and for a long way drove in a bus through the jungle. He had never seen big trees before, and when he sped along the road through a tunnel of green, with the trees towering above him, the sensation was thrilling; then he came to the waterfall; he stood at the edge of a great round pit and in front of him saw that huge mass of water, for it was just after the monsoon, falling from a prodigious height. It gave him an extraordinary emotion, he felt that he was the water, that he was falling like the water and that the water was himself; and he realized that he and the water were one. He is thirty-eight years old, fairly tall for an Indian of the Deccan, perhaps a couple of inches taller than I am, with black hair, naturally waving, that is turning grey, but his face has remained very young, with hardly a wrinkle on the forehead and no lines under the eyes; his eyes are large and swimming, his nose short, but well shaped and ever so slightly fleshy, his mouth is rather large, with full lips; his ears are small, set close to the head, but with long, fleshy lobes, like those, but of course less exaggerated, in the heads of Gautama. His face is clean-shaven, but his beard is heavy, and even after shaving it shows black through his dark, honey-coloured skin. He is not good-looking, but peculiarly attractive from the earnest candour of his expression. His teeth are excellent, very white and regular. His hands are larger than most Indians'.

He is dressed in a cotton dhoty of the cheapest material, a cotton shirt and a Gandhi cap; he wears the scarf that every Indian of condition carries and leather sandals on his bare feet. He speaks English fluently, though he has never been to England, and his voice is sonorous and pleasing. His sincerity is obvious and the goodness of his heart, but I was not so certain of his intelligence. Everything he thinks he has thought out for himself, and he does not know how many of the notions he has hammered out in suffering and meditation are lamentably commonplace. It is disconcerting when with deep feeling he gives utterance to platitudes of the utmost banality. On the other hand now and then he has a charming and even original thought.

He was arrested for a series of seditious articles which he wrote in the paper he owned, and sentenced to a year's imprisonment. He was put in a separate cell so that he should not contaminate the other prisoners by his conversation, but, though not forced to work, he asked to do so, and made carpets in the workroom with the others. He took his imprisonment very hard. He told me that he used to cry for hours at a time and sometimes would be seized with an irresistible desire to get out, and would beat at the iron bars of his cell door and try to break it open and scream till in exhaustion he threw himself on the mat and fell asleep. At the end of four months the prison food made him so ill that he was taken to the hospital, and spent there the remaining months of his imprisonment. It was then that he decided to renounce his possessions. But his trial had cost a lot of money and during his term in jail his paper did badly, so that when he was set free he found himself deeply in debt. It took him some years to pay his creditors. Then he called his employees together and gave them his paper, his machines, everything, on condition that they should pay his mother thirty rupees a month for her support and for that of his wife, his sister and his two children.

I tried to discover how his family took his decision. He was very casual about their feelings. 'They didn't like it,' he said, 'but I couldn't help that. You can't do what you think is right without causing somebody pain or inconvenience.' At his birth his horoscope was taken, and the astrologer said that he would either become a very rich, successful man, a king among men, or a sanyasin. For years his ambition had been to make a fortune and a great name for himself; but when he decided to renounce possession of everything he had, his mother, remembering what the astrologer had said, though grieved was not surprised. I asked him what he would answer when his son, on growing up, reproached him for bringing him into the world and instead of giving him the position that might have been his and a good education, had let him be brought up with only elementary knowledge so that he could be no more than a workman. He smiled quietly. 'I think he probably will reproach me,' he said, 'but he will have had a home to sleep in and food to eat, which I have provided. I do not see why just because you've brought a son into the world you must waste your life only that he should have a better one. You have rights as much as he has.'

He narrated an incident that took my fancy. The day after he had thus dispossessed himself of all he owned he went to see a friend who lived several miles out of Bangalore. He walked out, and on the way back, feeling tired, he jumped on a passing bus, but then suddenly recollected that he hadn't an anna in his pocket and was obliged to stop the bus and get out. I asked him where he lodged.

'If someone offers me shelter I sleep on the veranda, and if not, under a tree.'

'And food?'

'If someone offers me food I eat it, and if not I go without,' he answered simply.

I came to know him in rather a curious fashion. I was staying in Bombay for the second time and he wrote to me from Bangalore saying he would like to come and see me since he was assured I had something to say to him that it was important to him to know. I replied that I was a very ordinary person, a novelist and nothing else, and didn't think it could possibly be worth his while to travel for two days to see me. He came notwithstanding. I asked him how he had got the railway fare and he told me that he had gone to the station and waited. After some time he got into conversation with a man who was waiting to take the train and told him he was coming to see me, but hadn't the money to pay for a ticket. The man bought him one. I offered to pay for his return journey, but he wouldn't take money from me. 'I shall manage to get back somehow,' he smiled.

We had long talks on two successive days. I was wretchedly conscious all the time that he was expecting from me some high doctrine or at least a significant message. I had nothing to give him. He could not but have been disappointed, and it may be that I should have done better to fill him up with some highfalutin clap-trap. I couldn't bring myself to do it.

Goa. You drive through coconut groves among which you see here and there ruins of houses. On the lagoon sail fishing-boats, their lateen sails shining white in the brilliant sun. The churches are large and white, their façades decorated with honey-coloured stone pilasters. Inside they are large, bare, spacious, with pulpits in Portuguese baroque carved with the utmost elaboration and altar-pieces in the same style. In one at a side altar, a priest, a native, was saying mass with a dark-faced acolyte to serve him. There was no one to worship. In the Franciscan Church you are shown a wooden Christ on a crucifix and the guide tells you that six months before the destruction of the city it wept tears. In the cathedral they were holding a service, the organ was playing and in the organ loft there was a small choir of natives singing with a harshness in which somehow the Catholic chants acquired a mysteriously heathen, Indian character. It was strangely impressive to see these great empty churches in that deserted place and to know that day by day with not a soul to listen the priests said mass in them.

The priest. He came to see me at the hotel. He was a tall Indian, neither thin nor fat, with good, somewhat blunt features and large dark liquid eyes, with shining whites to them. He wore a cassock. At first he was very nervous and his hands moved restlessly, but I did what I could to put him at his ease, and presently his hands were still. He spoke very good English. He told me that he was of Brahmin family, his ancestor, a Brahmin, having been converted by one of the companions of St Francis Xavier. He was a man in the early thirties, of powerful physique and of a fine presence. His voice was rich and musical. He had been six years in Rome and during his stay in Europe had travelled much. He wanted to go back, but his mother was old and wished him to remain in Goa till she died. He taught in a school and preached. He spent much of his time converting the Sudras. He said it was hopeless now to try to do anything with the high-caste Hindus. I tried to get him to speak of religion. He told me that he thought Christianity was large enough to embrace all the other faiths, but regretted that Rome had not allowed the Indian Church to develop according to the native inclinations. I got the impression that he accepted the Christian dogmas as a discipline, but without fervour, and I am not sure that if one had been able to get to the bottom of his beliefs one would not have found that they were held with at least a certain scepticism. I had a feeling that even though there were four hundred years of Catholicism behind him he was still at heart a Vedantist. I wondered if to him the God of the Christians was not merged, if not in his mind, at least in some obscure depth of the unconscious, with the Brahman of the Upanishads. He told me that even among the Christians the caste system still obtained to this extent that none of them married out of his own caste. It would be unheard of that a Christian of Brahmin extraction should marry a Christian of Sudra extraction. He was not displeased to tell me that there was not in his veins a drop of white blood; his family had always kept resolutely pure. 'We're Christians,' he said to me, 'but first of all we're Hindus.' His attitude to Hinduism was tolerant and sympathetic.

The backwaters of Travancore. They are narrow canals, more or less artificial, that is to say natural stretches of water have been joined up by embanked channels to make a waterway from Trivandrum to Cochin. On each side grow coconuts, and thatched houses with mud roofs stand at the water's edge, each surrounded by its little compound in which grow bananas, papaya and sometimes a jack tree. Children play; women sit about, or pound rice; in frail boats, sometimes carrying loads of coconuts or leaves or provender for cattle, men and boys slowly paddle up and down: on the banks people fish. I saw one man with a bow and arrow and a little bundle of fish that he had shot. Everyone bathes. It is green, cool and quiet. You get a very curious impression of pastoral life, peaceful and primitive, and not too hard. Now and then a big barge passes, poled by two men from one town to another. Here and there is a modest little temple or a tiny chapel, for a large proportion of the population is Christian.

The river is grown over with the water hyacinth. The plants, with their delicate mauve flowers, rooted not in soil but in water, float along, and as your boat passes through, making a channel of clear water, they are pushed aside; but no sooner has it passed than they drift back with the stream and the breeze, and no trace that you have gone that way remains. So with us who have made some small stir in the world.

The Dewan. I had been told that he was not only an astute but an unscrupulous politician. Everyone agreed that he was as clever as he was crooked. He was a thickset, sturdy man, no taller than I, with alert but not very large eyes, a broad brow, a hooked nose, full lips and a small rounded chin. He had a thick crop of fuzzy hair. He was dressed in a white dhoty, a white tunic fitting close round the neck, and a white scarf; his feet were bare and he wore sandals which he slipped on and off. He had the geniality of the politician who for years has gone out of his way to be cordial with everyone he meets. He talked very good English, fluently, with a copious choice of words, and he put what he had to say plainly and with logical sequence. He had a resonant voice and an easy manner. He did not agree with a good deal that I said and corrected me with decision, but with the courtesy that took it for granted I was too intelligent to be affronted by contradiction. He was of course very busy, having all the affairs of the state in his charge, but seemed to have enough leisure to talk for the best part of an hour on Indian metaphysics and religion as though there were nothing that interested him more. He seemed well read not only in Indian literature, but in English, but there was no indication that he had any acquaintance with the literature or thought of other European countries.

When I began to speak of religion in India as being the basis of all their philosophy, he corrected me. 'No,' he said, 'that is not so; there is no religion in India in your sense of the word; there are systems of philosophy, and theism, Hindu theism, is one of its varieties.'

I asked him if educated, cultured Hindus had still an active belief in Karma and transmigration. He answered with emphasis. 'I absolutely believe in it myself with all the strength of my being. I am convinced that I have passed through innumerable lives before this one and that I shall have to pass through I do not know how many more before I secure release. Karma and transmigration are the only possible explanations I can see for the inequalities of men and for the evil of the world. Unless I believed in them I should think the world meaningless.'

I asked him if, believing this, the Hindu feared death less than the European. He took a little time to think of his answer, and, as I had already discovered was his way, while he was considering it, talked of something else so that I thought he was not going to answer. Then he said: 'The Indian is not like the Japanese who has been taught from his earliest years that life is of no value and that there are a number of reasons for which he must not hesitate for an instant to sacrifice it. The Indian does not fear death because it will take him away from life, he fears it because there is uncertainty in what condition he may be born next. He can have no assurance that he will be born a Brahmin, an angel or even a God, he may be born a Sudra, a dog or a worm. When he thinks of death it is the future he fears.'

The viña-player. He was a stoutish man of forty, clean-shaven, with all the front part of his head shaven too; his hair, long at the back, was tied in a knot. He was dressed in a dhoty and a collarless shirt. He sat on the floor to play. His instrument was highly decorated, carved in low relief and ending in a dragon's head. He played for a couple of hours, now and then breaking into a few bars of song, music hundreds of years old, but some much less, music of the last century when under a Maharajah of Travancore, himself an accomplished musician, there was great enthusiasm for the art. It is elaborate music, which requires all your attention, and I do not think I could have followed it at all if I hadn't had some acquaintance with modern music. It is slowly rhythmical and when your ear gets accustomed to it various and tuneful. Of late years the composers have been not a little influenced by modern music, European music, and it is queer in these Eastern melodies to discern a faint recollection of the bagpipes or the martial din of a military band.

A Hindu house. The owner was a judge who had inherited it from his fathers. He was dead. and I was received by his widow, a stout woman in white with white curly hair hanging down her back, and bare feet. You entered by a door in a blank wall and found yourself in a sort of loggia with a carved wooden ceiling of jackwood. It was decorated with lotus leaves and in the centre a bas-relief of Siva dancing. Then came a small dusty courtyard in which were growing crotons and cassias. Then the house. In front was a veranda with hanging eaves, showing the open woodwork of the roof, beautifully joined, and with a carved ceiling of a rich brown like that of the loggia. At each end was a raised part under which were receptacles in which the owner normally kept his clothes and which served as seats. Here he received his guests. At the back were two doors with rich locks and hinges of decorated brass; they led to two small dark rooms, with one bed in each, and in one of which the master of the house had slept. At one side was a closed aperture which led to a space in which the grain was kept. Going through a small door at the side you came into another courtyard; at the back of this were the women's apartments and on the sides the kitchen and other small rooms. I was shown into one room in which was some poor, shabby and old-fashioned European furniture.

The first courtyard at night would surely lose its dusty neglected aspect, and under the moon and the stars, cool and silent, form a romantic setting. I should have liked to listen there to the viña-player, his absorbed and serious face lit by the smoky flame of a brass lamp, its wick floating in coconut oil.

The Yogi. He was of average height for an Indian, of a dark honey colour, with close-cropped white hair and a close-cropped white beard. He was not stout, but plump. Though he wore nothing but a white loin-cloth he looked neat, very clean and almost dapper. He walked slowly, leaning on a stick, and he had a slight limp. His mouth was somewhat large, with thickish lips, and his eyes were neither so big nor so lustrous as are the eyes of most Indians; the whites were bloodshot. He bore himself with simplicity and at the same time with dignity. He was cheerful, smiling, polite; he did not give me the impression of a scholar, but rather of a sweet-natured old peasant. He came into the room in which I was lying down on a pallet bed, followed by two or three disciples, and after a few words of cordial greeting seated himself. I was not very well, having fainted a little time before, and he sat close to me. It was because he had been told that I was not well enough to go to the hall in which he ordinarily sat that he came to the little room into which I had been carried.

After the first few moments he ceased to look at me and with a sidelong stare of a peculiar fixity gazed as it were over my shoulder. His body was absolutely still, but one of his feet tapped now and then a little on the floor. He remained thus for perhaps a quarter of an hour, and they told me afterwards that he was concentrating in meditation on me. Then he broke off and asked me whether I wished to say anything to him or to ask him any questions. I was feeling weak and ill and said so, whereupon he smiled and said: 'Silence also is conversation.' He turned his head away again slightly and resumed his concentrated meditation, again looking as it were over my shoulder. He remained like this for perhaps another quarter of an hour, no one saying a word, the other persons in the room with their eyes riveted on him, and then got up, bowed, smiled a farewell and slowly, leaning on his stick, followed by his disciples, limped out of the room.

I don't know whether it was the result of rest or of the Yogi's meditation, but I felt very much better, and a little later I went into the hall where he sits by day and sleeps by night. It is a long bare room fifty feet long, I should think, and about half as broad. There are windows all round it, but the overhanging roof dims the light. The Yogi sat on a low dais on a tiger skin and in front of him was a small brazier in which incense was burning. Its scent was agreeable to the nostrils. Now and again a disciple came forward and lit another stick. The faithful sat on the floor. Some were reading; others meditated. Presently two strangers came in with a basket of fruit, prostrated themselves before the Yogi and presented their offering. He accepted it with a slight inclination of the head and motioned to a disciple to take it away; he spoke kindly for a little to the strangers and then with another little inclination of the head signified to them that they were to withdraw. They prostrated themselves again and went and sat among the rest of the faithful. Then the Yogi became abstracted in meditation, a little shiver seemed to pass through all who were there, and I tiptoed out of the hall.

I heard later that my fainting had given rise to fantastic rumours. The news of it was carried not only to various parts of India, but even reached America. It was ascribed by some to the awe that overcame me at the prospect of going into the presence of the holy man. Others said that his influence, acting on me before ever I saw him, had caused me to be rapt for several minutes into the infinite. When I was asked about it I was content to smile and shrug my shoulders. In point of fact that was neither the first nor the last time I have fainted. Doctors tell me it is due to an irrit-

ability of the solar plexus which presses my diaphragm against my
heart and that one day the pressure will continue a little too long.
One feels unwell for a few minutes and then one knows nothing
more till one regains consciousness – if one does.

Madura. The temple at night. There is always a noise in India.
People talk all day long at the top of their voices, but in the
temple they talk more loudly than ever. The row is terrific.
People pray and recite litanies, they call to one another, voci-
ferously discuss, quarrel or greet one another. There is nothing
that suggests reverence and yet there is a vehement overwhelming
sense of the divine that sends cold shivers down your spine.
In some strange way the gods there seem to be near and living.

The throng is dense, men, women and children. The men
are stripped to the waist, and their foreheads, and often their
arms and chests, are thickly smeared with the white ash of
burnt cow-dung. Many of them in the day-time, while going
about their ordinary affairs, wear European clothes, but here
they have discarded Western dress, Western civilization and
Western ways of thought. Here in the temple is the native
India that knows nothing of the West. You see them making
obeisance at one shrine or another and sometimes lying full
length on the ground, face downwards in the ritual attitude of
prostration.

You pass through long halls, the roof supported by sculp-
tured columns, and at the foot of each column is seated a religious
mendicant. Some are old and bearded, some terribly emaciated,
some are young, brawny and hirsute. Each has in front of him
a bowl for offerings or a small mat on which the faithful now
and again throw a copper coin. Some are clad in red, some are
almost naked. Some look at you vacantly as you pass, some are
reading, silently or aloud, and take no notice of the streaming
throng. Sitting on the floor, outside the adytum, is a group of
priests, the fore part of their skulls shaven, the hair at the back
tied in a knot, rather stout, their hairless brown chests and their
fleshy arms streaked with white ash. One, a scholar and a noted
holy man, in a red turban, with bracelets on his arms, and a

coloured dhoty, with a grey beard and an authoritative manner, comes followed by two or three pupils, utters a prayer at a shrine, and then, with the dignity of a man who is respected, the way cleared for him by his pupils, strides into the holy of holies.

The temple is lit by naked electric bulbs that hang from the ceiling and throw a harsh light on the sculpture, but where they do not penetrate render the darkness more mysterious. The impression you take away with you, notwithstanding that vast, noisy throng, or maybe because of it, is of something secret and terrible.

When I was leaving India people asked me which of all the sights I had seen had most impressed me. I answered as they expected me to answer. But it wasn't the Ta Mahal, the *ghats* of Benares, the temple at Madura or the mountains of Travancore that had most moved me; it was the peasant, terribly emaciated, with nothing to cover his nakedness but a rag round his middle the colour of the sun-baked earth he tilled, the peasant shivering in the cold of dawn, sweating in the heat of noon, working still as the sun set red over the parched fields, the starveling peasant toiling without cease in the north, in the south, in the east, in the west, toiling all over the vastness of India, toiling as he had toiled from father to son back, back for three thousand years when the Aryans had first descended upon the country, toiling for a scant subsistence, his only hope to keep body and soul together. That was the sight that had given me the most poignant emotion in India.

Wellington is supposed to have said that the Battle of Waterloo was won on the playing fields of Eton. It may be that the historians of the future will say that India was lost in the public schools of England.

1939

Lens. The *table d'hôte*. A long table at which sat a number of youngish men respectably dressed in dark clothes, but who gave

you the impression that they hadn't had a bath for some time.
They were school teachers, insurance clerks, shop-assistants and
what not. Most of them read the evening paper while they dined.
They ate their food greedily, a lot of bread, and drank *vin
ordinaire*. They talked little. Suddenly a man came in. '*Voilà
Jules*,' they cried, and seemed to wake up. Jules brought gaiety.
He was a thin man of thirty, with a pointed red face and a
comic look; you could well see him as a clown at the circus.
His fun consisted in throwing bread pellets at all and sundry,
and when he hit anybody, the person hit cried: *un obus qui tombe
du ciel*.

They were all on friendly terms with the waiter, whom they
tutoyé'd, and who *tutoyé*'d them. A little girl, the daughter of
the *patron*, sat on a bench knitting a foulard and they chaffed
her not unkindly; you got the sensation that they looked forward
to the time when they could make a pass at her.

The miners' village. Rows of little two-storey houses of red brick,
with roofs of red tiles and large windows. Each one has at the
back its bit of garden in which the miner grows vegetables and
flowers. A house has four rooms, a parlour in front, which is
hardly ever used, with a thick flowered lace curtain at the window,
a kitchen behind and two bedrooms above. In the parlour there
is a round table covered with a cloth, three or four straight-
backed chairs, and on the walls enlarged photographs of the
family. The family life is lived in the kitchen. A gun hangs on
the wall and pictures of film favourites. A stove, a radio, a table
covered with oil-cloth, and oil-cloth on the floor. A string is
stretched across to hang the washing on. A smell of cooking.
The radio goes from morning till night, Tito Rossi, the Lambeth
Walk, dance tunes. On washing-day a huge cauldron stands on
the stove.

When visitors come in they are offered a drink of rum. The
conversation turns on money and the cost of things, who has
married whom and what such a one is doing.

The miner comes downstairs in the morning and has his
breakfast of coffee and rum. He goes over to the sink and

washes his hands and face. He is dressed, all but his boots and coat, and these his wife hands him.

L.'s sister. A tall thin dark-haired woman, with fine features and fine eyes. She has lost two or three teeth. She is thirty-two, but looks fifty; she is haggard and her skin is dry and lined. She wears a black skirt and blouse and a blue apron. The four children are dirty, poorly dressed in odds and ends that their mother has made for them out of old clothes. One little girl has ear-ache and wears a scarf tied round her head. L.'s brother-in-law. He's thirty-five, but looks much older. He has a squarish, irregular, weather-beaten face, but a good-natured and amiable though rather obstinate look. He speaks seldom, and then slowly, in a pleasant voice. He is more at home with patois than with French. He has large, grimy hands and looks strong. His grey eyes have a soft, rather pathetic look accentuated by the coal dust on the lashes which no washing can remove.

The foreman. A merry soul, with a loud voice and a sort of fat Flemish joviality. He loves his comforts, his coffee and rum and his glass of wine. His wife is a large stout woman with untidy greying hair, a red face and a cheerful expression. She enjoys her food and for Christmas they had a real blow-out. She tells you how much the chicken cost and goes over the meal with gusto. They sat talking, listening to the radio and singing till four in the morning.

They have two sons. They didn't want the elder to become a miner and so made him a carpenter, but during his first week he had his right hand cut off by a circular saw, and now (a spectacled youth) he has some job in the mine. The younger son went down the mine without more ado.

Boys used to start at twelve, but now not till they are fourteen, and they work eight hours a day in three shifts at sorting out the stone from the coal. It is passed along on a moving pan and a little group of them side by side hurry to pick out the chips as the pan goes by. They look odd with tight-fitting caps on their heads and their blue overalls, their faces as black as their clothes, and the whites of their eyes shining.

A man hasn't the knowledge to become a skilled miner till he is thirty, and by forty-five he has lost the best of his strength, so that he has to do lighter work, for which he gets less money. At fifty-five he gets his pension, three thousand francs for himself and the same for his wife, but seldom lives to enjoy it for more than a year or two. He speaks of dying between fifty-five and sixty quite calmly, as something that is in the natural order of things.

He gets his house at a nominal rent of eight to ten francs a month and four hundred kilos of coal a month. He works five days a week for sixty francs a day and a supplement of twenty-five per cent, but if he is asked to work overtime and refuses he loses his supplement.

Medical attention is free, but he complains that the doctors neglect him; if they are busy they don't come till the day after they are called, and medical supplies are inadequate.

The miners are friendly, kindly, helpful people. They know that their work depends on the work of others and so a natural good fellowship exists between them. Some of them live an hour or more away from the mine and come in on their bikes. They are attached to their ugly little village and even if they can get a house near the mine won't leave it.

Besides the skilled miners who get out the coal, make the passages and do the tunnelling, there are the unskilled workmen who look after the electricity, drive the trucks that bring the coal from where it has been loaded to the lifts, and push the loaded trucks into the lift. The truck has to be uncoupled, pushed by hand along the curved rail and got into the lift. A man will push twelve hundred trucks into the lift in the course of a shift. It is hard work and he is paid twenty francs a day. Before the last strike he was only paid fourteen.

The lift is very shaky. It travels at a great rate, rattling fearfully, up and down. When it reaches the bottom the empty truck has to be pushed out again.

Chez Angelique. A smallish square room with a bar at the back of it and a lot of bottles on shelves. There are two or three square tables with a bench against the wall and chairs in front, and in the middle of the room a round table. Several miners are sitting at it and with them a heavily-built soldier in uniform on leave. One man is doing tricks with a piece of wool, a childish trick which thrills them, and they buy rounds of drinks on it. They are all friendly and cordial. At another table four men are playing cards. They talk little, mostly about the work and the price of things.

The family lives in a room behind the bar. There is a sick Pole in bed and half a dozen people are crowded round him. The air is foul.

The Poles look very different from the French. They have square heads and thick-set bodies and even through the black of the coal their skins seem white. They are on good terms with the French, but keep a good deal to themselves. They eat very sparingly, more so than the French, and put by money to send home to buy a farm with. They drink chiefly on public holidays and at marriages, when they have a great party and spend all they have. Then they economize for months to make up. They speak French haltingly, with a marked accent.

A bath is a serious business. The water is heated in the copper used for the household washing and in this the miner takes his bath. Young miners proud to show that they go down the mine walk about unwashed. When they are single they take a room, or a bed in a room, in a widow's house or in someone's who hasn't a large family. They go into Lens to go to the brothel, either by motor-bus or on their bike.

The tunnels are a little higher than an ordinary man's height. They are very long, lit coldly by naked bulbs, and a bitter wind blows down them. It is strange to walk along them and meet never a soul. They turn and twist, and one leads out of another, and you wonder how anyone can find his way; but the foreman told me he could do so blindfold.

It is wonderfully mysterious when you come suddenly upon a little group at work. You creep through a hole in the wall of the tunnel and scramble or crawl along a narrow passage, sometimes on all fours, till you come to where they are continuing the tunnel or actually mining the coal. The drill is so heavy that it needs two men to lift it, and the din it makes is infernal.

The light is dim, and the miners, stripped to the waist, with caps on to protect their heads, look hardly human.

Half-way through the day's shift they get half an hour off for lunch. They sit down on the coal dust and eat the food they have brought with them in a canister, a great lump of bread, buttered or with a stick of sausage inside it, and drink weak coffee out of a metal bottle.

The day's food. In the morning black coffee, bread-and-butter. At noon, when at home, soup, steak or veal, the vegetables that have gone to make the soup, and potatoes. They drink beer which is often made at home and is almost non-alcoholic; it has a peculiar taste that you have to get used to. At supper, coffee again and bread-and-butter, and if flush, a slice of ham.

In none of the houses is there any sign of comfort, nor does there seem any desire for it. They are content with their wages and all they ask is that things should remain as they are. Work, food, sleep, the radio: these are their lives.

The manager warned me that a visitor thinks the work much harder than it really is. Habit makes it, if not easy, at least tolerable. He is a young man, short, clean-shaven, dapper, with a prettyish wife with a long nose, in a red dress, and two children. He is enthusiastic about the business and seems intelligent, sympathetic and well-read. His wife's father, *procureur général* at Amiens, is staying with them, a smallish, elderly man, with a grey square beard. He is a fluent talker and tells you with great conviction what everyone has been saying for the last hundred years as though it were a considered opinion he has arrived at after intensive reflection. A thoroughly honest, worthy, narrow and boring man.

Murder on the Riviera. Jack M. was in bed with pneumonia when a telegram arrived telling him that his mother, Mrs Albert M., who had been living in a hotel at San Rafael, had been murdered. Since he could not move, his wife flew out in his place. Of course she was shocked, but at the same time could not but feel a blessed sense of relief. Her mother-in-law had made life almost intolerable to her. She found fault with Mary because she liked to go to parties and dances, because she spent good money on her clothes; she disapproved of the way she ran her house and brought up her children. What made it worse was that Jack admired and adored his mother. In his eyes she could do no wrong. Mary could never have stood the strain but for Mrs Albert's habit of spending every winter at San Rafael.

The plane put her down at Cannes, where an English lawyer, to whom Jack M. had wired, met her. As they drove to San Rafael he gave her the facts.

'You'll have to know them sometime. The local papers are full of the case.'

Mrs Albert had been found dead in her bed, strangled, and her money and her pearls had been stolen. She was stark naked.

'You know, the Riviera sometimes has an unfortunate effect on these lonely middle-aged women who come here from England and America.'

Mrs Albert was well-known at San Rafael. She was in the habit of frequenting bars and cafés where they danced, and it was with the lowest of the riff-raff that she hob-nobbed. She was a generous old girl always ready to stand drinks, and though they laughed at her they liked her. Two or three times a week she would take one of the roughs back to her hotel and he was always sure of a thousand francs in the morning. It was evidently one of her lovers who had killed her.

Mary listened to the story with consternation and yet with exultation. Now she would be able to get even with the woman who had tormented her for years. It would be a wonderful revenge to tell Jack that this pattern of all the virtues whom he had held up as a model for her to follow was just an old rip.

'Do they know who did it?' she asked.

'No, it might be any one of a dozen. She was pretty promiscuous.'

'It'll be a blow to my husband.'

'Need he ever know? They'd be glad to hush the whole thing up here and let it go for burglary and murder. A nasty scandal wouldn't do any good to a wintering-place like San Rafael.'

'Why should it be hushed up?'

'Well, for all your sakes and for your mother-in-law's. I daresay she led a pretty dull life in England. Are you going to blame her very much because she wanted to have a bit of fun before she died?'

Mary was silent for a long time. Then she said something that surprised herself.

'I hated the old bitch. I could have killed her myself and sometimes I wonder why I didn't. But now I know all I do know, for the first time since I married my husband I think I've got a sort of sneaking affection for her.'

Pasquier dying. He had a small café in one of the side streets of Nice, with a small, airless room at the back in which people danced. He owned or rented the house above the café, and you entered by a side door. He lived there, but he let the rooms for an hour or a night to the men who' had picked up a woman in the café. Now that Pasquier was so ill it was being run by his son, Edmond, and his son's wife. Edmond had married one of the women who frequented the café and Pasquier, outraged at the *mésalliance*, had turned them out of the house, but he was not one to let honour conflict with interest, and since Edmond was useful to him, he soon took him back. That night when I went in the place was crowded. The fleet were in and they were doing land-office business. I asked Edmond how his father was and he told me the doctor had given him up and he could not last more than a day or two longer. He asked me to go and see him. I went round, and Jeanne, the woman who showed clients to their room, took me up to him. He was lying in a huge four-poster, a little old man in a night-shirt, his face sallow and puffy, and his hands swollen.

'*Je suis foutu,*' he said to me.

'Nonsense,' I said with the false cheerfulness one puts on with the sick, 'you'll get well.'

'I'm not afraid. How is it downstairs? Full?'

'Crammed.'

He perked up.

'If I had twice the number of rooms I could fill them tonight.' He rang his bell. 'It's terrible I should have to lie here and can't look after things myself.' The maid came in. 'Go and knock on the doors,' he told her, 'and tell them to be quick. Others are waiting. *Mon Dieu*, it doesn't take all night to do what they've come here to do.' And when the maid went out: 'When I think of my poor wife I'm glad she's dead; she'd have died with shame when Edmond married a tart. And mind you, we gave him a good education. Do you know what they're going to do when I'm gone? They're going to clear the women out and let the rooms by the month to clerks and shop-assistants. They can't make money like that. And, why couldn't he marry a *bourgeoise*, the daughter of decent tradespeople, who understood that business is business? It's hard to lie here and know that this business I've built up will go to pot as soon as I'm dead and buried.' Two heavy tears rolled down his cheeks. 'And for why?' he sniffled. 'Because the dirty bitch wants to be respectable. Do people pay you money because they respect you? *Merde.*'

He died two or three days later. The hearse was loaded with flowers and quite a number of the girls who frequented the café went to the funeral. 'It shows that they have good hearts,' Edmond's wife said to me afterwards.

Romance. The Duke of York, a brother of George III, came to Monaco on his yacht and there fell very seriously ill. He asked the ruling prince to receive him and this the prince consented to do, but refused to receive the mistress whom the Duke had brought with him on the yacht. She took a house at Roquebrune and every day went out to the point to see if the flag was still flying over the palace. One day she saw it at half-mast and knew her lover was dead. She threw herself into the sea.

The other day, after dinner in Grosvenor Square, I listened to an author, no longer young, complaining of the small esteem in which men of letters are held in England to-day. He compared it unfavourably with the position they had in the eighteenth century when they were arbiters of taste in the coffee-houses and the munificence of patrons saved them from having to prostitute their gifts for filthy lucre. I wondered it didn't occur to him that in the eighteenth century, if he and I had been in that house at all we should have come up the back stairs, and if we had been given a meal it would have consisted of a tankard of beer and a cut off the cold joint in the housekeeper's room.

His name was Paul. He was a Belgian, and he murdered his wife. He was tried and sentenced to death. He took his condemnation very hard. He was terribly hysterical. He couldn't sleep. He was pitiably afraid. Alan was told to visit him to see whether he couldn't comfort him a little, and if not console him at least help him to be resigned to his fate. Alan went to see him every day. One day he told me that he wanted to read a book which wasn't in the prison library and asked me if I would buy it. Of course I said I would, and asked what it was. The answer astounded me. I couldn't think why a man should want so much to read that particular book before he was hanged. It was Sterne's *Sentimental Journey*.

Hotel bedrooms. In one of them there is a man who looks upon an hotel bedroom as a symbol of liberty. He thinks of the adventures he has had in such rooms, the pleasant meditations; and his thoughts are so peaceful and happy that he feels the moment can never be excelled and so takes an overdose of sleeping-pills. In another room is a woman who has wandered for years from hotel to hotel. To her it is misery. She has no home. If she isn't living in an hotel it is because she has shamed friends into asking her to stay with them for a week or two. They take her out of pity, they see her go with relief. She feels she can't bear the wretchedness of her life any longer, and so she too takes an overdose of her sleeping-pills. To the hotel people and the Press the mystery is insoluble. They suspect a romance. They look for a connection between the two, but can discover nothing.

He was a successful lawyer, and it was a shock to his family and his friends when he committed suicide. He was a breezy, energetic, exuberant man, and the last person you would have expected to do away with himself. He enjoyed life. His origins were humble, but for his services in the war he had been granted a baronetcy. He adored his only son, who would succeed to his title, follow him in his business, go into Parliament and make a name for himself. No one could guess why he had killed himself. He had arranged it so that it should look like an accident, and so it would have been considered except for a small oversight on his part. It was true that his wife was causing him a certain amount of anxiety. She was at the menopause and it had affected her brain, she was not mad enough to be put in an asylum, but certainly not sane. She suffered from severe melancholia. They didn't tell her that her husband had committed suicide, but only that he had been killed in a motor accident. She took it better than was expected. It was her doctor who broke the news to her. 'Thank God I told him when I did,' she said. 'If I hadn't I should never have had another moment's peace in my life.' The doctor wanted to know what she meant. After a while she told him: she had confessed to her husband that the son he doted on, the son on whom all his hopes were set, was not his.

Bermondsey. A plumber went to the house of some retired tradespeople to do some repairs. They lived in a semi-detached house in Kennington. He was a good-looking youth and their daughter fell in love with him. They met at nights in the road. But he felt that she was deeply conscious of the distance between them and he got it into his head that she treated him as a servant. He made up his mind that he'd get even with her. He put her in the family way. Her parents turned her out. The plumber refused to marry her, but she went to live with him, and after the child was born she went to work in a biscuit factory. The baby was farmed out. At the factory one of the workers fell in love with her and asked her to marry him. She knew the plumber didn't care two pins for her, so she left him; the plumber was furious with her, and when he found out that she was going to marry the other man he went to him and told him that he had had a child by her. The man then refused to have anything more to do with her.

Bermondsey. A man gassed in the war was living on a pension with his wife in two rooms on the ground floor of a three-storey house. They both belonged to a burial club. He had been ill for a long time and at last he realized he was dying and couldn't live more than a few days longer. He got his wife to consent to use the money she would get for his funeral on one last beano. They invited all their friends and had a grand supper with champagne. He died the night following. The money from the burial club was spent, but the friends clubbed together to give him a fine funeral; his widow wouldn't hear of it, and he was followed by all of them to his pauper's grave. Later in the day one of them went to see the widow and asked her to marry him. She was surprised, but after thinking it over for a little consented; but she felt it wouldn't be right to marry him before the year's mourning was out, so she suggested that until then he might come and live with her as a lodger.

Bermondsey. A man, an ex-soldier, and a girl working in a factory fall desperately in love with one another. He is unhappily married to a nagging, jealous wife. The pair elope and take lodgings in Stepney. By the papers the girl discovers to her horror that the man has killed his wife. He must inevitably be caught, but while they are hiding they give themselves over to their passion. She comes to understand that to avoid arrest he intends to kill himself and her too. She is frightened and wants to flee from him, but she loves him too much to tear herself away. She leaves it too late. The police come and he shoots her before shooting himself.

Bermondsey. Dan has been out of work for months. He is miserable and humiliated, and his brother Bert, who is in work, bullies him. He throws it in Dan's face that he keeps him. To take it out of him he makes him do odd jobs for him. Dan is so wretched that he feels he'd like to make an end of himself, and it requires all his mother's persuasion to get him to wait till something turns up. The mother, Mrs Bailey, is a charwoman who works in a Government office in Whitehall. She goes out at six in the morning and doesn't get back till six at night. One day Bert comes home and because Dan hasn't fetched his other shirt from the laundry and he wants to go out, he swears at him. They have a fight and Dan, smaller, weaker, ill fed, gets a thrashing. Mrs Bailey comes in and stops the fight. She roundly abuses Bert. He says he's sick of it all and he's going to be married. They are horrified; without his week's money, with Dan earning nothing, it's impossible for Mrs Bailey to support herself, Dan and the two younger children. It means starvation. They tell Bert he can't get married, at least not till Dan gets work; he says he must, his girl's going to have a baby. He flings out. They are all crying. Mrs Bailey goes down on her knees and makes the others, Dan and the two children, do so too, and she prays God to have mercy on them and help them. They are still praying when Bert comes back with the shirt he has just fetched for himself. He looks at them angrily.

'Oh, all right, all right,' he shouts. 'I'll give her ten bob to get rid of the little bastard.'

Mrs Bailey. She was a tallish woman, with reddish, untidy, scanty hair, and when she opened her mouth you saw that two of her front teeth were missing. One of her ears was partly torn off by her husband, and there was a scar on her forehead which was the result of a cut when once he had thrown her out of a window. He was a big, strong, brutal fellow who had been badly wounded in the war, and Mrs Bailey forgave him his violence because he was often in great pain. They had four children and they all went in terror of him. But Mrs Bailey had a strong sense of humour the real Cockney humour, and when she wasn't in fear of her life was full of fun. She loved a good laugh. At last Bailey died. I went to see her after his death and she said to me: 'He wasn't a bad man really. D'you know what he said to me? They was almost his last words. "I've given you hell, haven't I? You'll be glad to be rid of me." "No, I won't, Ned," I said to him, "you know I've always loved you." He gave me a funny look, and d'you know what he said? "You old cow," he said. That shows he loved me really, doesn't it? – calling me an old cow like that, I mean.'

These are a few of the notes I made when I intended to write a novel about the people of Bermondsey.

1940

I got into conversation the other day with a French officer, and of course we talked of the collapse of France. '*Et dire que nous avons été battus par des imbéciles,*' he said. His remark dismayed me. The French seem incapable of understanding that if they have been so shamefully defeated, it is not in spite of the Germans being stupid, but because on the contrary they are clever. Because the French were well-educated, good and witty talkers, they were silly enough to think that they alone were intelligent. Their self-conceit, which led them to despise everything that wasn't French, made them the most insular people in Europe. When they were in a mess they really believed that a *bon mot* could get them out of it. But when something goes wrong with your car it isn't a sound knowledge of the classics or a neat quip that'll make it go right; you want a mechanic for that, and in such a juncture his intelligence is the only one that counts, yours is stupidity. Was it so witless of the Germans to make themselves familiar with the methods of modern warfare and to provide themselves with modern armaments? Wasn't there cleverness in their organisation of the war machine so that it should function with efficiency? Didn't they show acumen when they informed themselves accurately on conditions in France so that they were able to take advantage of its disunity, unpreparedness and emotional instability? No, it isn't the Germans who were imbeciles in the war, it's the

French; but what hope can one cherish for the restoration of France when the French, overcome by such a catastrophe, still entertain so inept a vanity? The Allies can talk till they're blue in the face of the necessity of restoring France to her place as one of the great powers; they will never succeed till the French learn to look the truth in the face and see themselves as they are. And the first thing they must learn is not humility, that can do them no good, but common-sense.

1941

New York. H. G. has been here. He was looking old, tired and shrivelled. He was as perky as he has always been, but with something of an effort. His lectures were a failure. People couldn't hear what he said and didn't want to listen to what they could hear. They left in droves. He was hurt and disappointed. He couldn't understand why they were impatient with him for saying very much the same sort of thing as he had been saying for the last thirty years. The river has flowed on and left him high and dry on the bank. The writer has his little hour (if he's lucky), but an hour is soon past. After all, he's had it and he ought to be satisfied. It's only reasonable that others should have their turn. One would have thought it would be enough for H. G. to reflect on the great influence he had on a whole generation and how much he did to alter the climate of opinion. But he has always been too busy to be anything of a philosopher.

She feels in a terrifyingly commonplace way the most obvious emotions not only with sincerity, but with an almost unbelievable assurance that no one has ever felt them before. The ingenuousness of this middle-aged woman of the world is so ridiculous that it is not absurd but touching. She is as clever as she can stick, and so stupid that you could beat her.

One fusses about style. One tries to write better. One takes pains to be simple, clear and succinct. One aims at rhythm and balance.

One reads a sentence aloud to see that it sounds well. One sweats one's guts out. The fact remains that the four greatest novelists the world has ever known, Balzac, Dickens, Tolstoi and Dostoievsky, wrote their respective languages very indifferently. It proves that if you can tell stories, create character, devise incident, and if you have sincerity and passion, it doesn't matter a damn how you write. All the same it's better to write well than ill.

Sentimentality is only sentiment that rubs you up the wrong way.

The world has always been a place of turmoil. There have been short periods of peace and plenty, but they are exceptional, and because some of us have lived in such a period – the late years of the nineteenth century, the first decade of the twentieth – we have no right to look upon such a state as normal. Man is born unto trouble as the sparks fly upwards: that is normal, and we may just as well accept the fact. If we do, we can regard it with that mingling of resignation and humour which is probably our best defence.

Why is it that when you hear a young man talking arrant nonsense with assurance, being dogmatic and intolerant, you are angry and point out to him his foolishness and ignorance? Do you forget that at his age you were just as silly, dogmatic, arrogant and conceited? And when I say *you* of course I mean *I*.

He would be astounded if you told him he was a crook. He honestly looks upon a fifty-fifty proposition as seventy-five for himself and twenty-five for the other fellow.

Fundamentally man is not a rational animal. It is this that makes fiction so difficult to write; for the reader, or the spectator of a play, demands, at all events to-day, that he should behave as if he were. We feel dissatisfied when the persons of a story do not act from motives that we accept as sufficient. We expect their behaviour to be rational, and if it isn't we say: 'But people don't act like that.' Our demand for probability grows more and more stringent. We balk at coincidence and accident. We expect the characters that are presented to us invariably to behave like themselves.

The behaviour of the persons in *Othello*, of Othello himself principally, but to a less extent of almost everyone in the play, is wildly irrational. The critics have turned themselves inside out to show that it isn't. In vain. They would have done better to accept it as a grand example of the fundamental irrationality of man. I am quite ready to believe that contemporary theatregoers saw nothing improbable in the behaviour of any of the characters.

I don't know why it is that the religious never ascribe common-sense to God.

When I was young I pretended to know everything. It often got me into trouble and made me look a fool. I think one of the most useful discoveries I ever made was how easy it is to say: 'I don't know.' I never noticed that it made anyone think the worse of me. The only inconvenience is that there are people who have nothing better to do than to tell you at tedious length all about something of which you have confessed your ignorance. But there are quite a number of things that I don't *want* to know about.

The subjunctive. American writers use the subjunctive much more than we do. I suppose they are used to it and so it seems natural to them – to us it has always a slightly pedantic look – but I haven't noticed that they use it in conversation, and I suppose it is their teachers who teach them to use it in writing. I surmise that the primness of language which teachers inculcate is forced upon them by the general slovenliness and incorrectness of speech common to their pupils. They are kicking against the pricks; the subjunctive mood is in its death throes, and the best thing to do is to put it out of its misery as soon as possible. After all, writing is founded on common speech, and there's no reason to forget that out of the slovenliness and incorrectness which offend the pedagogue apt phrases and picturesque idioms arise. No American, either man or boy, would say: 'I'll come to see you if I be in town'; he'd say: 'I'll come and see you if I'm in town.' It's much better that he should write it too.

Of course there's a certain difficulty in deciding when you should drop a word or an expression that is correct in favour of one that is in common use. Lunch is the verb, luncheon the noun. But common usage had made lunch a noun too. No one would ask you to have luncheon with him unless he remembered that it was correct; he would naturally ask you to have lunch with him. I think the sensible writer will use the shorter word and let the other fall into desuetude. There are still people who will refuse to talk of a bus and insist on calling it an omnibus, but when they want a cab it never occurs to them to ask for a cabriolet.

I read somewhere that Rogers, the banker poet who was celebrated for his breakfast parties, said he hoped never to have at his table someone who spoke of balcŏny instead of balcōny.

Unless a novelist makes you believe in him he is done, and yet if he is entirely believable he may very well be dull. That (complete verisimilitude) is at least one reason why people turn to detective fiction. It has suspense, it excites their curiosity, it gives them a thrill; and in return for so much they make no great demand that it should be probable. They want to know who done it, and they are willing to accept the most unlikely and inadequate motive for who done it having done it.

There is no need for the writer to eat a whole sheep to be able to tell you what mutton tastes like. It is enough if he eats a cutlet. But he should do that.

We were spending the night at a small town in Texas. It was a convenient stopping-place for people driving across the continent, and the hotel was full. Everyone went to bed early. At ten o'clock a woman in one of the rooms put in a call to Washington, and in the frame house you could hear plainly every word she said. She wanted a Major Tompkins, but she didn't know his number; she told the operator that he was in the War Department. Presently she got on to Washington, and when the operator told her that she couldn't trace him, flew into a temper and said that everyone in Washington knew Major Tompkins. It was very important, she said, and she *had* to speak to him. She was cut off and in a few minutes tried again. She tried every quarter of an hour. She abused the local operator, what sort of a one-horse dump is this? She abused the Washington operator. She made more and more noise. Nobody could sleep. Indignant guests rang down to the office, and the night manager came up and tried to get her to be quiet. We listened to her angry replies to his mild expostulation and when, defeated, he left her she started once more to ring the exchange. She rang and rang. She shouted. Furious men in their dressing-gowns, dishevelled women in wrappers, went into the passage and banged on her door telling her to stop making so much noise so that they could sleep. She told them to go to hell with such variety of language as to excite the outraged indignation of the ladies. The manager was again appealed to and at his wits' end sent for the sheriff. The sheriff came, but he was no match for her and not knowing what else to do sent for a doctor. Meanwhile she rang and rang, screaming obscenities at the operator. The doctor came, saw her, shrugged his shoulders and said he could do nothing. The sheriff wanted him to take her to the hospital, but for some reason I couldn't understand, something to do with her being a transient from another state, and if she was crazy, as all these frantic people insisted, she might become a charge on the county, the doctor refused to act. She went on telephoning. She screamed that she must get Major Tompkins; it was a matter of life and death. At last she got him. It was four in the morning and no one in the hotel had shut an eye. 'Have you got Major Tompkins?' she asked the operator. 'You're quite sure you've got him? Is he on the line?' Then with concentrated fury, spacing out her words to make them more emphatic: 'Tell – Major – Tompkins – that – I don't – want to speak – to him.'

With that she banged the receiver down on to the cradle.

There is one queer thing about patriotism: it is a sentiment that doesn't travel. Many years ago I wrote a play called *Cæsar's*

Wife which was a success in England, but a failure elsewhere. It wasn't a bad play. To the inhabitants of other countries it seemed improbable and faintly absurd that English people should sacrifice themselves to what they considered was their duty to their country. I have noticed the same thing in the war plays of the present time. Granted that there is a lot of hokum in all of them, American audiences will swallow it when it deals with the heroism and self-sacrifice of Americans, but the same heroism, the same self-sacrifice in the English excite their ridicule rather than their sympathy. They are impatient with the courage of the English during the bombing of London; their discomfiture in Greece, a discomfiture expected by all who took part in the expedition, their hopeless stand in Crete, only excited their irritation.

South Carolina. The moan of the wind in the pine trees was like the distant singing of the coloured people, singing their sad song to a heedless or a helpless God.

I wonder if the form of a story isn't a sort of *memoria technica* that holds it in your memory. Why does one remember Guy de Maupassant's best stories, *Boule de Suif, La Maison Tellier, L'Héritage* so clearly after forty years? It is not only the anecdote. The anecdote is no better than in a thousand other stories one had read and forgotten. This reflection has been occasioned by a story of G's. It has been in several anthologies, and I think he was a trifle hurt that I didn't put it in mine. He writes with distinction, and he has the peculiar American felicity for describing the feel, the scent, the impression of an environment. The story was interesting and complicated; but it fell into two parts, each of which would have made a good story, and he hadn't had the sense of form to combine them into a unity.

I think you must make sure not to divide the interest in a story; Chekov, however haphazard his sometimes appear, took care never to do this. In fact, in a story as in a play, you must make up your mind what your point is and stick to it like grim death. That is just another way of saying that it must have form.

Some American Delusions.

(i) That there is no class-consciousness in the country.
(ii) That American coffee is good.
(iii) That Americans are business-like.
(iv) That Americans are highly-sexed and that red-heads are more highly-sexed than others.

Of all the hokum with which this country is riddled the most odd is the common notion that it is free of class distinctions. I was asked one day out West to lunch with a woman who, I was told, had twenty millions. I have never seen a duke in Europe treated with such deference as she was. You might have thought that every word that issued from her opulent lips was a hundred-dollar bill that the guests would be allowed to take away with them. It is true that there is a pretence that one man is as good as another, but it is only a pretence. A banker will talk in the club car of a train to a travelling salesman as though they were equal, but I am not aware that he will dream of asking him to his house. And in such communities as Charleston or Santa Barbara the travelling salesman's wife, however charming and cultivated, will never succeed in making her way into society. Social distinctions in the final analysis depend upon money. The great English lords of the eighteenth century were not treated by their inferiors with the obsequiousness which now turns our stomachs because of their titles, but because of their wealth, which, with the influence it gave them, enabled them to grant favours to their friends and dependants. With the industrialization of England they lost a great part of their wealth and with it their influence. If they have managed to maintain themselves in some measure as a class apart it is due to the innate conservatism of the English. But they no longer enjoy the same consideration. It was properly respectful dearly to love a lord when there was something to be got out of him, but now that he has nothing to give you it is contemptible.

But it is a mistake to suppose that class distinctions exist only in the upper and middle class of society. In England the wife of the skilled artisan looks upon herself as a cut above the wife of the common labourer and will not consort with her. I know of a mushroom city in the Far West which was built only a few years ago to house the employees of a great factory. White-collar workers and factory hands live in adjoining blocks in houses built on the same pattern and as like as peas; they eat the same canned goods, read the same papers, go to the same movies, drive the same automobiles; but the wives of the white-collar workers will not play bridge with the wives of the factory hands. It looks as though the existence of class distinctions is inseparable from life in the social state, and instead of denying its existence it would be more honest to admit it.

I wonder that the people who are concerned for the survival of democracy are not anxious at the inordinate power it gives to oratory. A man may be possessed of a disinterested desire to serve his country, he may have wisdom and prudence, courage and a knowledge of affairs, he will never achieve a political position in which he can exercise his powers unless he has also the gift of the gab. I was listening to some people the other day discussing the chances L. had of becoming prime minister and their opinion was unanimous that he had none because he was a poor speaker. I suppose they were right, but is it not frightening that the indispensable qualification a politician needs to conduct the complicated business of a modern nation is a voice that sounds well over the air or the knack of inventing striking phrases? It is only a happy accident if he combines these gifts with common-sense, integrity and foresight. The appeal of oratory is not to reason, but to emotion; one would have thought that when measures that may decide the fate of a nation are under consideration it was pure madness to allow opinion to be swayed by emotion rather than guided by reason. Democracy seldom had a ruder shock than when a phrase – you shall not crucify mankind upon a cross of gold – nearly put an ignorant and conceited fool in the White House.

Of course Mother's Day is an ingenious device of the manufacturers to sell their goods, but they surely wouldn't buy costly space in the newspapers to advertise this occasion for giving unless the public response were satisfactory. They are trading on a sentiment. I have a notion that family affection is a great deal stronger in America than with us. People are expected to feel it and doubtless do. I was surprised to hear that a busy man in a busy office was to be away for a week because he had gone with his wife to bury her mother in some place no farther from New York than Bristol is from London. In England he might have gone to the funeral, but would have come back at the latest next day. What surprised me was not only that he felt it necessary to absent himself for so long from his urgent affairs to support his wife in the distress which for all I know she felt, but that his employer, notwithstanding the inconvenience it caused him, looked upon it as right and proper. During this war I have seen instances of the passionate affection that exists between son and mother and between mother and son. Once at Pennsylvania Station, waiting for my train, I saw a group of draftees who were going to camp. There was one woman, a stout, homely little grey-haired woman, who clung to her boy, her arms clasped round his waist, with an expression on her face of despair. She might have been a mistress parting from her lover, yet the boy was only going into training and there was no chance of his being sent overseas for many months. In England that mother, if she had come to the station to see her son off at all, would have kissed him lightly when the gates were opened and said: 'Well, good-bye, old boy. Be good,' and with a smile and a wave of the hand walked away. I have seen soldiers in the U.S.O. clubs so homesick that they were pitiful.

In England mothers have been parting from their sons for three hundred years, sometimes knowing it was for ever, and have come to look upon it as too normal an event to make a fuss about. It is true that in the development of America families going West went together, and the hardship and danger they had to encounter may have strengthened the tie between them; but after all, thousands of adventurous young men went off alone, and there is no sign in the letters or memoirs of the time to indicate that their departure filled their parents with anguish.

There is nothing to show that the women left behind when the whalers went out from New Bedford and Nantucket bore the separation with anything but fortitude. Isn't this emotionalism something of recent origin? I don't suppose anyone doubts that the Americans of to-day are more emotional than the English. They weren't, as far as one can tell, a hundred years ago. How has this come about? I can only suppose through the admixture of blood which has prevailed during the last two or three generations. Emotion is communicative; the sentimentality of the German, the excitability of the Italian, the effervescence of the Irishman, the susceptivity of the Jew, have overcome the reticent self-control of the New Englander and the pride of the Virginian. The stiff upper lip now is a sign of stupid insensibility. It gives occasion to a sneer or a wisecrack.

I often think how much easier life would have been for me and how much time I should have saved if I had known the alphabet. I can never tell where I and J stand without saying G, H to myself first. I don't know whether P comes before R or after, and where T comes in has to this day remained something that I have never been able to get into my head.

There is nothing about which men lie so much as about their sexual powers. In this at least every man is, what in his heart he would like to be, a Casanova.

She was successful, well-off, admired; she had a host of friends. She should have been a very happy woman, but she wasn't, she was miserable, nervous and discontented. Psychoanalysts could do nothing for her. She couldn't tell them what ailed her, because she didn't know herself. She was in search of her tragedy. Then she fell in love with a young airman, many years younger than herself, and became his mistress. He was a test-pilot, and one day, when he was trying a machine, something went wrong and he crashed. He was killed before her eyes. Her friends were afraid she would commit suicide. Not at all. She became happy, fat and contented. She had had her tragedy.

It is curious how defenceless people are when confronted with their own frailties in others. The humbug is taken in by other people's humbug; the flatterer takes their flattery at its face value. The most abandoned liar I know once wrote to me in a fury because someone had told lies about her daughter. I don't know why I didn't write back to ask her if she thought she was the only abandoned liar in the world. R., who is an inveterate swanker, is invariably taken in by other people's swank. He is always trying to make himself out more important than he is, and not withstanding one disappointment after another, goes on placing implicit faith in the similar pretensions of others. Nothing ever made me more doubtful of T. E. Lawrence's genuineness than that he so heartily trusted two persons whom I knew to be bogus.

One of the things that must strike the foreigner in the United States is that whereas most men have a host of acquaintances, few have friends. They have business associates, playmates at the bridge table or on the golf links, buddies they fish or shoot or sail with, boon companions they drink with, comrades they fight with, but that is all. Of all the people I have met in America I only know two men who are close friends. They will arrange to dine together and spend the evening in desultory conversation because they enjoy one another's society. They have no secrets from one another and each is interested in the other's concerns because they are his. Now when you consider how sociable the Americans are, how amicable and cordial, this is very strange. The only explanation I can offer myself is that the pace of life in the United States is so great that few men have time for friendship. Leisure is needed for acquaintance to deepen into intimacy. Another possible explanation is that in America when a man marries his wife engulfs him. She demands his undivided attention and she makes his home his prison.

Women's friendships everywhere are unstable. They can never give their confidence in its entirety, and their closest intimacy is tempered with reserve, misgiving and suppression of the truth.

A friend indeed. She is middle-aged, but neat and trim and very smartly dressed, the kind of woman of whom you say: 'She must have been quite pretty when she was young'; but when you ask why she never married you are told: 'She's simply devoted to her mother.' She has a great capacity for sympathy. No one could be kinder. When your husband is being tried for fraud she will sit beside you all through the proceedings, and when he is sentenced to a term of imprisonment she will come and stay with you till you get used to the situation. If through some mischance you are suddenly ruined she will spend a week with you to help you to decide what to do, and if you're in Reno and suddenly feel you can't face the ordeal of going into court she'll hop on a plane and give you her support till you get your decree. But it is in the case of death that she is at her best. If your husband has died of coronary thrombosis, if your daughter has passed away in childbirth or your son been killed in a motor accident, she will pack a couple of suitcases and by train or air fly to be with you. Distance is no object. She will not be appalled by the rigours of the climate in North Dakota, nor deterred by the heat of summer in Texas; even the inopportune gaiety of Miami at the height of the season will not daunt her. She will not shrink if the tragic event is attended by an unwelcome publicity; she is very nice to the reporters and can't forgive herself that she forgot to ask them not to mention her name in their write-up. She will listen with unfailing patience as you tell her over and over again the sad details of your dear one's last moments. She will make the necessary arrangements. She will see to the flowers. She will answer the letters of condolence that you don't think you need answer yourself. She will pray by your side in church; she will stand by your side, sobbing, at the open grave. On your return from the cemetery she insists on your taking a rest and then, after a good dinner – 'You must keep up your strength, darling' – she suggests a game of gin-rummy. She always leaves the day after the funeral, she has a thousand things to do in New York, and 'You must try and pick up the threads, darling.' Back in the metropolis, though naturally exhausted after what she has gone through, she picks up the telephone and tells her friends, one after the other, how dreadful it has all been.

It is natural enough that Americans should resent it when Englishmen in America criticize, and the retort is obvious: 'If you don't like the country why don't you go away?' They don't make it; they brood in dudgeon. But what is hard is that when they criticize England, and you don't take offence, but are quite likely to agree with them, they ascribe it to your conceit. They take it as an affront, for they think you don't care. And you don't.

Of late I have been asked two or three times to write for the French papers and magazines that have come into existence in England and America since the fall of France. I have refused, but not from ill will, for I owe a great deal to France: it was France that educated me, France that taught me to value beauty, distinction, wit and good sense, France that taught me to write. I have spent many happy years in France. I have refused because I thought the sort of articles they wanted me to write would only be of disservice. A number of distinguished writers have since done what I would not do. To my mind they have written to no purpose. They have told the French that for long they were the most civilised people in Europe and that their culture was matchless; they have spoken of the grandeur of their history, the greatness of their literature and the super-excellence of their painting; they have told them that they live in a beautiful and fertile country and that Paris is an enchanting city that all the world has loved to visit. The French are only too well aware of all that. It has been their undoing, for it has caused them to conceive a grossly exaggerated opinion of themselves. At the beginning of the nineteenth century France was the richest and most highly populated country in Europe; the Napoleonic wars drained her wealth and decimated her people. For more than a hundred years now she has been a second-class power masquerading as a first-class one. It has been a double misfortune to her; first because it led her to pretensions she lacked the resources to maintain, and secondly because it caused the greater powers to fear ambitions which she could never in point of fact have realized. The war has made manifest what only the very astute saw. Let her face the truth and decide what she will do about it. She can resign herself to being a richer Spain, a more spacious Holland, or a resort place as delectable as Italy; but if that does not suffice her and she desires once more to become a first-class power it is in her own hands. She has a productive country, advantageously situated, and a quick-witted, brave and industrious people. But she must cease to depend upon the prestige of her past greatness; she must abandon her self-complacency; she must face facts with courage and realism. She must put the common welfare above the welfare of the individual. She must be prepared to learn from peoples she has too long despised that a nation cannot have strength without sacrifice, efficiency without integrity, and freedom without discipline. She were wise to turn a deaf ear to these gentlemen of letters, for it is not flattery that can help France, but truth. She alone can help herself.

I was surprised when a friend of mine told me he was going over a story he had just finished to put more subtlety into it; I didn't think it my business to suggest that you couldn't be subtle by taking thought. Subtlety is a quality of the mind, and if you have it you show it because you can't help it. It's like originality: no one can be original by trying. The original artist is only being himself; he puts things in what seems to him a perfectly normal and obvious way: because it's fresh and new to you you say he's original. He doesn't know what you mean. How stupid are those second-rate painters, for instance, who can't but put paint on their canvas in a dull and commonplace way and think to impress the world with their originality by placing meaningless and incongruous objects against an academic background.

I made up my mind long ago that life was too short to do anything for myself that I could pay others to do for me. I would now except shaving. I am amazed when I see busy men, who tell you their time is valuable, expose themselves on six days a week to the long, tedious and elaborate operation that American barbers have made of it.

I daresay it is very pleasant to be a member of a devoted and united family, but I have a notion that it is no help to the grown man when he goes out into the world. The mutual admiration which is common in such a family gives him an erroneous idea of his own capacity, and so makes it more difficult for him to cope with the rough-and-tumble of life. But if it is no more than disadvantageous to an ordinary man, to an artist it is fatal. The artist is a lone wolf. His way is solitary. It is to his own good that the pack should drive him out into the wilderness. The extravagant praise of doting relations for work that at best only shows promise can only injure him, for being persuaded that he has done well, he will not seek to do better. Self-complacency is the death of the artist.

It has not a little puzzled me to notice how greatly the spirit of adventure seems to have declined in this country. For after all it must have been the spirit of adventure that peopled it I know that great numbers were driven out of Europe by poverty, but many more stayed at home and endured their poverty; it was the adventurous who emigrated. I know that great numbers came so that they might enjoy religious or political freedom; they too must have had the spirit of adventure, for many more remained who were prepared to compromise with conditions that irked them. I know that of those who left the settled sea-board to make themselves homes in the Middle West many went with their families, but thousands upon thousands of men, young, middle-aged or old, went by themselves. They flocked to the minefields of Nevada and California. When Horace Greeley said: 'Go West, young man,' what was he doing but appealing to the young man's spirit of adventure? I have talked to a good many of these lads who are going to the war. Most of them go because they are obliged to, many from a sense of duty, but I have not found one who looked upon it as a thrilling adventure. You would think that their only ambition was to be left in peace in their own home town and get a job in an office or a store where they would be safe from risk.

Values. It is natural to hesitate when one comes to believe that a theory such as that values are absolute and independent of our minds is erroneous, when one knows it has been held by so many great philosophers. One would have thought that if values really were absolute and independent of our minds, the human race would have discovered by this time what they are and, taking them for granted, never think of wavering in their allegiance to them. But what values are esteemed depends on circumstances. They can change from one generation to another. The values prized by the Greeks of the Homeric age are not the same as those they prized in the Peloponnesian War. They differ in different countries. I don't know that the non-attachment of the Hindus has ever been held to be a value by the Europeans, nor that the humility which Christianity has regarded as a value has ever been regarded as such by the believers in other faiths. In my own lifetime I have seen values lose their worth. When I was young the conception of a gentleman had value; now not only what it stood for, but the word itself has become vaguely objectionable. Outside lavatories you will often see *Ladies* on the door of one, but *Men* on the door of another. If all that I hear and read is true the value of chastity in the unmarried woman has in the last thirty years become negligible in Anglo-Saxon countries. It is still important in Latin ones. But it is dishonest to assert that if moral values are not absolute they must depend on prejudices or preferences. It is admitted that language has grown up in response to biological needs. Why should moral values not have grown up in the same way? Does it not look likely that they have been developed in the evolution of the species because they were essential to its existence? If this war has shown anything it has shown that unless a nation cherishes certain values it will be destroyed. They are no less real because they have come to be cherished owing to their necessity for the survival not only of the state, but also of the individual.

When the war is won I passionately hope that we shall not be so foolish as to think it has been won because we possess virtues that our enemies lack. It will be a great error if we persuade ourselves that we are victorious because of our patriotism, our courage, our loyalty, our integrity, our disinterestedness; they would have availed us nothing unless we had had the power to produce great armaments and the means to train vast armies. Might has won, not right. All you can say of the virtues mentioned is that unless on the whole a nation practises them it will, as the example of France has shown, neglect or refuse to provide the instruments of defence which will enable it to repel a foe. It would be silly to deny that our enemies have some of the same virtues as we; they have at least courage, loyalty and patriotism. They have certain values that are different from ours; it is long odds that if they had achieved the world domination which was their ambition, in a hundred years these values of theirs would have been no less unquestioningly accepted than the values we cherish now are accepted by the unthinking in our countries. It is a cruel saying that might is right, and all our prejudices lead us to deny it, but it is true. The moral is that a nation must make very sure that it has the might to defend its own conception of right.

Aldous in the first of his *Seven Meditations* says: 'God *is*. That is the primordial fact. It is in order that we may discover this fact for ourselves, by direct experience, that we exist.' What a fool he makes out God to be!

It is a tough job those philosophers have who want to rank Beauty as one of the absolute values. When you call something beautiful all you mean is that it excites a specific state of feeling in you, but what that something is depends on all manner of circumstances. What sort of an absolute is it that is affected by personal idiosyncrasy, training, fashion, habit, sex and novelty? One would have thought that when once an object was recognized as beautiful it would contain enough of intrinsic worth to retain its beauty for us indefinitely. We know it doesn't. We get tired of it. Familiarity breeds not contempt perhaps, but indifference; and indifference is the death of the aesthetic emotion.

Beauty is a value, whatever its object may be, but it is only an essential value if it exalts the soul and so enables it to accept or to be in a fit emotional state to accept more important values. But what the dickens is the soul?

Certain sensations occasioned by external causes have the power to produce in you what is known as aesthetic emotion. But the odd thing about aesthetic emotion is that it may be produced by art of indifferent quality. There is no reason to suppose that it is less sincere, less geniune and less productive in the person who gets it from Balfe's *Bohemian Girl*, say, than in him who gets it from Beethoven's Fifth Symphony.

The theorists of art who decide that the absolute of beauty is what is generally held to be beautiful by a sensitive, educated and cultured taste are arrogant. Hazlitt was certainly a man of cultured, educated and sensitive taste; yet he put Correggio on a level with Titian. When they give examples of such artists as in their opinion have produced works whose beauty may be considered absolute they are apt to mention Shakespeare, Beethoven (or Bach if they are highbrows) and Cézanne. They are perhaps safe in the first two (or three) but how can they be certain that Cézanne will produce the same effect on succeeding generations as he does on ours? It may well be that our grandchildren will look upon him with the same cool indifference as we now look upon the painters, at one time so greatly admired, of the Barbizon School. I have seen in my own lifetime too many reversals of aesthetic judgement to place confidence in contemporary opinion. A thing of beauty is not, as Keats said, a joy for ever; it is a thing that excites in us a peculiar emotion at a particular moment, and if it does that it gives us all that beauty can give. It is absurd to despise people who don't share our aesthetic opinions. We all do.

It looks as though the physical characteristics of a race, and with them the ideal of beauty, can change within a generation or two. The beautiful Englishwoman of my youth had an ample bosom, a small waist and massive hips. She gave the promise of having many children. Now she is slim, her hips are slender, her breasts small and her legs long. Is it possible that she is admired for these traits because economic circumstances have made large families undesired, and that her approximation to the male figure pleases owing to its suggestion of sterility?

If you can go by pictures and photographs the American of the last century was gaunt and lanky, with marked features, a big nose, a long upper lip, a thin mouth and an aggressive chin. You would have to go far now to find anyone who resembled the Uncle Sam of English cartoonists. The American of to-day is plump, round-faced, and his small features are a trifle muzzy. He does not wear well. You can see any number of beautiful young persons in America; you do not see many who retain their good looks in middle age.

I have been reading Santayana again. It is a very pleasant exercise, but after you have finished a chapter and stop to ask yourself whether you are the better or the wiser for having read it you hardly know what to answer. He is commonly praised for his fine phrases, but a phrase is fine when it elucidates a meaning; his too often obscure it. He has great gifts, gifts of imagery, of metaphor, of apt simile and of brilliant illustration; but I do not know that philosophy needs the decoration of a luxuriance so lush. It distracts the reader's attention from the argument and he may well be left with an uneasy feeling that if that were more cogent it would have been stated in a manner less elaborate.

I think Santayana has acquired his reputation in America owing to the pathetically diffident persuasion of Americans that what is foreign must have a value greater than what is native. So they will offer you with pride French Camembert regardless of the fact that their own home-made product is just as good, and generally much better, than the imported. To my mind Santayana is a man who took the wrong turning. With his irony, his sharp tongue, common-sense and worldly wisdom, his sensitive understanding, I have a notion that he could have written semi-philosophical romances after the manner of Anatole France which it would have been an enduring delight to read. He had a wider culture than the Frenchman, a wit as keen, a less circumscribed horizon and an intelligence of a more delicate calibre. It was a loss to American literature when Santayana decided to become a philosopher rather than a novelist. As it is he is most profitably read in the little essays which Pearsall Smith extracted from his works.

Humility is a virtue that is enjoined upon us. So far as the artist is concerned, with good reason; indeed, when he compares what he has done with what he wanted to do, when he compares his disappointing efforts with the great masterpieces of the world, he finds it the easiest of virtues to practise. Unless he is humble he cannot hope to improve. Self-satisfaction is fatal to him. The strange thing is that we are embarrassed by humility in others. We are ill at ease when they humble themselves before us. I don't know why this should be unless it is that there is something servile in it which offends our sense of human dignity. When I was engaging two coloured maids to look after me the overseer of the plantation who produced them, as a final recommendation, said: 'They're good niggers, they're humble.' Sometimes when one of them hides her face with her fingers to speak to me or with a little nervous giggle asks if she can have something I've thrown away, I'm inclined to cry: 'For heaven's sake *don't* be so humble.'

Or is it that humility in others forces upon us the consciousness of our own unworthiness?

But why should man be humble when he comes face to face with God? Because God is better and wiser and more powerful than man? A poor reason. No better than that my maid should humble herself before me because I'm white, have more money and am better educated than she is. I should have thought it was God who would have cause to be humble when he reflects upon what an indifferent job he has made in the creation of a human being.

I don't know why critics expect writers always to do as well as they should have done. The writer seldom does what he wants to; he does the best he can. Shakespearian scholars would save themselves many a headache if when they come across something in the plays that is obviously unsatisfactory, instead of insisting against all reason that it is nothing of the kind, they admitted that here and there Shakespeare tripped. There is no reason that I can see to suppose that he was not well aware that the motivation in certain of the plays is so weak as to destroy the illusion. Why should the critics say that he didn't care? I should have said that there was evidence that he did. Why should he have put into Othello's mouth those lines beginning *That handkerchief did an Egyptian to my mother give* . . . unless it was because he was aware that the episode of the handkerchief was too thin to pass muster? I think it would save a lot of trouble to conclude that he tried to think of something better, and just couldn't.

He was a tall, heavily-built fellow, with a shock of wavy, golden hair that glistened in the sun, bright blue eyes and a friendly, open countenance. He had little education and his English was terrible. He had no trace of self-consciousness. He was unaffected, chatty and sociable. He was an airman. He was talking of his experiences. 'I never believed in religion before,' he said, 'but when I was in a jam I prayed. "O God," I said, "let me live till tomorrow." I just said it over and over again.'

She is a little woman with dark hair and dark eyes, with the prettiness of youth, and neat in her appearance. The vicissitudes of the war have brought her down to the deep South, but till then she had always lived in Portland, Oregon, and she measures everything by the standards, habits and way of living of that city. Whatever is different excites her dislike and contempt. She is happy in the knowledge that she is as good as anybody else and smarter (in the American sense) than most, but is painfully embarrassed when, as here, she is thrown into the society of persons who, she is uneasily conscious, belong to a higher class than her own. She is at once abashed and aggressive; abashed because she is afraid that they do not take her at her own valuation, and aggressive because she is determined not to let them put anything over on her. She was before her marriage secretary to a business man and never in her life till now had servants to wait on her. It fills her with a half-angry confusion; she thinks it undemocratic; but why she should imagine it more undemocratic to have someone to cook your dinner than to have someone to write your letters is not apparent. She resents the kindness of her hosts as patronage and accepts all that is done for her as her due because she has been forced to leave her home town. She dislikes Easterners; she thinks them stuck-up, stilted, condescending and supercilious; in fact she regards them with the same distaste as Americans regard the English. She compares them very unfavourably with the people of Portland, Oregon.

It will be lamentable if in selfishness, lack of foresight and stupidity the Allies after the war neglect in abhorrence of the German vices to practise their virtues. The Germans are ruthless and cruel, faithless to their word, treacherous and tyrannical, dishonest and corrupt. True, every word of it. They have taught their people habits of industry and discipline. They have taken pains to make the youth of their country strong, virile and brave. They have taught them willingly to sacrifice themselves to the common good. (It has little to do with the matter that their notion of the common good differs from ours.) They have made patriotism a powerful and active force. All these are good things and we should be wise to imitate them. People should read history. The people of the Italian republics thought they could maintain their liberty by buying off with hard cash the enemies who threatened them, and with mercenaries defend their frontiers. Their history proves that unless the citizens of a state are prepared to fight, unless they are willing to spend their money to provide sufficient armaments, they will lose their freedom. It is a trite statement that no one can enjoy freedom unless he is willing to surrender some part of it. It is always forgotten.

I am gratified when a friend slaps me on the back and tells me

I'm a fine fellow, but I do a little resent it when with his other hand he picks my pocket.

He's a crook and he's been in jail. He's in the army now and is very unhappy. He's just been promoted again and it has depressed him; he hates life because he says he is always thwarted, every ambition he has ever had has always been realized and he has nothing to live for.

Gushing, she said to me: 'What does it feel like to be famous?'

I suppose I've been asked the question twenty times and I never could think how to answer, but to-day, too late, it suddenly occurred to me.

'It's like having a string of pearls given you. It's nice, but after a while, if you think of it at all, it's only to wonder if they're real or cultured.'

And now that I have my reply ready I don't expect anyone will ever put the question to me again.

Plumbing. When you consider how indifferent Americans are to the quality and cooking of the food they put into their insides, it cannot but strike you as peculiar that they should take such pride in the mechanical appliances they use for its excretion.

How sad that life should be both tragic and trivial: a melodrama in which the noblest sentiments of men serve merely to stir the cheap emotions of a vulgar audience.

Let us eat, drink and be merry, for tomorrow we die. Yes, but we die wretchedly and in anguish: yet not always: sometimes we die sitting quietly in an arm-chair over a whisky and soda after a pleasant round of golf, or asleep in our beds without knowing anything about it. Then, I suppose, we have the laugh over those who have tried and tried again and never rested till the end overtook them with so much they wanted to do still undone.

They ascribe omnipotence and omniscience to him and I don't know what else; it seems to me so strange that they never credit him with common-sense or allow him tolerance. If he knew as much about human nature as I do he'd know how weak men are and how little control they have over their passions, he'd know how full of fear they are and how pitiful, he'd know how much goodness there is even in the worst and how much wickedness in the best. If he's capable of feeling he must be capable of remorse, and when he considers what a hash he's made in the creation of human kind can he feel anything but that? The wonder is that he does not make use of his omnipotence to annihilate himself. Perhaps that's just what he has done.

What use is knowledge if it doesn't lead to right action? But what is right action?

Anyone can take me in once: I don't mind that, I would rather be deceived than deceive, and it makes me laugh to have been made a fool of. But I take care not to let the same person take me in twice.

Why is it so wounding to have an ill turn done you by a friend? Naïvety or vanity?

A good rule for writers: do not explain overmuch.

G. K. He knew X. was a crook, but thought, whomever else he cheated, X. wouldn't cheat him. He didn't know that a crook is a crook first and a friend afterwards. And yet I find something horribly fascinating in X.'s crookedness. He ruined G. K. and fled to America to escape prosecution. I met him in New York dining at an expensive restaurant; he was as debonair, as amiable, cheery and sympathetic as he had ever been. He seemed honestly glad to see me. He was very much at his ease and the embarrassment was not on his side but on mine. I'm sure no qualms of conscience disturbed his night's rest.

One would have thought it easy to say thank you when someone has done you a service, and yet most people find it a difficult thing to say. I suppose because subconsciously their pride revolts at the notion that you have put them under an obligation.

I have just been reading again Russell's *Our Knowledge of the External World*. It may be that, as he says, philosophy doesn't offer, or attempt to offer, a solution of the problems of human destiny; it may be that it mustn't hope to find an answer to the practical problems of life; for philosophers have other fish to fry. But who then will tell us whether there is any sense in living and whether human existence is anything but a tragic – no, tragic is too noble a word – whether human existence is anything but a grotesque mischance?

No one can live long in America without noticing how prevalent is the vice of envy. It has unfortunate consequences, for it leads people to depreciate things that are in themselves good. How strange that it should be a sign of affectation, and even of degeneracy, to be well-mannered and well-dressed, to speak English with correctness and live with a certain elegance! A man who has been to a good boarding-school and to Harvard or Yale must walk very warily if he wants to avoid the antagonism of those who have not enjoyed these advantages. It is pitiful often to see a man of culture assume a heartiness of manner and use a style of language that are foreign to him in the vain hope that he will not be thought a stuffed shirt. None of this would matter very much if the envious wanted to raise themselves to the level of those they envy, but they don't; they want to drag them down to their own. Their ideal of the 'regular fellow' is a man with a hairy chest who eats pie in his shirtsleeves and belches.

Somewhere in *Trivia* Pearsall Smith remarks, not without complacency, that best sellers cast an envious eye on writers of greater literary distinction. He is in error. They regard them with cool indifference. The author of whom he is thinking belongs to a different class; he is only a best seller in a small way, but he has pretensions to be a man of letters and it is a mortification to him that critical opinion will not give him what he considers his due. Such was Hugh Walpole, and I have little doubt that he would have given all his popularity to gain the esteem of the intelligentsia. He knocked humbly at their doors and besought them to let him in, and it was a bitterness to him that they only laughed. The real best seller is harrassed by no such desires. I knew the late Charles Garvice. He was read by every servant-girl, every shop-girl in England and by a great many people besides. Once at the Garrick I heard him asked how many copies of his books had been sold. At first he would not tell. 'Oh, it's not worth talking about,' he said, but at last, pressed, with a little gesture of impatience, he said: 'Seven millions.' He was a modest, unassuming, well-mannered man. I am convinced that when he sat down at his desk to turn out another of his innumerable books, he wrote as one inspired, with all his heart and soul.

For this is the point: no one can write a best seller by trying to. He must write with complete sincerity; the clichés that make you laugh, the hackneyed characters, the well-worn situations, the commonplace story that excites your derision, seem neither hackneyed, well worn nor commonplace to him. On the contrary he thinks them fresh and true. He is as intently absorbed in the creatures of his invention as Flaubert ever was in Madame Bovary. Years ago Edward Knoblock and I decided to collaborate on a picture. It was a hair-raising melodrama, and we piled thrilling incident upon thrilling incident, and as one thing after another occurred to us we laughed till our sides ached. It took us a fortnight and we had a grand time. It was a competent piece of work, well constructed and exciting; but we could never get anyone to produce it. The persons to whom we submitted it one and all said the same thing: 'It looks as though you had written it with your tongue in your cheek.' And that of course is exactly what we had done. The conclusion is obvious: you cannot write anything that will convince unless you are yourself convinced. The best seller sells because he writes with his heart's blood. He is so framed that he honestly shares the aspirations, the prejudices, the sentiments, the outlook of the great mass of the public. He gives them what they want because that is what he wants himself. They are quick to discern the least trace of insincerity and will have nothing to do with it.

One of the misfortunes of human beings is that they continue to have sexual desires long after they are sexually desirable.

315

I suppose it is not improper that they should gratify them, but I think they would do better not to talk about it.

He told me that his wife was rather silent and that he wished he could get her to talk. 'Good heavens,' I said, 'start reading a newspaper. That'll immediately set her chattering like a magpie.'

For centuries satirists have been holding up to ridicule the ageing woman who pursues a reluctant youth: the ageing woman continues indefatigably to pursue the reluctant youth.

She is not a stupid woman; indeed, she is a clever one. She neither looks at the paper nor listens to the radio, for, says she, since she can do nothing about the war she can't see why she should bother about it. She honestly can't understand why you should want to read the news rather than hear her talk about herself.

I gave her an advance copy of my book to read. She was enthusiastic in the praise of it, and every word of praise she uttered was a mortification to me. I had to exercise all my self-control not to tell her to hold her silly tongue, and instead to pretend to be gratified and flattered. If there was no more in it than she saw, then all the thought I had given to it, all the reading I had done, all the pains I had taken were waste. I try to persuade myself that she had only seen vanity and shallowness in it because she is a vain and shallow woman. It may be that you only get out of a book what you put into it and see in it only what you are. So it may be that you can only realize the serenity of the *Phaedo* if there is at least some serenity in you, and the nobility of *Paradise Lost* if you are not yourself quite devoid of nobility. The notion tallies with that old one of mine that the writer of fiction can only adequately create characters that are aspects of himself. Others he describes, he does not create, and they seldom carry conviction. And if this is true it follows that by studying the characters with which an author has best succeeded, which he has presented with most sympathy and understanding, you should be able to get a more complete idea of his nature than any biography can give you.

1944

By way of postcript. Yesterday I was seventy years old. As one enters upon each succeeding decade it is natural, though perhaps irrational, to look upon it as a significant event. When I was thirty my brother said to me: 'Now you are a boy no longer, you are a man and you must be a man.' When I was forty I said to myself: 'That is the end of youth.' On my fiftieth birthday I said: 'It's no good fooling myself, this is middle age and I may just as well accept it.' At sixty I said: 'Now it's time to put my affairs in order, for this is the threshold of old age and I must settle my accounts.' I decided to withdraw from the theatre and I wrote *The Summing Up*, in which I tried to review for my own comfort what I had learnt of life and literature, what I had done and what satisfaction it had brought me. But of all anniversaries I think the seventieth is the most momentous. One has reached the three score years and ten which one is accustomed to accept as the allotted span of man, and one can but look upon such years as remain to one as uncertain contingencies stolen while old Time with his scythe has his head turned the other way. At seventy one is no longer on the threshold of old age. One is just an old man.

On the continent of Europe they have an amiable custom when a man who has achieved some distinction reaches that age. His friends, his colleagues, his disciples (if he has any) join together to write a volume of essays in his honour. In England we give our eminent men no such flattering mark of our esteem. At the utmost we give a dinner, and we don't do that unless he is very eminent indeed. Such a dinner I attended when H. G. Wells attained his seventieth year. Hundreds of people came to it. Bernard Shaw, a magnificent figure with his height, his white beard and white hair, his clean skin and bright eyes, made a speech. He stood very erect, his arms crossed, and with his puckish humour said many things highly embarrassing to the guest of the evening and to sundry of his hearers. It was a most amusing discourse delivered in a resonant voice with admirable elocution, and his Irish brogue pointed and at the same time mitigated his malice. H. G., his nose in the manuscript, read his speech in a high-pitched voice. He spoke peevishly of his advanced age, and not without a natural querulousness protested against the notion any of those present might have that the anniversary, with the attendant banquet, indicated any willingness on his part to set a term to his activities. He protested that he was as ready as ever to set the world to rights.

My own birthday passed without ceremony. I worked as usual in the morning and in the afternoon went for a walk in the solitary woods behind my house. I have never been able to discover what it is that gives these woods their mysterious attractiveness. They are like no woods I have ever known. Their silence seems more intense than any other silence. The live oaks with their massive foliage are festooned with the grey of the Spanish moss as if with a ragged shroud, the gum trees at this season are bare of leaf and the clustered berries of the wild China tree are dried and yellow; here and there tall pines, their rich green flaming, tower over the lower trees. There is a strangeness about these bedraggled, abandoned woods, and though you walk alone you do not feel alone, for you have an eerie feeling that unseen beings, neither human nor inhuman, flutter about you. A shadowy something seems to slink from behind a tree trunk and watch you silently as you pass. There is a sense of suspense as though all about you there were a lying in wait for something to come.

I went back to my house, made myself a cup of tea and read till dinner time. After dinner I read again, played two or three games of patience, listened to the news on the radio and took a detective story to bed with me. I finished it and went to sleep. Except for a few words to my coloured maids I had not spoken to a soul all day.

So I passed my seventieth birthday and so I would have wished to pass it. I mused.

Two or three years ago I was walking with Liza and she spoke, I don't know why, of the horror with which the thought of old age filled her.

'Don't forget,' I told her, 'that when you're old you won't have the desire to do various things that make life pleasant to you now. Old age has its compensations.'

'What?' she asked.

'Well, you need hardly ever do anything you don't want to. You can enjoy music, art and literature, differently from when you were young, but in that different way as keenly. You can get a good deal of fun out of observing the course of events in which you are no longer intimately concerned. If your pleasures are not so vivid your pains also have lost their sting.'

I could see that all this seemed cold comfort, and even as I spoke I realized that it afforded a somewhat grey prospect. When later I came to think it over, it occurred to me that the greatest compensation of old age is its freedom of spirit. I suppose that is accompanied by a certain indifference to many of the things that men in their prime think important. Another compensation is that it liberates you from envy, hatred and malice. I do not believe that I envy anyone. I have made the most I could of such gifts as nature provided me with; I do not envy the greater gifts of others; I have had a great deal of success; I do not envy the success of others. I am quite willing to vacate the little niche I have occupied so long and let another step into it. I no longer mind what people think of me. They can take me or leave me. I am mildly pleased when they appear to like me and undisturbed if I know they don't. I have long known that there is something in me that antagonises certain persons; I think it very natural, no one can like everyone; and their ill will interests rather than discomposes me. I am only curious to know what it is in me that is antipathetic to them. Nor do I mind what they think of me as a writer. On the whole I have done what I set out to do, and the rest does not concern me. I have never much cared for the notoriety which surrounds the successful writer and which many of us are simple enough to mistake for fame, and I have often wished that I had written under a pseudonym so that I might have passed through the world unnoticed. I did indeed write my first novel under one, and only put my own name to it because my publisher warned me that the book might be violently attacked and I did not wish to hide myself under a made-up name. I suppose few authors can help cherishing a secret hope that they will not be entirely forgotten the moment they die, and I have occasionally amused myself by weighing the chances I have of survival for a brief period.

My best book is generally supposed to be *Of Human Bondage*. Its sales prove that it is still widely read, and it was published thirty years ago. That is a long life for a novel. But posterity is little inclined to occupy itself with works of great length, and I take it that with the passing of the present generation, which very much to my own surprise has found it significant, it will be forgotten along with many other better books. I think that one or two of my comedies may retain for some time a kind of pale life, for they are written in the tradition of English comedy and on that account may find a place in the long line that began with the Restoration dramatists and in the plays of Noel Coward continues to please. It may be that they will secure me a line or two in the histories of the English theatre. I think a few of my best stories will find their way into anthologies for a good many years to come if only because some of them deal with circumstances and places to which the passage of time and the growth of civilization will give a romantic glamour. This is slender baggage, two or three plays and a dozen short stories, with which to set out on a journey to the future, but it is better than nothing. And if I am mistaken and I am forgotten a month after my death I shall know nothing about it.

Ten years ago I made my final bow on the stage (metaphorically speaking, for after my first plays I refused to expose myself to the indignity of this proceeding); the Press and my friends thought I did not mean it and in a year or so would emerge from my retirement; but I never have, nor have I had any inclination to do so. Some years ago I decided to write four more novels and then have done with fiction also. One I have written. (I do not count a war novel that I wrote as part of the war work I was asked to do in America and which I found a weariness to do), but I think it unlikely now that I shall write the other three. One was to be a miracle story set in sixteenth-century Spain; the second, a story of Machiavelli's stay with Cesare Borgia in the Romagna, which gave him the best of his material for *The Prince*, and I proposed to interweave with their conversations the material on which he founded his play *Mandragola*. Knowing how often the author makes up his fiction from incidents of his own experience, trifling perhaps and made interesting or dramatic only by his power of creation, I thought it would be amusing to reverse the process and from the play guess at the events that may have occasioned it. I meant to end up with a novel about a working-class family in the slums of Bermondsey. I thought it would form a pleasing termination to my career to finish with the same sort of story of the shiftless poor of London as I had begun with fifty years before. But I am content now to keep these three novels as an amusement for my idle reveries. That is how the author gets most delight out of his books; when once he has written them they are his no longer and he can no more entertain himself with the conversations and actions of the persons of his fancy. Nor do I think I am likely at the age of seventy or over to write anything of any great value. Incentive fails, energy fails, invention fails. The histories of literature with pitying sympathy sometimes, but more often with a curt indifference, dismiss the works of even the greatest writers' old age, and I have myself sadly witnessed the lamentable falling off of talented authors among my friends who went on writing when their powers were but a shadow of what they had been. The best of the communications an author has to make is to his own generation, and he is wise to let the generation that succeeds his choose its own exponents. They will do it whether he lets them or not. His language will be Greek to them. I do not think I can write anything more that will add to the pattern I have sought to make of my life and its activities. I have fulfilled myself and I am very willing to call it a day.

One sign that calls my attention to the notion that I am wise to do so is that whereas I have always lived more in the future than in the present, I have for some time now found myself more and more occupied with the past. Perhaps it is but natural when the future must inevitably be so short and the past is so long. I have always made plans ahead and generally carried them out; but who can make plans now? Who can tell what next year or the year after will bring, what one's circumstances will be and if it will be possible to live as one lived before? The sailing-boat in which I used to like to lounge about on the blue waters of the Mediterranean has been seized by the Germans, my car has been taken by the Italians, my house has been occupied by the Italians and now by the Germans, and my furniture, books and pictures, if they have not been looted, are scattered here and there. But no one can be more indifferent to all this than I. I have enjoyed every luxury that man can desire, and a couple of rooms to myself, three meals a day and access to a good library will sufficiently satisfy my wants.

My reveries tend often to be concerned with my long past youth. I have done various things I regret, but I make an effort not to let them fret me; I say to myself that is it not I who did them, but the different I that I was then. I injured some, but since I could not repair the injuries I had done I have tried to make amends by benefiting others. At times I reflect somewhat ruefully on the opportunities for sexual congress that I missed when I was of an age to enjoy them; but I know that I couldn't help missing them, for I was always squeamish, and when it came to the point a physical repulsion often prevented me from entering upon an adventure that beforehand had fired my imagination with desire. I have been more chaste than I wished to be. Most people talk too much and old age is loquacious. Though I have always been more disposed to listen than to talk, it has seemed to me of late that I was falling into the defect of garrulity, and I no sooner noticed it than I took care to correct it. For the old man is on sufferance and he must walk warily. He should try not to make a nuisance of himself. He is indiscreet to force his company on the young, for he puts them under a constraint, they cannot be quite themselves with him. and he must be obtuse if he does not detect that his departure will be a relief to them. If he has made some stir in the world they will on occasion seek his society, but he is foolish should he fail to see that it is not for its own sake, but that they may go and prattle about it afterwards with friends of their own age. To them he is a mountain you have climbed not for the fun of the ascent or for the view you may get from the top, but so that you may recount your exploit when you have come down again. The old man is well advised to frequent the society of his contemporaries, and he is lucky if he can get any amusement out of that. It is certainly depressing to be bidden to a party where there is no one but has one foot in the grave. Fools don't become less foolish when they grow old, and an old fool is infinitely more tiresome than a young one. I don't know which are more intolerable, the old people who have refused to surrender to the assault of time and behave with a nauseous frivolity, or those fast-rooted in times gone by who have no patience with a world that has refused to stand still with them. These things being so, it might seem a poor lookout for the old man, when the young do not want his company and he finds that of his contemporaries tedious. Nothing remains to him then but his own, and I look upon it as singularly fortunate that none has ever been so enduringly satisfactory to me as mine. I have never liked large gatherings of my fellow creatures, and I regard it as not the least of the compensations of old age that I can make it an excuse either to refuse to go to parties or slink away quietly when they have ceased to entertain me. Now that solitude is more and more forced upon me I am more and more content with it. Last year I spent some weeks by myself in a little house on the banks of the Combahee river, seeing no one, and I was neither lonely nor bored. It was indeed with reluctance that I returned to New York when the heat and the anopheles obliged me to abandon my retreat.

It is strange how long it can take one to become aware of the benefits a kindly nature has bestowed on one. It is only recently that it occurred to me how lucky I was never to have suffered from head-aches, stomach-aches or tooth-aches. I read the other day that Cardan in his autobiography, written when he was approaching eighty, congratulated himself on still having fifteen teeth. I have just counted mine and find that I have twenty-six. I have had many severe illnesses, tuberculosis, dysentery, malaria and I know not what, but I have neither drunk too much nor eaten too much, and I am sound in wind and limb. It is evident that one cannot expect to get much satisfaction out of old age unless one has fairly good health; nor unless one has an adequate income. It need not be a large one, for one's wants are few. Vice is expensive, and in old age it is easy to be virtuous. But to be poor and old is bad; to be dependent on others for the necessities of life is worse: I am grateful for the favour of the public which enables me not only to live in comfort, but to gratify my whims and to provide for those who have claims upon me. Old men are inclined to be avaricious. They are prone to use their money to retain their power over those dependent on them. I do not find in myself any impulse to succumb to these infirmities. I have a good memory, except for names and faces, and I do not forget what I have read. The disadvantage of this is that having read all the great novels of the world two or three times I can no longer read them with relish. There are few modern novels that excite my interest, and I do not know what I should do for relaxation were it not for the innumerable detective stories that so engagingly pass the time and once read pass straight out of one's mind. I have never cared to read books on subjects that were in no way my concern, and I still cannot bring myself to read books of entertainment or instruction about people or places that mean nothing to me. I do not want to know the history of Siam or the manners and customs of the Esquimaux, I do not want to read a life of Manzoni, and my curiosity about stout Cortez is satisfied with the fact that he stood upon a peak in Darien. I can still read with pleasure the poets that I read in my youth and with interest the poets of to-day. I am glad to have lived long enough to read the later poems of Yeats and Eliot. I can read everything that pertains to Dr Johnson and almost everything that pertains to Coleridge, Byron and Shelley. Old age robs one of the thrill one had when first one read the great masterpieces of the world; that one can never recapture. It is sad, indeed, to reread something that at one time had made one feel like Keats's Watcher of the Skies and be forced to the conclusion that after all it's not so much. But there is one subject with which I can still occupy myself with my old excitement, and that is philosophy, not the philosophy that is disputatious and aridly technical – 'Vain is the word of a philosopher which does not heal any suffering of man' – but the philosophy that treats the problems that confront us all. Plato, Aristotle (who they say is dry, but in whom if you have a sense of humour you can find quite a lot to amuse you), Plotinus and Spinoza, with sundry moderns, among whom Bradley and Whitehead, never cease to entertain me and incite me to reflection. After all, they and the Greek tragedians deal with the only things that are important to man. They exalt and tranquillize. To read them is to sail with a gentle breeze in an inland sea studded with a thousand isles.

Ten years ago I set down haltingly in *The Summing Up* such impressions and thoughts as experience, reading and meditations had occasioned in me concerning God, immortality and the meaning and worth of life, and I do not know that on these matters I have since then found cause to change my mind. If I had to write it over again I should try to deal a little less superficially with the pressing subject of values and perhaps find something less haphazard to say about intuition, a subject upon which certain philosophers have reared an imposing edifice of surmise, but which seems to me to offer as insecure a foundation for any structure more substantial than a Castle in Spain as a ping-pong ball wavering on a jet of water in a shooting-gallery.

Now that I am ten years nearer to death I look forward to it with no more apprehension than I did then. There are indeed days when I feel that I have done everything too often, known too many people, read too many books, seen too many pictures, statues, churches and fine houses, and listened to too much music. I do not know whether God exists or not. None of the arguments that have been adduced to prove his existence carries conviction, and belief must rest, as Epicurus put it long ago, on immediate apprehension. That immediate apprehension I have never had. Nor has anyone satisfactorily explained the compatibility of evil with an all-powerful and all-good God. For a while I was attracted to the Hindu conception of that mysterious neuter which is existence, knowledge and bliss, without beginning, without end, and I should be more inclined to believe in that than in any other God that human wishes have devised. But I think it no more than an impressive fantasy. It is impossible logically to deduce the multiplicity of the world from the ultimate cause. When I consider the vastness of the universe, with its innumerable stars and its spaces measured by thousands upon thousands of light years, I am overwhelmed with awe, but my imagination cannot conceive a creator of it. I am willing enough to accept the existence of the universe as an enigma the wit of man cannot hope to solve. So far as the existence of life is concerned I am not disinclined to credit the notion that there is a psychophysical stuff in which is the germ of life and that the psychic side of this is the source of the complex business of evolution. But what the object of it all is, if any, what the meaning of it all is if any, is as dark to me as it ever was. All I know is that nothing philosophers, theologians or mystics have said about it persuades me. But if God exists and he concerns himself with the affairs of humanity, then surely he must have sufficient common-sense to take a lenient view, as lenient a view as a reasonable man takes, of the weakness of human beings.

And what of the soul? The Hindus call it the Atman, and they think it has existed from eternity and will continue to exist to eternity. It is easier to believe that than that it is created with the conception or birth of the individual. They think it is of the nature of Absolute Reality, and having emanated from that will at long last return to it. It is a pleasing fancy; no one can know that it is anything more. It entails the belief in transmigration, which in turn offers the only plausible explanation for the existence of evil that human ingenuity has conceived, for it supposes that evil is the retribution for past error. It does not explain why an all-wise and all-good creator should have been willing or even able to produce error.

But what is the soul? From Plato onwards many answers have been given to this question, and most of them are but modifications of his conjectures. We use the word constantly, and it must be presumed that we mean something by it. Christianity has accepted it as an article of faith that the soul is a simple spiritual substance created by God and immortal. One may not believe that and yet attach some signification to the word. When I ask myself what I mean by it I can only answer that I mean by it my consciousness of myself, the I in me, the personality which is me; and that personality is compounded of my thoughts, my feelings, my experiences and the accidents of my body. I think many people shrink from the notion that the accidents of the body can have an effect on the constitution of the soul. There is nothing of which for my own part I am more assured. My soul would have been quite different if I had not stammered or if I had been four or five inches taller; I am slightly prognathous; in my childhood they did not know that this could be remedied by a gold band worn while the jaw is still malleable; if they had, my countenance would have borne a different cast, the reaction towards me of my fellows would have been different and therefore my disposition, my attitude to them, would have been different too. But what sort of thing is this soul that can be modified by a dental apparatus? We all know how greatly changed our lives would have been if we had not by what seems mere chance met such and such a person or if we had not been at a particular moment at a particular place; and so our character, and so our soul, would have been other than they are.

For whether the soul is a conglomeration of qualities, affections, idiosyncrasies, I know not what, or a simple spiritual substance, character is its sensible manifestation. I suppose everyone would agree that suffering, mental or physical, has its effect on the character. I have known men who when poor and unrecognized were envious, harsh and mean, but on achieving success became kindly and magnanimous. Is it not strange that a bit of money in the bank and a taste of fame should give them greatness of soul? Contrariwise I have known men who were decent and honourable, in illness or penury become lying, deceitful, querulous and malevolent. I find it then impossible to believe that the soul thus contingent on the accidents of the body can exist in separation from it. When you see the dead it can hardly fail to occur to you that they do look awfully dead.

I have been asked on occasion whether I would like to live my life over again. On the whole it has been a pretty good life, perhaps better than most people's, but I should see no point in repeating it. It would be as idle as to read again a detective story that you have read before. But supposing there were such a thing as reincarnation, belief in which is explicitly held by three quarters of the human race, and one could choose whether or no one would enter upon a new life on earth, I have in the past sometimes thought that I should be willing to try the experiment on the chance that I might enjoy experiences which circumstances and my own idiosyncrasies, spiritual and corporeal, have prevented me from enjoying, and learn the many things that I have not had the time or the occasion to learn. But now I should refuse. I have had enough. I neither believe in immortality nor desire it. I should like to die quickly and painlessly, and I am content to be assured that with my last breath my soul, with its aspirations and its weaknesses, will dissolve into nothingness. I have taken to heart what Epicurus wrote to Menoeceus: 'Become accustomed to the belief that death is nothing to us. For all good and evil consists in sensation, but death is deprivation of sensation. And therefore a right understanding that death is nothing to us makes the mortality of life enjoyable, not because it adds to it an infinite span of time, but because it takes away the craving for immortality. For there is nothing terrible in life for the man who has truly comprehended that there is nothing terrible in not living.'

With these words and on this day I think it fitting to put an end to this book.

It is five years since I wrote the above piece. I have not altered it, though I have since written three of the four novels of which I spoke; the fourth I shall leave unwritten. When I came back to England after my long sojourn in the United States and revisited the part of London in which I proposed to situate my story and renewed my acquaintance with the people some of whom were to serve as models for my characters I found that great changes had taken place. Bermondsey was no longer the Bermondsey I had known. The war had destroyed much; there had been grave loss of life; but there was no longer the unemployment the fear of which had hung, a black cloud, over the lives of my friends, and they dwelt no longer in bug-ridden tenements, but in neat and tidy council flats. They had a radio and a piano and went to the movies twice a week. They were no longer members of the proletariat, but of the petty bourgeoisie. But these changes, all to the good, were not the only ones I found. The spirit of the people was different. Whereas in the bad old days, notwithstanding the hardships and privation they endured, they were gay and friendly, now their lives were sadly embittered by envy, hatred and malice. They had not been discontented with their lot; now they were filled with resentment against those who enjoyed advantages of which they were deprived. They were sullen and dissatisfied. The mother of a family, a charwoman by occupation, whom I had known for many years, told me: 'They've cleaned up the slums and the dirt, and all the happiness and joy has gone with it.' I entered upon a world that was strange to me. I have no doubt that it still offers ample material for a novel, but that which I had in mind was a picture of conditions that have ceased to exist, and I see no point in writing it.

During the last five years I have perhaps learnt a little more than I knew before. Through a chance encounter with an eminent biologist I was led to make myself at least superficially acquainted with the philosophy of organism. It is an instructive and absorbing subject. It liberates the spirit. Men of science seem to be agreed that at some remote period this earth of ours will cease to support even the most elementary forms of life; but long before this state is reached the human race will have become extinct, as have so many species of living creatures which could not adapt themselves to a changing environment. The conclusion can hardly escape one that then all this business of evolution will have been singularly futile and, indeed, that the process that led to the creation of man was a stupendous absurdity on the part of nature, stupendous in the sense that the volcano at Kilauea in eruption or the Mississippi in flood is stupendous, but an absurdity all the same. For no sensible person can deny that throughout the history of the world the sum of unhappiness has been far, far greater than the sum of happiness. Only in brief periods has man lived save in continual fear and danger of violent death, and it is not only in the savage state, as Hobbes asserted, that his life has been solitary, poor, nasty, brutish and short. Throughout the ages many have found in the belief in a life to come an adequate compensation for the troubles of their brief sojourn in a world of sorrow. They are the lucky ones. Faith, to those who have it, solves difficulties which reason finds insoluble. Some have ascribed to art a value which is its own justification and persuaded themselves that the wretched lot of the common run of men was not too high a price to pay for the radiant productions of painter and poet.

I look askance at such an attitude. It seems to me that the philosophers were right who claimed that the value of art lies in its effects and from this drew the corollary that its value lies not in beauty, but in right action. For an effect is idle unless it is effective. If art is no more than a pleasure, no matter how spiritual, it is of no great consequence: it is like the sculptures on the capitals of columns that support a mighty arch; they delight the eye by their grace and variety, but serve no functional purpose. Art, unless it leads to right action, is no more than the opium of an intelligentsia.

It is not in art then that one may hope to find some assuagement to the pessimism that long ago found immortal expression in the Book of Ecclesiastes. I think there is in the heroic courage with which man confronts the irrationality of the world a beauty greater than the beauty of art. I find it in the defiant gesture of Paddy Finucane when, plunging to his death, he transmitted the message to the airmen in his squadron: 'This is it, chaps.' I find it in the cool determination of Captain Oates when he went out to his death in the arctic night rather than be a burden to his comrades. I find it in the loyalty of Helen Vagliano, a woman not very young, not very pretty, not very intelligent, who suffered hellish torture and accepted death, for a country not her own, rather than betray her friends. In a famous passage Pascal wrote: '*L'homme n'est qu'un roseau, le plus foible de la nature, mais c'est un roseau pensant. Il ne faut pas que l'univers entier s'arme pour l'écraser. Une vapeur, une goutte d'eau, suffit pour le tuer. Mais quand l'univers l'écraseroit, l'homme seroit encore plus noble que ce qui le tue, parce qu'il meurt; et l'avantage que l'univers a sur lui, l'univers n'en sait rien. Toute notre dignité consiste donc en la pensée.*' Is that true? Surely not. I think there is some disparagement to-day in the notion of dignity, and I believe that the French word is better translated into English by nobility. There is a nobility which does not proceed from thought. It is more elemental. It depends neither on culture nor breeding. It has its roots among the most primitive instincts of the human being. Faced with it, God, if he had created man, might hide his head in shame. It may be that in the knowledge that man for all his weakness and sin is capable on occasion of such splendour of spirit, one may find some refuge from despair.

But these are grave subjects for which, even if I had the capacity to deal with them, this is not the place. For I am like a passenger waiting for his ship at a war-time port. I do not know on which day it will sail, but I am ready to embark at a moment's notice. I leave the sights of the city unvisited. I do not want to see the fine new speedway along which I shall never drive, nor the grand new theatre, with all its modern appliances, in which I shall never sit. I read the papers and flip the pages of a magazine, but when someone offers to lend

me a book I refuse because I may not have time to finish it,
and in any case with this journey before me I am not of a mind
to interest myself in it. I strike up acquaintances at the bar
or the card-table, but I do not try to make friends with people
from whom I shall so soon be parted. I am on the wing.

FOR THE BEST IN PAPERBACKS, LOOK FOR THE

In every corner of the world, on every subject under the sun, Penguin represents quality and variety – the very best in publishing today.

For complete information about books available from Penguin – including Pelicans, Puffins, Peregrines and Penguin Classics – and how to order them, write to us at the appropriate address below. Please note that for copyright reasons the selection of books varies from country to country.

In the United Kingdom: For a complete list of books available from Penguin in the U.K., please write to *Dept E.P., Penguin Books Ltd, Harmondsworth, Middlesex, UB7 0DA*

In the United States: For a complete list of books available from Penguin in the U.S., please write to *Dept BA, Penguin, 299 Murray Hill Parkway, East Rutherford, New Jersey 07073*

In Canada: For a complete list of books available from Penguin in Canada, please write to *Penguin Books Canada Ltd, 2801 John Street, Markham, Ontario L3R 1B4*

In Australia: For a complete list of books available from Penguin in Australia, please write to the *Marketing Department, Penguin Books Australia Ltd, P.O. Box 257, Ringwood, Victoria 3134*

In New Zealand: For a complete list of books available from Penguin in New Zealand, please write to the *Marketing Department, Penguin Books (NZ) Ltd, Private Bag, Takapuna, Auckland 9*

In India: For a complete list of books available from Penguin, please write to *Penguin Overseas Ltd, 706 Eros Apartments, 56 Nehru Place, New Delhi, 110019*

In Holland: For a complete list of books available from Penguin in Holland, please write to *Penguin Books Nederland B.V., Postbus 195, NL–1380AD Weesp, Netherlands*

In Germany: For a complete list of books available from Penguin, please write to *Penguin Books Ltd, Friedrichstrasse 10 – 12, D–6000 Frankfurt Main 1, Federal Republic of Germany*

In Spain: For a complete list of books available from Penguin in Spain, please write to *Longman Penguin España, Calle San Nicolas 15, E–28013 Madrid, Spain*

FOR THE BEST IN PAPERBACKS, LOOK FOR THE

THE PENGUIN TRAVEL LIBRARY – A SELECTION

Hindoo Holiday   J. R. Ackerley
The Flight of Ikaros   Kevin Andrews
The Path to Rome   Hilaire Belloc
Looking for Dilmun   Geoffrey Bibby
First Russia, then Tibet   Robert Byron
Granite Island   Dorothy Carrington
The Worst Journey in the World   Apsley Cherry-Garrard
Hashish   Henry de Monfreid
Passages from Arabia Deserta   C. M. Doughty
Siren Land   Norman Douglas
Brazilian Adventure   Peter Fleming
The Hill of Devi   E. M. Forster
Journey to Kars   Philip Glazebrook
Pattern of Islands   Arthur Grimble
Writings from Japan   Lafcadio Hearn
A Little Tour in France   Henry James
Mornings in Mexico   D. H. Lawrence
Mani   Patrick Leigh Fermor
Stones of Florence and **Venice Observed**   Mary McCarthy
They went to Portugal   Rose Macaulay
Colossus of Maroussi   Henry Miller
Spain   Jan Morris
The Big Red Train Ride   Eric Newby
The Grand Irish Tour   Peter Somerville-Large
Marsh Arabs   Wilfred Thesiger
The Sea and The Jungle   H. M. Tomlinson
The House of Exile   Nora Wain
Ninety-Two Days   Evelyn Waugh

FOR THE BEST IN PAPERBACKS, LOOK FOR THE

THE PENGUIN LIVES AND LETTERS SERIES

A series of diaries and letters, journals and memoirs

William Allingham: A Diary, 1824–1889 Introduced by John Julius Norwich

Arnold Bennett: The Journals Edited by Frank Swinnerton

Lord Byron: Selected Letters and Journals Edited by Peter Gunn

The Daughters of Karl Marx: Family Correspondence 1866–98 With a Commentary and Notes by Olga Meier

Earthly Paradise Colette

The Letters of Rachel Henning Edited by David Adams with a Foreword and Drawings by Norman Lindsay

Lord Hervey's Memoirs Edited by Romney Sedgwick

Julia: A Portrait of Julia Strachey By Herself and Frances Partridge

Memoirs of the Forties By Julian Maclaren-Ross, with a new Introduction by Alan Ross

Harold Nicolson: Diaries and Letters: 1930–64 Edited and Condensed by Stanley Olson

The Pastons: The Letter of a Family in the Wars of the Roses Edited by Richard Barber

Queen Victoria in her Letters and Journals A Selection by Christopher Hibbert

The Quest for Corvo: An Experiment in Biography By A. J. A. Symons

Saint-Simon at Versailles Selected and Translated from the Memoirs of M. le Duc de Saint-Simon by Lucy Norton

Osbert Sitwell: Left Hand, Right Hand! Abridged and Introduced by Patrick Taylor-Martin

Evelyn Waugh: Diaries Edited by Michael Davie